P9-CKF-355

BREAD ALONE

BREAD ALONE

BOLD FRESH LOAVES FROM YOUR OWN HANDS

DANIEL LEADER
JUDITH BLAHNIK

WILLIAM MORROW AND COMPANY, INC.
New York

Copyright © 1993 by Daniel Leader

Line drawings copyright © 1993 by Jan Haber

Color photographs copyright © 1993 by Mark Antman

All rights reserved. No part of this book may be reproduced or utilized in any form
or by any means, electronic or mechanical, including photocopying, recording, or by
any information storage or retrieval system, without permission in writing from the
Publisher. Inquiries should be addressed to Permissions Department, William Morrow
and Company, Inc., 1350 Avenue of the Americas, New York, N.Y. 10019.

It is the policy of William Morrow and Company, Inc., and its imprints and affiliates,
recognizing the importance of preserving what has been written, to print the books we
publish on acid-free paper, and we exert our best efforts to that end.

BREAD ALONE

ISBN 0-688-09261-6

Library of Congress Catalog Card Number 92-47236

Printed in the United States of America

First Edition

6 7 8 9 10

BOOK DESIGN BY CHERYL CARRINGTON / CARRINGTON DESIGN

641.915
LEA
1993

TO
MY WIFE, SHARON,
WHOSE PATIENCE, SUPPORT,
AND WISDOM
INSPIRES ME EVERY DAY

CONTENTS

FOREWORD

Bread is a metaphor for life. Indeed, learning to create a satisfying loaf of homemade bread can be compared to the quest for the secret to a joyful life, an ideal marriage, eternal happiness. The goal may never be totally achieved, but the search inevitably equips us with critical lessons in life.

We all begin with the same basic ingredients—flour, water, and leavening—measuring, mixing, kneading, witnessing the bread's rise, and finally its journey in and out of the oven. The more we bake, the better we get, the more adventuresome, audacious, creative we are. And when we succeed, we inevitably conceive a thoroughly personal loaf that resembles no other.

Along the way, we learn a good deal about perseverance and patience, about failure and success. And there is no joy like the exhilaration a baker feels as that honey-colored, fragrant, crackling loaf comes from the oven. Ready to slice. Ready to share.

Daniel Leader says it all, when he declares that "every loaf of bread has a soul." Even though I live in Paris, where good bread is not hard to find, I bake sourdough bread nearly every day. Not out of necessity, but because I am driven by a passion. A passion for the fragrance, the feel, the look of a handmade loaf—golden, crusty, wholesome bread that exudes contentment and well-being.

Baking bread keeps you honest. The very act of kneading is a form of meditation. The entire process resembles a personal ballet performance. Dough does not allow you to cheat, nor does it relinquish total control. Consciously or unconsciously, we submit to the changing ambience of our surroundings, as heat, cold, drafts, altitude, and temperature changes the structure of our loaf. In the end, each loaf is like a small miracle, a birth, an accomplishment, an outward sign that we are nurturing ourselves and those around us.

I travel around the world with my sourdough starter—baking bread wherever anyone will let me into their kitchens—never making the same loaf twice. As I seek the perfect loaf, I also hope to make each loaf special, different, impossible to duplicate. I toss in flaxseed, sesame seed, oats, or cornmeal, according to season, whim, what's found in the larder. I make round loaves, long loaves, and for very special occasions, a crownlike *couronne*. It is my own way of keeping a small part of every modern, high-tech day just a little bit "handmade."

Growing up in Milwaukee, my mother baked bread often—always on Saturday, always two at a time, and always giant, white, American-style loaves that rose like mushroom clouds from rectangular pans. By example, she gave me confidence in the kitchen, taught me not to be afraid of yeast (I don't ever remember a loaf of hers failing to rise), introduced me to the joyful fragrance of dough as it springs to life within the warm shelter of the oven. When guests came for dinner, there were always homemade dinner rolls, "refrigerator rolls" she called them, for the yeasty, cream-colored dough rose slowly, overnight, in the damp, cool darkness of the refrigerator.

Consider the fact that bread is but flour, water, leavening, and the intervention of man. Wine is only grapes and the intervention of man. Cheese is nothing more than milk and the intervention of man. All are primary, fermented foods that are alive and continue to grow as they age. And they supply us with just about all the nurturing we need to lead a healthy, happy life.

So bake your own bread, with your own personality, with Daniel Leader's able assistance. He takes you by the hand, helping you to form loaves of many sizes, shapes, and flavors. He teaches you to be yourself in your own kitchen, showing how to let bread baking suit your life-style, not vice versa.

As Leader suggests, "Dough is a living thing, but not a monster." Don't be afraid of it. Learn from it. Accept the rewards that come from repetition, from kneading, and from baking a loaf over and over and over again.

As you bake, play out your passions, show off your idiosyncrasies, test your creative juices in the small, contained, private place that is your kitchen. One day, perhaps when you least expect it, that bread will be your bread, like none other, crackling, moist, and memorable.

Daniel Leader wrote *Bread Alone* for you, the everyday baker. This is neither a textbook nor a treatise for pioneer commercial bakers but rather a kindly, gentle, friendly, meticulously written book designed to make you comfortable in your own kitchen. Hold Daniel Leader's hand, take his advice, and soon you, too, will be fetching landmark loaves from your very own oven.

—PATRICIA WELLS
Paris, 1993

ACKNOWLEDGMENTS

The conception of this book was, as most conceptions are, an absolute high point. It was the labor and delivery that caused the trouble. However, I am personally and professionally indebted to many people for their ability to see beyond the uncertainty and to believe in my ability to finish this book and have it be the book that I envisioned.

Thank You, Maria Guarnaschelli, you were the spark that ignited this project and my ability to do it. I am truly grateful to have you on my side.

Pat Wells, whose book, *The Food Lover's Guide to Paris,* sits in tatters on my bookshelf, a testimony to the wonders that I found between the covers. Your dedication to the artisan tradition has exposed the world to its threatened extinction. I feel honored to have your well-chosen words grace the pages of my book.

To the entire staff at Bread Alone. Without your continued support and hard work I would never have been able to leave the bakery, much less travel, do research, spend hours writing and rewriting and even more hours testing and photographing. Every loaf of bread baked at Bread Alone is made possible by the dedication of a great staff.

For the nuts and bolts of the book I have many people to thank. First, my coauthor, Judith Blahnik. We began this project as total strangers and have traveled the rough road to bookdom and are now, I can honestly say, friends. (It doesn't hurt that we share the same birthday, either.) To the crew of bakers who worked on the recipes, including Carol Guthrie, Peggy Cullen, and Toy Dupree. Pulling the final manuscript together to make a book took the able hands and minds of many. Thank you all, especially, Cheryl Carrington, the designer of the book, Chas Edwards, Maria's able assistant, and Skip Dye.

A big thank you and sigh of relief to Rick Rodgers, who took the final recipes and whipped them into perfect shape. To Judith Weber and Nat Sobel, Green Market customers and agents of the highest order, and Mark Antman who first photographed the building of our brick ovens and whose delicious photos make me smile when I see them.

Of course, I wouldn't be the baker that I am without the serious infusion of a real live Frenchman. I have two, André LeFort, master oven builder, and Basil Kamir, whose *boulangerie* Le Moulin de la Vierge inspires me to this day. My other source of French inspiration comes from Bernard Ganauchaud, who I thank for his generous advice to me on the baking of my bread. Other *boulangers* whom I must mention are poet and baker Max Poilâne, Bernard Lebon, Roland Amon, Steve Sullivan, and the mad Noel Comess.

To all of the customers of Bread Alone; I would be lost without you, and to Nancy Jenkins whose article spurred this project on.

To Bert and Moira Shaw, whose love and support I cherish. To Jane Keller for her ideas and Tom Oliverie for helping to keep the bakery running all these years. To Bob Green who has nothing better to do all day but come to the bakery and shake things up. The doors would be closed without you.

And, of course, to the chief tasters and main critics, my children: Liv, an expert on manners; Nels, my official timekeeper; Octavia, whose love of dessert rivals my own; and to Noah, whose little smile brightens up the room.

AN INTRODUCTION

Two hundred and thirty big country loaves are just about ready to come out of the oven. Five more minutes, I think to myself—any longer would burn some, and any less would leave others raw and doughy. I stand in front of the oven and wait. It's the only time I'll have to stand still, and I like it. I take the chance to admire the oven for maybe the thousandth time. I love looking at it—tall, wide, deep, beautifully solid red brick, with a wood fire that emits soft inescapable heat. Forty minutes ago these breads were loaded into the oven; the last flames have died, but I can still feel the burn of the heat. Sometimes it's so intense it turns the arched bricks of the hearth inside ash-white. To weather it, I work in tanktop, shorts, and sneakers—winter, spring, summer, and fall.

I can't see how the breads are doing now, but I want to. Any one of the four rectangular iron doors would easily swing open if I tapped on it with the paddle end of my fourteen-foot-long baker's peel. But I resist. I don't want to disrupt the balance of heat, time, and baking inside. The aroma from the oven is tender-sweet, not at all the strong toasted smell that signals burning crust. A few more minutes, I say to myself. I wait.

I glance at my hands curled around the smooth handle of the peel. As usual, they are gloved with flour. There's flour under my fingernails and the same creamy dust coats every hair on my arms up to my elbows. My palms have become like dough itself, warm and soft. Almost every baker I've met for the first time has shook my hand with the same kind of smooth and dusty palm I have now.

The fragrance in the air has changed somewhat—not so sweet, slightly toasted. I tip open a door and the bright hearth light illuminates the breads, a sea of round caramel-colored loaves, each one domed and glowing. A vision of abundance, they sit on the brick hearth in neat rows, looking so swollen they could explode. I pull one out and look at it carefully. Its vibrant reddish-brown crust has expanded beautifully. I turn it over and give the bottom a thump with my finger: the sound is hollow. Done to perfection. The loaf is very hot, so I quickly place it on the cooling rack. As I do, I hear its crust begin to crackle and pop. All the loaves will do the same, as the hot and puffy crusts contract slightly when they meet the cooler air.

I begin to work quickly, sliding the peel under as many loaves as possible at a time, then pulling them out and sliding them onto the wire cooling racks nearby. I have to hustle to get the breads out before they toast too dark, because even with the doors open, the hearth and oven remain extremely hot and the breads will continue to bake. Heat pours out into the room while I work near the open face of the oven, shoving the long-handled peel deeper each time to retrieve more loaves. They are so hot it feels as if I'm pulling fire from fire. If I can keep a consistent rhythm going, I'll get to the loaves in the back just at the right moment. They always take a little longer to bake than the breads in front.

Halfway through I examine another loaf.

It has a very good color and aroma, but an odd knot on the top makes it imperfectly round. It makes me smile, and I place it on the rack with the others. There will be many more like it.

Fifteen minutes later the cooling racks are full and crackling with new breads. Not one burned or toasted too dark. I take the one that has been cooling the longest and hold it up to my face with both hands. The sweet wheat fragrance makes my mouth water. I press with my thumbs until the crust fractures and a sweet grain aroma rises from within. I share the loaf with the other bakers.

The vacant hearth floor has cooled some and the cavernous oven, looking like the open mouth of a hungry animal, awaits the next doughy raw loaves. With a weathered wrought-iron hook, I open the damper to the oven, remove the empty cast-iron water bucket, and lift the heavy iron collar into its housing over the firebox; this will direct the flames into the oven for the next firing. Next, I open the firebox door and immediately feel the rush of coal-red heat on my legs. I take a shovel and level the piles of burning embers. Then I go through the back door of the bakery to the woodpile outside. The chilly autumn air invigorates my hot skin. There's a wheelbarrow sitting nearby, and eventually I've piled it high with split logs for a fresh fire. When I stoke the coals in the firebox with the new wood, the logs explode into flames.

I am hypnotized by the fire—a rich, primitive, organic power. I stare into it as it grows and gains force, and my imagination is fed by the flames. Sometimes I see memories come alive in the quick strokes of fire—times I've spent with people around other fires in other places. Sometimes I stare and work through a problem I have to solve: How will I pay the miller this month, why is the sourdough so sluggish? But today I'm not thinking anything. I'm feeling.

I'm not sure what the feeling is exactly, but luck comes the closest. If my life were a fable or myth, I would love the role I've been cast in—the village baker. I'm happy producing hearty breads in the tradition of European village bakers. These are large hand-formed loaves made only from organic flour, yeast, water, and salt—nothing else. There are never any oils or fats, sugar, or preservatives in my breads—just bread alone. Delicious country-looking loaves, thick crusted and dusted with flour, cracked wheat, or oats. I don't know anyone who can resist picking one up with both hands and smelling it, touching it. When the loaf makes it home, it is cut into large slices to eat with soups and stews, torn apart in small bits to mop up sauces and gravies, or sliced thin for whole-meal sandwiches.

I make breads that are golden or caramel-colored with chewy crusts and moist grain flavor. They are eye-catching because of their rustic simplicity—exactly like the loaves that mesmerized me as a boy.

While most kids were taken with the five-and-dime window toy display in town, when I was six years old the shop that captivated me was the deli, where large rye loaves were stacked haphazardly whole and naked-brown in the window. That delicatessen in suburban Buffalo, New York, would be the closest I'd come to a real traditional bakery for several years. But now every day I produce a large collection of breads that replicate Old World breads that have been made for centuries: large sourdough ryes, rich and dark raisin-pumpernickel loaves, French *pain au levain,*

big round whole wheat with walnuts, crusty *baguettes,* high and airy peasant breads, nutty farm breads from Scandinavia, wheat-berry and cracked-rye breads from Sweden, and tapered sourdough loaves studded with currants. When all the various shapes and crust colors are heaped together and presented in willow baskets, the breads are irresistible to the eye—a symbol of abundance, good health, and simple hospitality.

When I was older, and I was traveling alone in France for the first time, I stopped for a late lunch in a small town on the road from Paris to Lyons. The restaurant was empty owing, I suppose, to the late hour. Feeling a little uncomfortable, I seated myself at a small table on the edge of the room. Then a woman came from the kitchen carrying a harvest basket full of fresh loaves of all kinds of breads. There was seeded rye, *levain,* wheat loaves studded with hazelnuts, golden loaves of raisins and sesame seed, black breads, herbed rolls, and *baguettes.* She offered me my choice of breads for the meal, and from that moment on all my discomfort melted. I was home.

Old-fashioned loaves that look and taste like somebody cared about them can bring me home no matter where I am. On that same first trip to Europe I set out to Eurail it from Amsterdam to Paris. I was glued to my seat as I watched the stunning country landscape of Holland pass by my window. Hours later I still hadn't moved an inch. As the sun was setting over the pasturelands of northern France, my head filled with ironic images of war and the bloody battles once fought on this lush and passive countryside. When darkness fell, I was hungry and began to make my way through several crowded passenger cars to the dining car. The mixture of languages and accents I heard from the passengers made me feel acutely displaced. But when I stood at the entry to the dining car and saw the white linen tables set with baskets of fresh country breads, I was home again. I eagerly sat down at a table with a friendly couple who told me they were from Brussels and two other travelers who were from Paris. We ate wheaty country bread, pâté, and soup, and then mopped our plates with tufts of bread after the garlicky roast chicken. There was rich walnut bread and cheese afterwards, and we talked until ours was the last table still set with linen and breadbasket. My companions all spoke a little English, and the Parisians did not wince at my broken French. Again, I was home.

On another morning in Paris, in a deserted backdoor alley on the Left Bank, I was startled by a small paneled truck that came speeding around the corner, taking the turn on two wheels. It whizzed past me, then stopped abruptly. A stodgy little man leapt out, trotted to the rear, and flung open the two doors on the back of the truck. Inside, stacked neatly from bottom to top and wall to wall, were hundreds of golden *baguettes*. All of them seemed to be looking right at me. Their sweet just-baked smell wafted under my nose and the beauty of such a delicate cargo caught my breath. I stood still in my tracks and watched. The delivery man pulled out one slender loaf at a time until he had an armload. Then he trotted through the back entrance of a shop and disappeared. In the quiet of the alley I stood gazing. All those *baguettes* stacked, crammed really, were graceful and lively. The feeling washed over me again. I was home, this time as if surprised by an old friend on the street.

I try to bake breads that continue to have that effect on me: beautiful loaves that look, feel, and taste like someone took time and really cared about them. That is a distinct characteristic of Old World breads. Looking at one of these special breads and holding it in my hands incites a memory—not a clear and real memory, but the feeling of remembering, the feeling of sweet longing. The simple whole loaf is a momentary link to the long-gone past tucked away inside of me, inside of all of us.

The paradox is that the more I focus on making a simple loaf of good bread, the larger my world gets. On one hand a baker's life is solitary; we often work alone, many times while everyone else is sleeping. And the demands of producing daily bread keep us tied to a routine that encloses our lives. But my world has exploded. I want to know everything I can about the bread before it becomes bread. So I've traveled to the farms to meet the farmers who grow the grain. I've followed the grain to the miller and watched as the flour is processed. I've traveled to the big cities of Europe, and to so many tiny towns I can't remember, just to eat good bread. I spend time with other bakers, I travel to them or they travel here. We talk endlessly about the quality of flour, the fermentation of the dough, the fire, and the hearth. Recently, the corporate world of supermarkets has asked me to consult, as more and more are building their own bakeries, and culinary schools have asked me to teach the essentials of fine breadmaking.

So before my world expands or explodes beyond my own reach, I'm writing it down. Here is *Bread Alone*, a description of my world as a global village baker. In these pages you will read about my commitment to making good bread by beginning with organic flours. I describe farms and harvests I have visited, and

I help you locate organic flour for your own breads. You'll read about other bakers—my friends who live in Paris, California, Brooklyn, Vermont, and many small towns and villages. They have become my friends and their shared experiences have shaped my own passion for simple, traditional breads.

Here, too, are all the recipes I've collected, borrowed, adapted, and created over the years. The most important ingredients in all my recipes, however, you won't find listed with the flour, water, yeast, and salt. (Even the best flour can do only so much.) The two unwritten ingredients for all my recipes are your patience and slow fermentation of the dough. With any fine wine, beer, or good cheese, the impressive final taste is due to careful fermentation. So it is that slow fermentation of dough is the ingredient within the process that makes my breads taste and look so good. As dough becomes fine bread, its flavor and character are determined by the kind of fermentation it goes through.

I will guide you through the process, teaching you traditional techniques of making a *poolish*, then the dough, then fermenting the dough in a variety of ways, and finally baking your own beautiful loaves. I will also teach you a simple method for making a classic *levain* (the French sourdough starter) and a sourdough rye starter. And I have given you more than two dozen sourdough breads and *pain au levain* to try, as well as many delicious breads that can be made without sourdough starters.

If you bring an attitude of love and patience and make these breads slowly and caringly, you won't find them difficult. But neither will you find baking these breads an ordinary food chore, as the whole procedure is alive and full of surprising rewards. With a little willingness on your part, you will produce high, crusty loaves with nutlike flavor and aroma— breads you will want to make again and again. These are the breads that made a reputation for me, and I hope they will do the same for you—fresh, bold loaves from the earth, the grain, the flour, the slow risings, and finally from your own hands and hearth. They will look and taste like you cared, and they will call you and those you care about home.

THE BAKERY

THE STORY OF BREAD ALONE

My bakery stands on a battered service road alongside Route 28, in the wooded foothills of the Catskills in upstate New York. You might say we're smack in the middle of nowhere. We are up in the country, out in the sticks, a spot on the road two hours north of New York City that most motorists speed by on their way to ski areas or to the nearby tourist town of Woodstock. Boiceville is our town of residence, and it's so small that I've only met a handful of people outside the area who have ever heard of it.

When the three morning bakers check in at 4:00 A.M., each has likely driven the car on a solitary, dark winding road. Each sets to work under bright lights, with the pitch-dark of the surrounding woods pressing against the windows. The sounds of crickets rise from the crevices in the warm foundation beneath the oven, and reggae music pounds from the bakers' tape deck.

The first task is to measure flour from fifty-pound sacks and pour it into large electric mixer bowls fitted with paddles. The bakers then add portions of sourdough starter, cracked wheat grains, and cracked rye. They measure off water at the proper temperature, add salt, and mix until the dough is kneaded. Then they lift the dough in pieces and place it in vats, where it will ferment several hours before the bakers on the next shift create the final mixed-grain loaves.

ALBUQUERQUE ACADEMY
LIBRARY

Just before daybreak the air inside the bakery is perfumed with the earthy fragrance of fermenting sourdough. The bakers have opened the vats of ready *levain* dough, and they begin to weigh and cut it into loaf-size amounts. The heavy dough yields as serrated blades slice through, popping bubbles of trapped gas. When all the dough has been measured, the three bakers stand at the bench and begin the long, skilled process of forming the loaves. Their hands know exactly what to do while their eyes gaze out the window. I've yet to see a baker not mesmerized by the coming of dawn at the bakery. Those who work in the middle of the night wait for the arrival of light, and even the men packing our trucks on the loading dock stop to watch the dawn.

The hills surrounding us are thick with groves of maple, oak, and birch, and in the winter-gray months the sunrise is spectacular. The naked white birch are first to emerge from the pitch black, appearing timidly like an apparition. The deep blue light of dawn grows lighter and brighter until the sun lifts over the ridge and brilliant shafts of yellow light pierce the thick woods, creating striking black silhouettes of the tall, barren trees.

Day has begun. The newly formed loaves of *pain au levain* rest in canvas-lined baskets where they will rise one more time, while the bakers haul in wood from the pile outside and prepare to fire the oven. Freshly baked loaves will be ready for our first customers when the doors open at 7:00.

Our daily customers are part of a deeply rooted rural community. Many are descendants of the dairymen and farmers who for a hundred years or more supplied the markets of New York City. That agricultural community has disappeared, but in the past few years a local rebirth of small farmers has begun to take place. Scattered throughout the Hudson Valley are new wineries, goat farms producing fine cheeses, and small vegetable and herb farms. Bread Alone is part of that revival.

There is a parking area in front of the bakery, and from the desk in my office I like to watch customers come and go. A car pulls in, tires making a rolling crunch sound on the gravel. I see the familiar face of an old man who's been buying bread here twice a week for nine years. I watch as he slips inside the bakery doors. When I look up again, he's slowly descending the stairs, and he's carrying one of our largest white paper bags filled with breads. I know what he has bought; it's always whole wheat walnut loaf and currant buns. It's Friday afternoon and he's stocking up for the weekend.

I lean back, watch, and take in the simple pleasure of seeing someone going home with bread. It's the moment that completes the process—grain, flour, water, yeast, or sourdough; the dough, the baker's hands, the fire of the brick ovens; the aroma of breads on the hearth; and finally someone with the loaf in his hands. It is the close-to-the-source quality of this experience that lured me into the food world. And it's only after a very complicated trip—a life full of complex turns—that I have come back to treasure such simple pleasure, right where I started.

When I was a little boy, my grandfather took me to the wholesale food market on the outskirts of Buffalo, my hometown. In the pre-dawn hours, local farmers and distributors converged there twice a week with trucks and railway cars. Bundles, bags, baskets, and crates of fresh produce sat stacked on truckbeds and loading docks, ready for sale and movement to the several hundred markets in the upstate area. The growers and businessmen raced excitedly through all the fresh cargo, dickering over prices, while forklifts and workers quickly unloaded pallets of boxes and burlap bags. The energy was intense, the atmosphere chaotic. The perishable goods had to move fast. Deals were made quickly.

In earlier days my grandfather would have done great business on such a morning. He was a burlap-bag maker, supplying new bags to the farmers and taking old ones for repair. Paper and plastic retired him.

Nearby was an open-air market, and as light dawned I could see tailgates and tables filled with fresh fruits and vegetables for sale, with the farmers who grew them standing nearby. It was exhilarating for me—rubbing the dirt from a potato, smelling the melons, listening to my grandfather bargain for several bags of apples. A great sense of well-being came over me as I took an apple from the farmer's crate, rubbed it on my sleeve the way my grandfather always did, and ate it—simply ate it. I knew where it came from and how it got there. It was all incredibly immediate, and I felt connected to it all.

In college, when I started to cook, the pleasure for me then was finding the freshest ingredients at the Saturday farmers' market at the State Capitol in Madison, Wisconsin. I bought tomatoes just off the vine, corn from a farmer's stand, cheese made at the dairy on the outskirts of town. Preparing simple meals from food grown close to home made me feel whole and connected to where I was living. It was this romance with food and wholeness that led me to study to be a chef. My dream: to court local farmers, selecting their best produce, then prepare and serve simple meals in a homey atmosphere.

I put myself through the Culinary Institute of America as fast as the school would allow, and I landed my first job as a chef at Le Veau d'Or in New York City. It was a cozy bistro, featuring the kind of fare I liked—simple French country *cassoulets*, soups, and stews. I began to move up quickly, changing jobs regularly, moving from restaurant to restaurant—each time stepping up to more responsibility and prestige.

With each advance, however, I got further and further from my dream. Manhattan seemed to be the farthest possible place from local farmers. I was so busy, I couldn't be precise about the selection of fresh produce and meats. I had no idea where they were grown and under what conditions or by whom. The sophisticated restaurants I was working in were more like stages than homey refuges, and the meals I prepared were foods for performance—overpriced entrées made to look dazzling, served with fancy sauces. The patrons came to be entertained and stimulated. So each night was another opening, another show. And while I was garnering respect and notoriety, I was slowly giving up what I really wanted to do—offer fresh, honest meals in classicly simple surroundings.

After my first child, Liv, was born, I began to settle for keeping a busy schedule among the noise, congestion, and crowds of the city. But each time I went to Europe to study or visit, I found myself in the tiny countryside kitchens. I would wander in open-air markets and find myself in the bakeries—watching as the flour and water became bread, watching the muscular hands of the baker, watching the intent faces of customers selecting their loaves, watching the breads be carried away in sacks.

Each time I came back to New York, I knew I had to find a way to get my life back to the basics. Perhaps a bakery of my own, perhaps a small country inn, maybe a little restaurant in a quiet spot. With the first extra cash in the bank I bought a small summer cottage near Woodstock, New York. Weekend escapes to the quiet of the Catskills alleviated some of the city pressures. For relaxation, I read the work of Helen and Scott Nearing, and became enthralled with their accounts of how they built their house from stones they gathered from the land, how they grew their own food.

I then landed the job of chef de cuisine at the Water Club in New York City. It was an enviable position, but as the months went by I was torn between feeling grateful for the job and being suffocated by it. The food was still high performance and the restaurant scene still too chaotic. After a few months I decided to find my niche outside the complicated kitchens of the very complicated city. When my son Nels was born, so was the resolve to become a baker—a country baker. Bread Alone was born, too.

There was a building for sale on Route 28 near my summer house. I bought it for an unbelievably cheap price, but I prolonged the closing as long as I could while I tried to figure out what I needed. Should the oven come first or the mixer; a staff, a phone, or a business plan?

I decided to research ovens first. I had no doubt that I wanted a traditional wood-fired brick oven because I had seen the brick oven of Bernard Lebon in Paris, one of only fifty left in the city, and had tasted the wonderful breads the hearth produced. I had also spent time visiting my friends Jules and Helen Rabin in Vermont and raved about the breads they turned out from the brick oven in their backyard.

A local mason and I began to draw up plans. We decided that the oven would be made of stones, which we eventually would carry one by one from the stream across from my house. I closed on the sale of the building and, while the masons worked, spent nights and weekends in New York City at D & G bakery on Mulberry Street, in the heart of Little Italy. Theirs was a brick coal-fired oven, but it gave me a chance to get the feel of a traditional oven and to get used to working with huge amounts of fermenting dough.

When the oven was ready, I bought a used mixer and a baker's bench at a shop in the restaurant supply district on the Bowery. We named ourselves Bread Alone, fired the oven, mixed our first dough, and began to bake. It was all done very unscientifically—a scoop of flour, water in various amounts, guestimated baking times—and we baked a lot of bad bread those first months. There were yeasty loaves that fermented too quickly at too high a temperature, tough breads that were overbaked, and wet doughy breads that were underbaked. My "must have" oven turned out to be capricious and unpredictable; it wouldn't hold heat well or provide steam.

But I kept at it. Each morning I'd get up at 3:00 A.M. and bake. I became a little more precise about weighing ingredients and timing fermentation. By 10:00, I'd load the bread into the back of my Mazda hatchback. I searched for customers, going off to markets, fine food shops, delis, restaurants—anywhere I thought I could sell the bread. I had no trouble. People were eager for the fresh, simple, and honest character of our bread.

I was dissatisfied, however. The *pain au levain* was *too* sour, the wheat walnut loaf was flat-tasting, and none of our loaves had the eye-catching beauty or vibrant flavor of those breads I had tasted in Europe. I wanted to reproduce the rich and hearty traditional Old World breads: large wheaty round loaves, thick crusted and studded with walnuts; *pain au levain* with a fine sour tone without a dominating bite; high and light country loaves with crisp golden crusts; and robust farm breads fragrant with the smell of the earth and chewy with cracked wheat and rye.

I became a hound for information on Old World baking techniques and traditions, making it a point to visit bakers who were making the kinds of breads I wanted to bake. Wherever I traveled, if the breads in a shop window caught my eye, I dropped in and introduced myself, then asked to see the oven and meet the baker. One old baker in Amsterdam told me that the success of his breads was due to the organic flour he imported from central France. A woman in Monaco made me a delicious *pissaladière,* a famous Provençale onion pizza. Then she told me it was the water in the region that made her dough taste so good. In a Brooklyn shop where the front window was packed with exciting-looking rows of loaves, a passionate third-generation Italian baker told me that every loaf of bread has a soul. He baked his breads in a coal-fired brick-hearth oven because, he insisted, without the hearth the soul of the bread withers.

Whenever I heard of an old-fashioned baker, I wrote a letter or called and made plans to visit. I talked to dozens of sons and grandsons of bakers who ran small one-baker–one-oven shops in Italy, France, Denmark, California, Vermont, Michigan, New Hampshire, and New York. But instead of discovering the "secret formula" for traditional breads, I accumulated more opinions than there are breads. The bakers in the Pyrenees said an authentic hearty loaf could only be made with mountain water and baked at high altitudes. Some Parisian bakers told me truly great *pain au levain* could only be produced in a brick oven, while a Jewish baker in the Williamsburg section of Brooklyn said it was not the oven but the freshness of the whole-grain rye flour that produced good bread. "Ordinary flour yields ordinary bread," he insisted. There were young New Wave "old-fashioned" bakers in Berkeley, Los Angeles, and Paris who also bowed to high-quality flour, but they emphasized that the secret lay in the length of time and the temperature during fermentation of the dough.

I had already built a traditional wood-fired oven at my bakery, and I was using local Catskill Mountain water in the breads. So I began to question the quality of the flour I was using. It was pretty unspecial—much like the flour available on most supermarket shelves. Then it became apparent that I was trying to make Old World breads using New World flour. The wheat berry had been stripped of most of its outer bran layer and ground in high-speed steel mills, a process that destroys most of the nutrition and much of the wheat taste.

I had to have flour from grain grown the way it had grown two centuries ago—before New World techniques added chemical fertilizers to soil and sprays to plants—and when the whole grain of wheat was ground slowly between two heavy millstones. I wanted flour that hadn't been denuded of its nutritional components, bleached white, then enriched with vitamins. I wanted a flour as close to the natural state of the grain as possible. Good flour from good earth.

The search wasn't difficult. I discovered a small but lively network here in the United States of organic farmers who grow acres of wheat in soil fed with organic manures, not synthetic agents. There were stone millers, too, who milled the grain the old-fashioned way between heavy stones. I called one of these millers in Minnesota and ordered a ton of fresh organic stone-ground flour. The breads I produced started to acquire that hearty European character and deep taste I had been searching for. Next, I began to experiment with fermentation, letting some doughs ferment longer at lower temperatures. This had an even more pronounced effect on the flavor of my breads.

Through trial and error and living a day at a time—one dollar ahead of the bills—the bakery business grew. We continued to experiment with organic flour; I was always on the phone with a new miller somewhere. And we continued to experiment with fermentation of the dough, allowing some dough to ferment at lower temperatures, some at higher. The breads were becoming star attractions.

It took five years to build a solid clientele, and about that long to master our moody and idiosyncratic oven. We were finally feeling somewhat secure when I made plans for an extended trip to Paris—

a trip that was intended to be one of those times away when I would connect with other bakers and strengthen my ties. However, it was in fact a trip that changed the bakery and my life dramatically.

One afternoon in Paris I stood talking with my friend the baker Basil Kamir, in front of the brick oven in the basement of his bakery, Le Moulin de la Vierge on rue Vercingétorix. A hundred loaves had just come from the oven. They crackled as they cooled in willow baskets, and I watched as the tiny cracks appeared in the thick crusts. The pronounced aroma of sourdough wafted to my head. It permeated the air and stayed in my clothes until the next laundry.

When André LeFort, the famous oven mason whom I had yet to meet, descended the stairs, Basil was quick to introduce me as *un boulanger Américaine.* His tone was tongue-in-cheek amazement as if it were a small wonder that America could produce a real baker.

I had heard of LeFort and of his fine work. He had rebuilt the oven for the celebrated Lionel Poilâne. I felt honored to meet him, and told him so as we shook hands in front of the iron plate on Basil's oven wall, which read *"Jean LeFort et Fils."* Then Basil popped a sudden question.

"So, André, do you want to go to America and build Dan an oven like mine? Imagine a LeFort in the United States! Wouldn't that be something?"

I laughed at the question and the total improbability of it. André didn't laugh.

"But I don't have a passport," André said, looking seriously at Basil.

"Oh, don't worry about the passport," Basil said, comforting André and putting his arm around his shoulder. He knew André had never been to America, had never been far from Paris at all.

"And who would take care of Madame, my cat, and the bird?" André went on, truly concerned.

I really had no idea or hope of ever replacing the old stone oven at Bread Alone. After all, I had spent five difficult years learning to deal with its limitations. Even to imagine having an oven built by LeFort was like dreaming of a move up from a Volkswagen van in need of a valve job to a Rolls-Royce. But because Basil is rarely serious about anything, always setting up jokes, it was easy for me to be a player in the scene that was unfolding. I added my bit.

"Do you think," I asked Basil, "if Mssr. LeFort comes over to build one oven, might he just as well build two?"

"Well, what do you think, André," Basil laughed, "will you build one or two ovens for Dan?"

André smiled at us both and said, "Well it is a long way, a very great distance to travel. I may as well build two ovens."

"So would you build them end-to-end?" I asked.

"Side-by-side," André said, matter-of-factly, "side-by-side would be good."

When we shook hands to say goodbye, the play was over and yet by some quirk I felt a real agreement had been made.

The next day Basil helped André fill out his passport application. I returned to New York to tell everyone that soon a Frenchman they had never heard of was coming to the bakery to build two new ovens. When they asked what would happen to the old oven, I told them we would tear it down. When they asked how much this project would cost, and I told them that I didn't know because André and I had never talked money, they told me I had lost my mind. In a way I had lost my mind. There are those moments when you lose your mind, but come to your senses. Moving on instincts and sixth and seventh senses only, I trusted that this vague arrangement with LeFort for two new ovens would unfold in its own way. It seemed oddly fine that I had no further details.

In a few months I returned to Paris and shopped with André for materials. I wrote checks all over France ordering over ten tons of brick and ironwork. Eight thousand dollars worth of materials filled a cargo container to be shipped to New York City, and still André and I hadn't made a formal deal. I had no idea how much the project would cost.

Meanwhile back in Boiceville the local planning board was fighting my proposal to build the ovens. Bread Alone was making headlines: "Local Baker Fights Town Planners For Oven." When it came to the final vote, fortunately the board locked in a tie—fortunate because the bylaws stated that a tie is a pass.

I won the right to build only shortly before André LeFort arrived ready to work. We threw a crew together, and in six months André and his crew built the two ovens side-by-side, as he had promised. And the cost? $100,000.

From that day on, the entire life of the bakery changed dramatically. First, the other bakers and I had to learn how to use the fiery new ovens. Great puffbacks of flame singed many eyebrows. But the big change was in the breads. With two solid, reassuring ovens that produced even heat and steam, the enthusiasm and expertise of all the bakers began to grow. The bakers working here with me in those days experimented freely, developing greater flavor and character in the breads that have become the stars of the Bread Alone family. We now have a repertoire of thirteen traditional breads, from husky peasant loaves to *pain au levain* to *baguettes* and walnut breads. I owe a lot to the devotion and imaginations of those bakers.

Soon after the new ovens were finished, we were able to bake more and more bread and began selling from trucks at the open-air farmers' greenmarkets in New York City. This was a dream come true! At last our freshly baked loaves were available to the ordinary working people of the city. Up until then, we had only been selling over the counter at the bakery and wholesale to fancy food shops, restaurants, and some health food stores and markets. Now I got to be a player in the hustle and bustle of the open market, right alongside the farmers and growers who set up stands and opened up their trucks. We arrived at 6:00 A.M., were set up by 7:00, and I hustled bread all day long.

The Bread Alone bakery is now twice the size of the original building. André's ovens are in plain view from the bread counter. There's a small café in front where customers can have cappuccino, stay a while, talk with each other, and smell the bread baking. The staff has grown slowly and steadily. High-school kids have come in the door looking for work; many have learned baking, gone off to France to study, and have returned. Graduates from my alma mater, the Culinary Institute, also come knocking to develop their baking skills. From a Mazda hatchback delivering a few bags of bread, we've grown to a small fleet of trucks making daily deliveries to Boston, New Jersey, and New York.

The most important element in my life as a baker—the people I bake for—has grown stronger and richer each year. My customers who travel Route 28 every day for fresh bread have nourished my heart as well as my business. They have become so attached to fresh bread from Bread Alone that they won't be daunted by weather, circumstance, or other inconvenience.

One day during the mess and chaos of our rebuilding and expansion, for about a half-hour the entrance to the retail area was blocked by scaffolding. Truly a temporary disturbance. Yet two older women climbed up the loading dock and over stacks of flour sacks to get in to buy two loaves of bread. Then they climbed over the flour sacks again, luckily one of the bakers insisted on helping them down off the five-foot loading dock. During the same half-hour a man stole around to the back of the bakery, jumped a wide ravine of rainwater runoff, scaled a steep pile of gravel, and came through the backdoor. His prize? One baguette. That's all he wanted. He bought it from the back side of the counter and left the same way he came.

I like that kind of passion for bread, not just because it's good for business but because there's something magical and paradoxical about it. I still don't get it myself. A desire for something as simple as a loaf of good-tasting, freshly baked bread makes one willing to take a long drive on a country road or climb over a stack of flour sacks.

My life as a professional baker is far from simple; in fact, I'm busier now than I ever was as a chef. Running the business is very demanding. I can get scattered, spread thin, and lose touch with the simplicity that I crave. So when I need to come down to earth, I hang around the customers at the bakery. I eavesdrop. I hear old customers talk to each other about the bakery as if it's a child they have watched grow. They remember the old oven, the creaking screen door, the shop cat.

New customers smile, taking obvious pleasure as they look for the first time at the loaves for sale sitting in baskets. They throw back their heads and inhale the warm yeasty smell of baking bread and they sigh out loud. They ask questions of the woman behind the counter, and they compare prices. Excited to be in the bakery that baked the bread, and paying the baker who shaped the loaf, they are part of an old and natural chain of events. They are like me, the little boy at the open market with his grandfather, connected for a moment to the source of something good.

I melt a bit, then. My cramping concerns about schedules ebb gently, leaving me free for a moment to also feel the connection to simple bread alone.

THE HARVEST

ORGANIC FARMERS AND THEIR GRAINS

From the moment I found good-tasting results from using organic flours, I wanted to know more about the farms that grew the grains for those flours. Until I saw and understood for myself what organic farming was, who the farmers were and how they grew better grain, I would feel unsettled. Part of my process as a baker would be missing, as if the loaf could never feel whole unless I was connected to every facet of making it. I had to go. I also thought the farmers and I might have something in common: old-fashioned oddities in a New Age world. So one August I set out.

My miller, Marc Schwartz, arranged visits for me with his grain farmers. I was met by him and Prescott Bergh, his organic farm certifier, in Minneapolis. We had lunch in the airport while I waited for my next flight out. After hello came my first question: What does a certifier do? He told me that the flour I was using at Bread Alone came from grains grown in fields that were tracked and studied for at least three years before they could be certified organic.

"That's when I do what I do," he said. "For three years, I keep a detailed history of the fields, beginning with all sprays ever used on the soil, and I take soil samples to measure any residue from pesticides used in the past. Then I suggest to the farmer specific nontoxic combatants for weeds and pests, and I help him devise a crop rotation plan to boost the fertility of the soil.''

Prescott emphasized that the soil's fertility—its ability to nourish and sustain life—is the constant concern and first responsibility of the farmer. Organic farmers are keenly aware that to get much from the soil, you must give much to it. It must be well-nourished in order to produce nourishing grains. During some seasons that often means letting a field rest or planting a cover crop (''green manure''), thereby rendering the field unprofitable for that season. Organic fields are fertilized by naturally occurring substances—composted materials, aged animal manures, and green manures. The soil becomes moist, rich, and loose. The roots of the grain plant can then grow deep, and the plant structure is strong. When the grain is harvested and cleaned, it is stored without the use of fumigants, irradiation, or synthetic agents. The result is a grain with a wholesome full-bodied taste. Like a tomato or a carrot grown in your own garden, the grain has a flavor that is strong and clear.

Commercial fields, on the other hand, are treated with pesticides to fight bugs, herbicides to combat weeds, fungicides to inhibit the growth of fungi, and synthetic and chemical fertilizers. The young crop of grain is sprayed repeatedly throughout the growing season and sprayed again when it is harvested and stored.

Many of these chemicals were developed to help farmers produce large, foolproof crops, and for a long time they seemed to work. Beautiful vegetables and fruits abounded, filling supermarket shelves. However, the presence of chemicals does not end with the harvest. Many of the commercial chemicals do their work systemically; they enter the plant's internal system through leaves or roots and remain there. The grain after harvest is cleaned, but it is never washed as one would scrub an apple, so the residue of synthetic chemicals often remains both inside and out. The effect of these residues on the body and on the planet is the subject of international concern and constant debate. I simply don't like ingesting them. But more to the point, I don't like the flat-tasting, characterless grain that comes from a commercially grown plant. The chemical procedures seem to rob the grain of its potential for a full and rich homegrown taste.

The talk with Marc and Prescott renewed my own commitment to using organically grown wheat, and I was super-charged about meeting the farmers and seeing their fields. I said goodbye to Marc and Prescott and boarded my connecting flight to Bismarck. I was about to see the great grain lands of North Dakota and Montana. I rented a car and headed west from Bismarck to Mandan, then I would go north to Stanton, Hazen, and Zap. Ten minutes outside of Mandan I was in a new world—one I had only heard about. For the first time in my life I was surrounded on all four sides by rolling grain spanning the horizon. I sped alone on a thin string of road that barely parted an endless terrain of sunflowers and alfalfa, forests of bright green corn, and stands of wheat, oats, and millet. For two hours I drove with only the whistle of the wind through the open windows, the heady fragrance of the grain, and those extending horizons of gold, yellow, orange, and green. Close to Stanton I was delighted to discover that the harvest had already begun in some fields. Huge combines rolled slowly and silently in the distance through windswept fields, snipping stalks and leaving them in neat rows to dry. The waving grains, the rolling blades, and the small figure of the farmer atop the big machine created a natural ballet of man, machine, wind, and wheat.

By the time I reached Stanton I was reeling from the experience. But then I had to put my mind to work following Marc's exact directions to the farm of Janice and Marshall Kargus, my first hosts. "Don't miss a landmark or a turn," Marc had warned. "It could mean two days in the wrong direction."

Stanton was a tiny town; it had a church, a general store, and a handful of houses. I turned left just outside the town and traveled the precise 22.3 miles, past the covered school-bus stop and over a small bridge, then took the first dirt road I came to. For five miles down this road, which was tightly bordered by fields of high grain, I had to drive with the windows up to keep the road dust out. Sweating from the heat of the relentless sun, I wondered if I might be passing into yet another world. There was one more turn, into the Kargus driveway, and another two miles of dirt road. Finally I could see the house. It was dwarfed by the wide horizon and obscured by four large round grain silos clumped together near the front.

Janice and Marshall Kargus live with their six children in the small house planted on the windward side of a hill. They overlook seven hundred acres of organic wheat, rye, alfalfa, and lentils, spread out in neat fields. And Marshall farms it all by himself.

Janice, who had a warm and strong handshake and the far-reaching eyes of a pioneer, met me and pointed me toward her husband. I walked down the long tractor path past a field of freshly cut alfalfa—the shafts lay drying in long windrows and the wild green scent of newly mown hay was thick in the air. Hot gusts of wind stirred up small whirlwinds of dirt and sent bits of chaff careening through the air.

Marshall had just finished working on the combine, readying it for the next day's wheat harvest. "It was a bargain at auction," he said, jumping down off the huge machine. "With some coddling, it'll hold up for the whole harvest." We shook hands. "Ah, so this is a baker's hand," he said gripping my smooth palm with his calloused one. "The baker comes to visit the farmer," he added smiling.

"Finally!" I said.

Marshall gestured toward a deep and wide field of golden wheat and we walked into it. I immediately felt the spongy soil give way under my feet. "We'll harvest this field last," he said, "in about two weeks." We stopped for a moment in golden stalks that touched just under my rib cage. Marshall pulled the head off one stalk and carefully counted the rows of grain. "I get a certain number of grain berries per stalk, which gives me a number per acre," he said, looking over the wind-bent grasses around us. "I'd guess forty-five bushels per acre for this crop." He squinted into the clear late-afternoon sky and added, "That's if these skies hold up." He told me that around harvesttime there wasn't a farmer or a friend of a farmer who didn't watch the weather carefully. "There's a lot of praying going on around here right now. This warm dry weather is exactly what we need. One big rain and the harvest is an impossible mess."

We trudged through rustling wheat until the stalks measured high on my chest. I felt the heat radiating from the thick forest of grain around me. "This is the field that we'll harvest tomorrow," he said. I almost knew it before he had said it because a pungent grassy fragrance made the whole field smell ripe. A family of partridge suddenly flew up out of the stalks, startling me. Marshall told me the fields were full of birds that eat the insects and worms that thrive in the organic soil.

Marshall's dad had been a cattle rancher, but Marshall had always wanted to grow grain. "There's something about producing such a bounty," he said. "Look at all of this. You get much more per square foot wheat farming than you do cattle farming. And cattle are noisy. Listen," he said. We were quiet for several moments, listening only to the wind through the wheat.

Marshall farmed commercial fields at first, until Janice became sick from the sprays and his children developed allergies. He turned to organic farming in order to get out of harm's way, and in the process discovered it was the only way to take better care of the land.

To show me the difference between an organic field and a commercial one, he drove me to his neighbor, a commercial farmer.

Ingredients: *left column, from top:* cracked rye, rye berries, cracked wheat, whole wheat berries; *second column, from top:* fine semolina flour, buckwheat flour, old-fashioned oats, blue cornmeal, coarse ground cornmeal; *third column, from top:* fine rye flour; medium ground, medium-shade rye flour; fine whole wheat flour; medium ground whole wheat flour; coarse ground whole wheat flour; *fourth column, from top:* all-purpose flour, unbleached flour with germ, homemade 20% flour, processed 20% flour; *fifth column, from top:* coarse sea salt, fine sea salt, baker's yeast, Fleischmann's Active Dry Yeast, Fleischmann's Square Yeast; *sixth column, from top:* cardamom seeds, cardamom pods, one vanilla bean

Poolish (page 64)
just mixed

1 hour old

2–3 hours old

5–6 hours, fully
developed

Classic Country-Style Hearth family: *long loaf in center*: Country-Style Hearth Loaf with Herbs and Onions (page 82); *below long loaf, left to right*: two currant rolls, two cumin rolls, Breakfast Loaf with Sesame Seeds and Raisins (page 93), Classic Country-Style Hearth Loaf (page 64), 100 Percent Whole Wheat Cumin Loaf (page 106), Country-Style Hearth Loaf with Dried Figs, Cognac, and Hazelnuts (page 75); *immediately above long loaf, left to right*: Fougasse with Olives (page 205), Country-Style Hearth Loaf with Sun-dried Tomatoes and Thyme (page 79), Wheat and Whole Berry Bread (page 90), Wheat Walnut Loaf (page 99); *top row, left to right*: My Personal Favorite *Pain au Levain* (page 205), Buttermilk Currant Loaf (page 103), Country-Style Hearth Loaf with Cornmeal, Cilantro, and Coarse Pepper (page 72)

Left and bottom: Classic Country-Style Hearth Loaf (page 64). Notice the bubbly texture in the grain of the loaf, a trademark of the *poolish*.

Coarse-Grain Norwegian Farm Loaf (page 86)

Summer picnic in the Catskill Mountains, New York. *Top:* Classic Country-Style Hearth Loaf with Herbs and Onions (page 82); *on tray, from left:* 100 Percent Whole Wheat Cumin Loaf (page 106), Country-Style Hearth Loaf with Sun-dried Tomatoes and Thyme (page 79), Country-Style Hearth Loaf with Dried Figs, Cognac, and Hazelnuts (page 75)

Top left: Wheat Walnut Loaf (page 99); *top right:* 100 Percent Whole Wheat Cumin Loaf (page 106); *bottom left:* Breakfast Loaf with Sesame Seeds and Raisins (page 93); *bottom right:* Country-Style Hearth Loaf with Dried Figs, Cognac, and Hazelnuts (page 75)

Freshly baked
Buttermilk Currant
Loaves (page 103). The
currants make the
poolish denser.

Bernard Lebon at his
bakery, *Au Panetier* in
Paris, loading *couche*
raised loaves onto a
peel.

The sourdough rye family: *top row, left to right:* Summer Herb Rye (page 150), Sourdough Rye with Currants loaf (page 141), Sourdough Rye with Caraway Seeds (page 128), Coarse-Grained Rye with Cracked Rye Berries (page 131); *middle row, left to right:* Rye with Havarti Cheese (page 157), Finnish Sour Rye Bread (page 164), Sourdough Rye with Potato (page 147), *upper:* Dark Pumpernickel with Raisins (page 137), *lower:* Sourdough Rye with Onion (page 144); *bottom row, left to right:* Lemon Dill Rye (page 160), Vollkornbrot (page 170), 100 Percent Whole Rye (page 167), Sourdough Rye Buns with Currants (page 141), Danish Light Rye (page 134)

Sourdough Rye with Caraway Seeds
(page 128) and sliced Swiss cheese

Dark Pumpernickel with
Raisins (page 137)
cooling on rack

Slices of Vollkornbrot (page 170) with smoked trout, onion, lettuce, tomato, capers, and dill

Dan removing breads from the brick oven at Bread Alone Bakery. Sourdough Rye with Caraway Seeds (page 128) in foreground

Boulanger Basil Kamir in front
of his bakery, Paris

Bakery storefront, Paris

A well-ripened *levain* starter ready to be used (page 185). The bubbly, extremely elastic texture is characteristic of a well-ripened *levain*.

A table full of Basil's *Pain au Levain* (page 189) resting during the second fermentation.

A family of traditional *Pain au Levain: top: Pain au Levain* with Olives and Rosemary (page 193); *middle, on left:* several loaves of Basil's *Pain au Levain* (page 189); *bottom: Fougasse* with Olives (page 208); *center:* Basil's *Pain au Levain* (scored differently); *all breads on right:* several loaves of *Pain au Levain* with Walnuts (page 202)

Fougasse with Olives (page 208) and *Pain au Levain* (page 189) at Le Moulin de la Vierge, rue Vercingétorix, Paris. The oven was built about 1860 by Jean LeFort and Sons.

Close-up of sliced Basil's *Pain au Levain* (page 189).

My Personal Favorite *Pain au Levain* (page 205)

Two four-pound loaves: My Personal Favorite *Pain au Levain* on peel

My Personal Favorite
Pain au Levain loaves
cooling

French baker dusting sourdough
loaves in canvas-lined French willow
baskets. The razor in his mouth is
at the ready for scoring the crusts.

Basil's *Pain au Levain* (page 189) cooling on rack. Raising the dough in German willow baskets causes the coil pattern on the finished breads.

Fougasse with Olives (page 208).
Background poster by Milton Glaser

San Francisco
Sourdough (page 212)

Classic Baguettes
(page 226) being scored
before baking and on
wooden peel straight
from oven

Classic Baguettes baking in ancient oven in southern France

Pain Normande (page 251) with Granny Smith apples and a handmade Laguiole knife

Chocolate-Apricot Kugelhopf (page 258) with dried apricots, coffee beans, and grated chocolate

Semolina Sesame Rolls (page 270) with sesame seeds, semolina and wheat flours, and unbaked semolina dough

Focaccia: counterclockwise from top left: Classic Olive Oil and Salt Topping (page 280), Garlic and Toasted Almond Topping (page 281), Tomato, Olive, Ricotta, and Fresh Herb Topping (page 281), olive oil and rosemary topping

Quick breads in Bread Alone Café: *front:* Angel Biscuits (page 307) and *back:* Savory Drop Biscuits (page 309); *in basket, front to back:* Provolone Sage Corn Loaf (page 316), Lemon Anise Tea Loaf (page 314), Dried Pear, Port, and Poppy Seed Loaf (page 313), Banana Buckwheat Bread (page 312); *on tray:* Vanilla Bean Butter Loaf (page 310)

Equipment: *left column, from top:* oblong baking basket on a baking stone, French-style rolling pin, six-quart ceramic mixing bowl, heavy-duty standing electric mixer; *second column, from top:* French willow basket on baker's peel, four dry measuring cups next to a rubber spatula, four-cup liquid measuring cup, kitchen scale; *third column, from top:* kitchen timer, serrated knife; pastry brush *(left)* and two-quart plastic container with lid, razor blade, dough knife *(left)*, and measuring spoons, two-cup liquid measuring cup *(left)* and oven thermometer, spritzer bottle *(left)*, long-stemmed thermometer *(top)* and room thermometer; *right column, from top:* kugelhopf mold, biscuit cutter, large brioche mold, 9" × 5" loaf pan *(top)* and 8" × 4" loaf pan on a wire cooling rack

There, the earth feeding the wheat was harder and crusty underfoot. There was no rustle of birds among the grain. When I asked why, Marshall said that his neighbor's land had suffered from commercial methods, that he hadn't rotated his crops or planted a cover crop to allow the soil to rest. I reached down as Marshall did and scooped up a handful of the topsoil. It blew from my hand like so much dust. "If we don't take care of the land and take care of it now, who will?" Marshall said. "Who will make sure the soil stays rich and moist and fertile?"

The next day we were up before dawn. Marshall drove the combine, which slowly snapped stalks of wheat, shook the grain berries loose, and spewed them out into the dump truck that Janice drove alongside. The long empty shafts lay collapsed in rows where the day before they had stood growing and ripe. When the wheat berries piled too high in one spot in the truck, my job was to jump in and shovel them even. I loved the feel of the berries around my ankles then up to my knees, the sight of bits of wheat chaff swirling in the wind clouding the air, and the unbelievably wild smell of freshly cut stalks.

I watched Marshall chew a handful of berries. "This is how to tell if it's a good protein wheat," he said. "Spit out the bran," he instructed, as I tried a mouthful. "Then spit out anything that doesn't feel chewy—that's the starch. What you have left is protein. Good gluten." He told me that farmers at harvest will chew it like gum all day long.

When the truck was full of grain, Janice backed it up to one of the silos at the house, and I shoveled the grain into the auger that funneled it into the silo. We worked all day, stopping only for lunch and then continuing until there was no more sunlight. That night I collapsed into sleep, and the next morning as Marshall and Janice headed into the fields, I set out to meet the other farmers on my list. I promised to return and stay longer, which I have done several times since.

Next, I headed southwest to look up two brothers, a farming team. "Oh, you want the Renner brothers' place," said the waitress behind the counter, "Brunell and Bob." I had stopped at a tiny diner in western North Dakota near Dickenson to ask directions. She drew a map on the back of a paper place mat, and when I paid for my coffee, she told me a hailstorm had come through the day before, that she had heard it hurt the Renners' corn crop, but that she hoped it hadn't hurt the wheat; and would I give them her and Harry's best when I saw them? I assumed Harry was her husband, the man at the grill.

I found the farm a half-hour later and the two men, each about fortysomething, were wading in calf-high fields of wheat. "Dwarf wheat," Brunell Renner said after we met. "This is about as big as it gets." They had a good growing season and were looking forward to a bountiful harvest. How different it felt to be taking small, careful steps through the grain field after trudging in the thick heat of the Kargus fields. Except for the hailstorm that had riddled their popcorn crop with holes, they had no bad luck. They were pleased to get the greetings from the diner folk in town.

Brunell and Bob Renner have been organic farmers all their farming lives, and they told me they've had to put up and deal with worse things than a hailstorm. Fortunately, their experiment with dwarf wheat is paying off. Each season they are able to grow more wheat per acre than they had grown with standard wheat. And the grain is just as protein-rich. My visit with them was brief. Since their harvest was two days off, I spent the night, and the next morning I left for my farthest destination, eastern Montana and my next host, Karl Swenson.

By the time I drove into the small town near Miles City, in the grain belly of Montana, I was keenly aware that things had not been going well in this farming community. The fields looked stunted and dry. Tumbleweeds blew across empty streets of town and the train station and several shops were boarded up.

The diner, however, being knowledge-central in these farming towns, was open and busy: several pickup trucks were parked out front. Inside I sat at the counter, ordered some breakfast, and listened. Several tables were full of men eating pancakes and eggs, and talking harvest—weather, combines, silos. The local morning news came on the television set, which sat on top of the cigarette machine. The commodities report listing the falling prices of grains drew moans from everybody. Then I listened to three men sitting at the counter near me try to make a deal with a farmer sitting with them. They were freelance harvesters—kind of a Have-Combine-Will-Travel service. When the crop was ready, they said, they'd show up with their combines and harvest for the farmer. The farmer said he wasn't sure his wheat would make it to harvest.

Then the news reported "yet another loss of another farm to the bank." The video footage showed a farmer leaving his house with the marshal. The entire diner was silent. No one spoke or moved; there was no tinkling of glasses or silverware, nothing. The waitress stood still and the cook stepped closer to the television. I heard somebody speak under his breath, "No one east of the Mississippi can know what it's like."

I got directions to the Swenson farm, this time from one of the patrons. And in a little while I was approaching the tractor barn where Karl Swenson was working. He is a tall red-faced Norwegian, and was wearing faded coveralls. He had been organic farming for a dozen years, he told me.

"It hasn't been good here," he said, explaining the general despondency in the air. "We've had two years of grasshoppers. For two years in a row we have lost the harvest to them." We walked in one of his fields. The morning sun was bright in a clear blue sky. "Finally, this year the grasshoppers aren't so bad," he said. We rustled as we walked through the waist-high plants, and hundreds of grasshoppers suddenly sprang up in a cloud so thick it grayed the air for a moment. I was astounded that Karl thought this display of plague wasn't "so bad." He said that during the first year the grasshoppers were so dense that daytime was as dark as night. He blamed the commercial farming techniques for the grasshopper proliferation. "Those farmers don't rotate crops," he said. "And they never let the field sit." He told me this is why the insects had a steady and predictable place to live and breed. Swenson was hoping at best for a meager harvest, and was looking forward to the next season.

At the bakery that fall and winter I used flour stone-ground from Marshall Kargus's grain and from the Renner brothers' dwarf wheat harvest. And things did get better for Karl Swenson. One year later I bought flour stone-ground from his first full harvest in three years.

In the early hours at the bakery, while I wait for the breads to rise and for the ovens to come to temperature, I think about those farmers and all the other organic farmers who have taken on the stewardship of our farmlands. They are the country's caretakers.

I'm a thousand miles away from the grain lands now, but the closer I stay to using only flour from whole grain grown in simple, organic partnership with the environment, the better my breads taste and look. And I feel connected to the whole process of making a loaf of bread, from the earth to the grain, to the flour to the dough, to the fire, and finally to the loaf. That makes me happy. I'm part of it *all*.

When you and I buy organic flour, we produce good-tasting breads *and* we support these farmers, the stewards of our land. We become stewards of the stewards, taking care of a vital source of ours, the vibrant good earth and grain.

▇ THE GRAIN ▇

I can't resist. I'm in my own bakery, walking by a large bin filled with thousands of tiny wheat berries. I plunge. Both hands go deep, up to my elbows. A tingle rushes up my arms and I feel the delight I always feel as I scoop up from deep within the bin. Slowly, very slowly, my hands emerge overflowing. I inhale. The fragrance is earthy, sweet. It's the very aroma that compels young children to make mud pies and their parents to take long walks after a heavy rain. There are hundreds and hundreds of perfectly formed grains spilling from my cupped palms. I feel like a man playing in gold.

I'm definitely not the first to take in the pleasure and power of the grain. The Pharaohs of Ancient Egypt were entombed with jars of barley grains to sustain their lives in the next world. The Greeks honored Demeter, the goddess who gave (or didn't give) an abundance of growing grain. The Aztecs built temples in which they stored grain. For 6,000 years agrarian and nomadic cultures and tribes have built entire economic, spritual, and political systems based on the power of a tiny grain.

I have stood in the wheat fields of North Dakota where stalks grow shoulder high and the heat and fragrance from the plants could seemingly make one drunk. Out there, the prize of the plant—the tiny wheat berry—is hidden, protected by the tough outer husk. Thirty to forty such berries are tucked in ten to fifteen neat symmetrical rows on the head of one slender stalk of grain. During the harvest, the berries are shook from their husks, and eventually thousands of bushels of the naked grains fill huge truck bins to the brim.

Wheat and other grains have grown wild all over the world for 50,000 years. But somewhere around the time of the Paleolithic peoples someone used the grain from a wild crop to plant a field, and thus wheat farming began.

Here in the United States there are particularily fertile growing areas in Kansas, Iowa, Minnesota, North and South Dakota, and Montana—the Grain Belt. Vast open areas ensure plenty of room for abundant fields, and a fairly predictable moderate rainfall creates fertile soil that's neither too dry nor too moist. When the soil is just dry enough, wheat, rye, barley, oats, and corn thrive. The plant sends its roots deep down in search of a little more moisture. This develops strong plants as well as plumper, healthier grain berries.

WHEAT

Wheat is the grain that is the backbone of most yeast breads. A wheat berry (the actual seed that is clustered on the stalk) is an edible power package. Within just one wheat berry is the near perfect balance of nutrients that so efficiently sustained our ancestors. Up to 19 percent of the berry is protein, the remainder being nutritionally valuable complex carbohydrates.

There are three major parts of the berry: the bran, the germ, and the endosperm.

The *bran* is the thin, shiny outer skin of the berry. It consists mainly of cellulose, an indigestible fiber that is good for our digestive system.

The *wheat germ* is the embryo of the berry. It is rich in protein and oil. Since this oil can turn rancid easily, it is especially important to refrigerate wheat germ or any flour that includes the germ in its makeup such as whole wheat flour or organic white flour with germ. (See Buying and Storing Organic Stone-Ground Flours, page 48.)

The *endosperm* nourishes the berry, and makes up the bulk of the grain. When the entire berry is ground, including the bran, germ, and endosperm, the result is whole wheat flour. When the bran and wheat germ are removed, the endosperm that remains is ground to make white flour.

While the endosperm is mainly starch, it also contains the proteins glutenin and gliadin. When these two proteins are moistened, they bond together to form a superprotein called gluten. Gluten provides "muscle" for a yeast dough, a highly valued baking quality. When the dough is kneaded, the gluten develops, forming thin, flexible, weblike strands in the dough. The muscular strands stretch and expand, trapping carbon dioxide as the dough rises during fermentation.

Doughs with well-developed webs of gluten will rise well, producing high, expansive breads with good flavor. Wheat is the only grain that provides such a high proportion of gluten, therefore it is an essential ingredient in making traditional breads.

Wheat has two growing seasons. The wheat planted in the spring produces a hard red berry like the ones I have stored in bins in my bakery. Since this wheat has a long growing period, it develops strength and is quite hearty. It is actually called hard red spring wheat, even though it is harvested in the early fall. The grain is very high in protein—from 12 to 14 percent.

Wheat planted in winter and harvested in spring produces a softer berry with a lower (10 to 11 percent) protein content. This grain is called soft red winter wheat.

Whole wheat berries are available in bulk at your local natural foods store. (Many cooks simmer the whole grains as a nutrition-packed side dish.) Brands that are simply marked "hard wheat berries" are usually the high-protein spring wheat berries. These are often stirred into bread doughs to add extra protein, fiber, and a strong wheaty flavor to the loaf as well as a substantially delicious chew to the crumb. They are usually softened by soaking overnight in water.

Cracked wheat is exactly what the name suggests: the whole berry, coarsely cracked. I also keep a bin of it at the bakery to add to doughs and sprinkle on crusts. It gives the final loaf a rustic look, a delectable habit-forming chew, and extra nutty flavor. It, too, is available at natural foods stores. (Don't get it mixed up with bulgur, which is cracked wheat that has been parcooked by steam, then dried and packaged.)

RYE

Rye has always grown amid wheat, being a heartier and more insistent plant—a weed, really. At one time Eastern European farmers tried to remove it from cultivated wheat crops, but eventually they gave up as the rye persisted, growing faster than they could remove it. They began simply to harvest it with the wheat, milled the combined grains, and called the end product "rye flour." While rye still manages to grow renegade with wheat, it is most often cultivated on its own. Today's rye flour is 100 percent rye without the adulterating wheat.

Rye contains very little gluten, so rye breads are often created using a high proportion of gluten-strong wheat flour to assure a well-risen loaf. Breads that are completely rye will not rise very much, but they will have a hearty, intriguing flavor. Be warned that dough with rye flour behaves differently from regular wheat doughs; it will be very tacky and rise at leisure. Do not add too much additional flour to these doughs if they feel sticky, or you will get a heavy, sodden loaf. Very sticky doughs will be easiest to manipulate if you use a dough knife as an aid to turning and kneading the dough. As long as the dough is not sticking excessively to your work counter, it is firm enough.

Rye berries are the dark brown whole grains from the rye stalks. Although each grain delivers only 7 percent protein and virtually no gluten, the fragrant benefit of adding rye to breads is remarkable. I will open the bin of cracked rye at the bakery just to catch a whiff of wild fields pungent with a tangy soured smell that teases my nostrils. I will add the soaked softened whole grain and the cracked rye berries to breads for the extra nutrition, distinct toasted aroma, and subtle bite in flavor.

Cracked rye is not as easy to find in natural foods stores as cracked wheat. Some mills grind whole rye berries, bran and all, to a very coarse meal, which is often called *pumpernickel rye flour.* (Pumpernickel bread does not come from the "pumpernickel" grain. The name derives from a German, Herr Pumpernickel, who popularized this dark, hearty bread many years ago.) However, beware, because each miller will grind pumpernickel to a different coarseness, and the berries may be ground into a medium-coarse flour rather than a meal. If you can't find cracked rye at the store, the most reliable way to prepare it is to use a grain mill, passing the berries through the coarsest setting. Or use a blender, electric coffee grinder, or food processor fitted with the metal chopping blade to process the berries in small batches, allowing the machine to run a minute or two to be sure the grains are cracked to less than ⅛ inch long. The nontechnological method uses a heavy cast-iron frying pan to crush the berries on a hard work surface.

OTHER GRAINS

While wheat and rye make up the bulk (literally) of my breads, I will often accent their flavors with other grains.

Corn is native to the Americas. According to archeologists, the Aztecs grew sacred forests of the yellow grain. The kernel, just like the wheat berry, is a whole package of complex carbohydrates. Cornmeal comes in a variety of colors, the shade determined by local availability and preference. For example, Yankees and much of the rest of the country cook with yellow cornmeal, yet Southerners like white cornmeal and southwestern Native Americans use blue cornmeal. The yellow and blue are the most flavorful, but you may have to add a little more fat to the recipe if you use the blue variety. Cornmeal adds a rich, sweet taste to the crumb and gives a rugged look to the crust.

Cornmeal is a very important grain to bakers. To discourage the shaped loaves from sticking to the work area while they rise, dust the surface lightly with cornmeal first. If finely ground wheat flour is used, it can be absorbed into the dough, making the loaves difficult to transfer to the peel. The cornmeal won't be absorbed, and the loaves won't stick. Semolina also works in the same manner.

Oats came to the New World with the early Puritan settlers and quickly took root. The grain is called the groat, and is packed with B vitamins, vitamin E, minerals and iron, a great deal of soluble fiber, and a fair amount of protein. I use cracked groat (also called steel-cut oats), which have been dried, then sliced lengthwise. Like wheat and rye berries, these are soaked before adding to doughs; they contribute a particular sweet and nutlike flavor, and a woody fragrance with crunch. I also sprinkle the familiar rolled oats, which is often cooked into oatmeal, on top of some breads for a classic country appearance. Instant or quick oatmeals are too delicate for my bread recipes.

Buckwheat is actually a grasslike herb, related to sorrel, and is appreciated by Eastern European bakers for its slightly sour flavor. Buckwheat flour is an attractive tan color, speckled with dark brown. I use it in my Banana Buckwheat Bread (page 312), but you can add it to yeast breads, too. Substitute no more than 20 percent of buckwheat for regular wheat in the recipe. If you add more, the taste will be too strong and will overpower the other flavors, especially if combined with rye. If you wish to experiment with different flours, this "20 percent" rule applies, since more than that will affect the gluten content in the bread, resulting in a heavy loaf.

▪▪ STONE MILLING ▪▪

They are two round granite stones the size and shape of truck tires. Each weighs several hundred pounds and is cold to the touch. Fitted with hardware, one rotates slowly while pressed heavily against the other. When the miller layers whole grains between the stones, the first turns produce great cracking sounds as the berries are broken into thousands of coarse chunks. That rough meal falls from the outer edges and down through the center hole of the grinding stones and is collected beneath. It is ground again and again until it is the textured flour that the miller wants—some coarse, some very fine.

When I open a sack of stone-milled flour, a wheaty aroma is at first subtle then very strong, permeating the air in seconds. I can't help but grab a handful of the fresh flour; it's moist between my fingers and nutty sweet on my tongue.

Stone milling is the oldest, slowest, and best method of grinding whole grains into the dense and creamy flour I use for my breads. It is a gentle and cool process that preserves every good part of the grain—the entire berry is homogeneously transformed into flour. All the protein, oils, and vitamins from the germ, all the sugars and starches from the endosperm, and the tiny bits of bran are there in the final wheaty fresh flour. High in nutrients and rich in protein, it has powerful bread-making qualities.

These stone mills exist all over the United States. Some are so old that the turning of the stones is still powered by water flowing in a stream or by wind turning a windmill. Some ancient mills turn because a horse or a mule, walking in circles, is attached to the pole that turns the rod that rotates the stones. But because of the growing popularity of good-tasting flour, more and more new stone mills are popping up near large urban areas. The new mills may have several pairs of stones electrically motorized.

A stone miller buys grain by the bushel from farmers. He then grinds it only when he feels he can sell the flour because the oils in the germ make the flour perishable. One of the millers I use is in nearby Syracuse. I know that when I get a shipment from him, the wheat has been ground perhaps only the day before he sent it to me.

The very existence of stone mills was threatened in the middle of this century by the high-speed roller mills commonly used by commercial flour makers. Steel rollers or hammers mill the grain at a remarkably high speed. More machines remove the germ and all bits of bran from the flour. Operating at high temperatures, the mills destroy many of the vitamins in the berry. The flour is bleached white with chemicals, bromated with potassium, enriched with minerals and some of the vitamins lost in the milling, and finally packaged. This treatment guarantees a long shelf life because the perishable oils in the germ have been removed. It also promises an abundance of flour on supermarket shelves because roller milling is fast. Unfortunately, it creates a flour that to me tastes and feels like dust.

The stone mills, however, like the tortoise in the fabled race with the hare, do their work slowly and surely. The natural coolness of the stones never robs the grain of its vitamins or essential oils, so the flour the miller sends me is fresh, full of nutlike flavor, and has the nutritional power of the whole berry.

The Appendix lists mills and millers that grind organic grains and that will ship via mail order, if your local natural foods store doesn't already carry them. If you can get to know the millers, they will help your baking and your breads.

▪▪ INGREDIENTS ▪▪

THE FLOUR

Organic, stone-ground wheat produces rich flour that varies in color from dark brown, to light caramel, to very light beige or cream—but it is never bright white. I strongly urge you to search out these excellent flours; they make unsurpassable breads. On the following pages I have supplied brand names for each type of flour used in the book; if you can't find them at your local natural foods store, many can be mail ordered from the list on page 322. They are the only kinds of flour I use at my bakery, and once you have tried them, you will immediately see a marked improvement in your bread baking.

This does not mean that you can't make these breads with ordinary supermarket flour! I do believe, however, that if you're going to take the time and put forth the effort to bake with just four basic ingredients—flour, water, yeast, and salt—you should get the best!

The very best all-around bread flour is from organic and stoneground wheat because it contains the most gluten—the superprotein that gives resilience and toothsomeness to baked loaves.

Flour can be ground from either hard red spring or soft red winter wheat. I use wheat flour, either whole wheat or unbleached white, ground from hard red spring wheat in all my traditional country breads because the protein count is higher—12 to 14 percent for every four ounces of flour. More protein generally means more gluten, which means my breads will be high, thick-crusted, and full of fresh grain flavor.

Soft red winter wheat flour, with its lower protein count (10 to 11 percent), is blended with high-protein flour to make a lighter all-purpose flour that is best for more delicate quick breads and pastries.

Short of sending your flour out to a laboratory for analysis, or interrogating your miller, how do you determine the protein and gluten content of your flour? The information is listed on the nutritional analysis label located on the side of most packaged flours. But be sure the figures are for four ounces of flour. For example, some brands give the analysis for only 2 ounces, so you must multiply that number times two to get the correct percentage—if the protein count is 7 grams for two ounces, multiply by 2 to get fourteen grams for four ounces. This is an important detail because it's easy to misread the label and assume your flour has only 7 grams of protein (too weak for bread making), when actually it has 14 grams (perfect for yeast breads).

An excellent miller will offer coarse, medium, and fine grinds of their flours. However, most of you will be able only to find medium grind, which is an acceptable, all-around coarseness for all of my breads. Again, you get outstanding results from organic, stoneground flours.

After the explanation of each type of flour, specific brands are listed. Each miller will often have a different name for the same kind of flour. Whenever you're in doubt, call the miller and ask him! Mail order sources for the different flours are listed on page 322.

WHOLE WHEAT FLOURS

Stone-ground coarse whole wheat flour is ground from 100 percent of the whole wheat berry, creating a heady light-brown flour. For bread making, be sure the flour has been ground from hard red spring wheat berries. The flour feels gritty when rubbed between your fingers, and the bran is visible in large flecks. During fermentation, these bran flecks help the dough rise because they trap carbon dioxide.

Coarse whole wheat flour produces a bold, chewy, country-style bread like my Coarse-Grain Norwegian Farm Loaf (page 86). It has a full, wheaty flavor and aroma. When I mix the coarse wheat flour with its rye equivalent, as in many of my sourdough ryes, the bread gets the best of both worlds—the dominant tang of rye and the muscular chew of whole wheat.

Coarse whole wheat flour is sometimes labeled Graham flour, named after Dr. Sylvester Graham, a man ahead of his time who prescribed whole-grain flours for healthy digestive tracks. (Yes, he's also the Graham of Graham crackers.) Unfortunately, like other varieties of the milling business, you can't be guaranteed that your miller's Graham flour will be sufficiently coarse. If you can't locate coarse whole wheat flour, a medium or fine grind is acceptable.

FLOUR BRANDS

Giusto's Whole Wheat Hi Protein Coarse Flour

Great Valley Hard Whole Wheat (not organic)

Weisenberger's Whole Wheat Flour (hard and coarse; not organic)

Stone-ground fine whole wheat flour also utilizes the entire red spring wheat berry. It is ground more finely than the coarse variety, and will be smooth and creamy to the touch. This is the grind of whole wheat flour you may be most familiar with, since it is the grind found in supermarket brands and in bulk at natural foods store.

FLOUR BRANDS

Giusto's Whole Wheat Hi Protein Fine Flour

Walnut Acres Whole Wheat Bread Flour

Arrowhead Mills Whole Wheat Flour

Pillsbury, Gold Medal, King Arthur, Hecker's, Hodgson Mills, and Ceresota are all supermarket brands of finely ground whole wheat flour, although none are organic and only some are stone-ground.

UNBLEACHED WHITE FLOURS

Stone-ground unbleached white wheat flour with germ is another high-protein (12 to 14 percent) flour made from hard red spring wheat. It is ground wheat flour with all the bran sifted off, but with all the germ remaining. As the sifted flour is stored and ages, it naturally "bleaches" and lightens in color. It was found that aged, bleached flour was easier to manipulate into a dough, so commercial bakeries began to demand the whitened flour. To accommodate this need without the lengthy aging period, chemical methods of bleaching were developed.

I *never* use the stark-white chemically bleached flours. I insist on the cream-colored, naturally bleached variety, which is called "unbleached" merely because it isn't treated with bleaching chemicals. It makes a fine partner with the heavier whole wheat flours, producing light breads with a hearty character. I also mix it with sourdough starter to create a San Francisco sourdough loaf that is extremely light.

When you buy unbleached white (or bread) flour in bulk at the natural foods store, this is normally what you are getting. Supermarket "bread" flour may be unbleached, but it is often conditioned with bromates to bake into light and airy loaves—not the robust, textured breads I love.

Unbleached white flour *without* germ is easy to find, but it may be a little tricky to locate brands with germ. You can make your own by stirring 1 tablespoon of raw or toasted wheat germ into each cup of unbleached white flour.

FLOUR BRANDS

Old Savannah Community Mills Unbleached White Flour with Germ

Arrowhead Mills Unbleached White Flour (without germ)

Great Valley Mills Unbleached Hard Wheat (with germ)

Weisenberger's Unbleached Flour (without germ)

Giusto's Unbleached Hi Protein Hi Gluten Flour (without germ)

Pillsbury, Gold Medal, King Arthur, Hecker's, Hodgson Mills and Ceresota are all supermarket brands of unbleached white flour without germ, although none is organic and only some are stone ground.

Stone-ground all-purpose white wheat flour looks and feels like the bread flour described above. However, it has a low protein count of 10 to 11 percent. It is a mixture of hard red spring and soft winter wheat flours. All of the bran and practically all of the germ has been removed, so it is a very light flour. I use it for delicate breads like the Honey Brioche Loaves (page 240) and quick breads.

This is *not* the whole wheat pastry flour you will see in many natural foods stores, which cannot be used as a substitute, as its protein count is very low. Conversely, the so-called unbleached all-purpose supermarket flours have high protein counts and are best used for bread making. I hate to endorse the overtreated, adulterated supermarket bleached all-purpose flours, but I grudgingly admit that they will do in a pinch. I encourage you to mail order an excellent unbleached all-purpose flour, or ask your natural foods store to order some.

FLOUR BRANDS

Weisenberger Mills All-Purpose White Flour (not organic)

Tuthilltown 1786 Grist Mill All-Purpose Flour (not organic)

Walnut Acres Unbleached All-Purpose Flour Blend

Giusto's Unbleached All-Purpose Flour

Great Valley Farms recommends mixing 70 percent of their Unbleached Hard Wheat Flour with 30 percent of their Unbleached Soft Wheat Flour to create all-purpose flour.

Semolina flour is a granular flour made from durum, a variety of hard wheat, with the bran and germ removed. The term "semolina" refers to the texture of the flour, which is similar to finely ground cornmeal. Like cornmeal, it can be used to sprinkle on the work surface to keep proofing loaves from sticking. Many cooks believe that semolina flour makes the best pasta, so you will often find it labeled "pasta flour." *Durum flour,* which is not used in this book, is a whole grain version with the traditional powderlike flour texture.

FLOUR BRANDS

Giusto's Semolina #1 (not organic)

Great Valley Mills Semolina Flour (not organic)

Weisenberger's Semolina Flour (not organic)

20 PERCENT BRAN WHEAT FLOUR WITH GERM

Stone-ground 20 percent bran wheat flour with germ falls somewhere between whole wheat and unbleached white flour. It is stone-ground from hard red spring berries. Eighty percent of the bran has been sifted off by the miller during the milling process, leaving 20 percent of the bran and all of the germ. It is a high- (12 to 14 percent) protein flour, and feels silkier and smoother than finely ground whole wheat flour. The taste of the wheat grain is fresh, but subtle. I combine it with coarse whole wheat flour to yield breads like my Classic Country-Style Hearth Loaf (page 64), which has a pronounced nutty flavor but a very light and airy crumb. It works fantastically on its own, too, producing chewy *baguettes* and a number of classic French breads, including *Pain au Levain* (page 189).

Unfortunately, you won't find this excellent flour labeled as such, as each mill gives it a proprietary name. I have deciphered the different brands below. The bad news is that you will probably have to mail order it, as few natural foods stores carry it. The good news is, you can make it yourself.

To make your own 20 percent bran wheat flour with germ, combine 3 parts unbleached white flour (preferably with germ) with 1 part stone-ground whole wheat flour, preferably medium or fine grind. This is easiest to do in large batches—3 pounds white flour to 1 pound whole wheat—and mixed with your hands in a transparent glass or clear plastic container so you can see that your blending is thorough. Store the homemade 20 percent bran flour in a covered container as you would any whole-grain flour (see page 48).

FLOUR BRANDS

Giusto's Old Mill Reduced Bran Flour

Walnut Acres Unbleached Bread Flour

RYE FLOURS

I use two grinds of rye flour for my recipes, and both are created from whole rye berries. As I stated before, *coarse rye flour* is often labeled "pumpernickel," indicating that the whole rye berries have been roughly processed into a meallike flour. *Fine rye flour* is smooth textured, like the fine whole wheat flour. If you find medium grind rye flour, it is fine as a substitute for either of the other two varieties.

Rye flour can sometimes be designated by color—light, medium, or dark—depending on the amount of bran processed out. They come in coarse, medium, and fine grinds. Most off-the-shelf varieties of rye flour are medium shade, medium grind, which is an excellent middle-of-the-road flour that can be used in all of these recipes. But

WHAT IS "ALL-PURPOSE" FLOUR?

All-purpose flour is named such because the miller wants to convince the baker that this particular flour will make all baked goods equally well. Theoretically, it should make everything from breads to cookies to cakes to pies, and everything in between, because it is a blend of both hard spring and soft winter wheat. But you should pick the proper individual flour to do each job, using hard high-protein flours for hearty breads and lighter all-purpose flours for more tender loaves, cookies, and quick breads. By checking the nutritional labels, you will find that many unbleached all-purpose flours—such as Hecker's, King Arthur, Pillsbury, Gold Medal, and Hodgson Mills—are actually bread flours, rendering the term useless.

FLOUR IS LIKE LIFE— ONLY MORE SO!

When I first started baking with organic flours I wasn't prepared for the surprises. After all, commercial flours, even though they never taste very good as a rule, manage to behave predictably and are durable. Organic flours may, on the other hand, deliver a full earthy taste one season and a subtle wheaty tang the next, depending on how the growing season progressed and how

dark, medium-grind flours, when you can locate them, will give the fullest taste. I don't recommend light ("white rye") flours in any of my recipes, but I list them here to avoid confusion if you order from a mill's catalogue.

FLOUR BRANDS

Giusto's Organic White Rye Flour (light shade, fine grind)

Great Valley Mills White Rye Flour (light shade, fine grind, not organic)

Tuthilltown 1788 Grist Mill Rye Flour (medium shade, medium grind, not organic)

Weisenberger's Rye Flour (medium shade, medium grind, not organic)

Walnut Acres Rye Flour (medium shade, fine grind)

Giusto's Organic Whole Rye Flour (medium shade, fine grind)

Great Valley Mills Dark Rye Flour (dark shade, fine grind, not organic)

Great Valley Mills Pumpernickel Rye Flour (dark shade, coarse grind with added wheat bran, not organic)

Tuthilltown 1788 Grist Mill Pumpernickel Flour (dark shade, very coarse grind, not organic)

BUYING AND STORING ORGANIC STONE-GROUND FLOURS

Buy the freshest flour you can, close to the time you want to use it. Buy from a stone miller, direct by mail order (see page 322), a local whole-grain bakery, or a natural foods store. If you are lucky enough to live in an area with different millers, shop around and try different mills, as flour differs in taste and texture, not only from mill to mill but from harvest to harvest. Speak with authority, using the flour terminology you've acquired from the preceding material, and he or she will give you what you want.

For do-it-yourselfers who want the absolute freshest flour possible, I highly recommend any one of the home mills available. Grind your own coarse or fine whole wheat or rye flour from hard spring wheat berries. Of course, unbleached white flour cannot be produced in a home mill. An excellent mill is available by mail order from Walnut Acres; see page 324.

Organic stone-ground whole-grain flour is full of essential oils and can become rancid in warm temperatures. When shopping in natural foods stores, choose a store that keeps its flours refrigerated or shelved in a cool section. Read the label carefully to be sure you are getting what you are paying for—stone-ground, organic flour—and check the nutritional analysis to guarantee the protein count and gluten amount. Unfortunately, the label won't tell you when the flour was milled, so pick a shop with a fast turnover in flour sales to ensure you are getting the freshest flour possible.

Store whole-grain flours in a cool (40° to 60°F.) place such as the refrigerator or a cool cellar or basement. This keeps the oils from turning rancid, which can happen within two months if left at room temperature. If stored in the refrigerator, keep the flour in an airtight container to avoid unwanted odors.

YEAST

When you bake bread, the minute you add yeast or sourdough starter and water to the flour, a whole series of dramatic changes is triggered. The process of flour transforming itself into bread has begun. Look at it as a living thing that you must treat with care.

Yeast in any form—moist, dry, or wild—is a living community of one-celled microorganisms of the fungus type. The yeast cells are plants that amass on benevolent hosts in order to feed and reproduce. Wild yeast is all around us. The fine white film you see on the surface of fresh grapes is yeast. Louis Pasteur first discovered that this "dust" on the grape was not only alive but also the principal factor in fermentation of the grape. Without these living cells, he observed, no fermentation can take place.

There can be as many as 30 to 60 billion cells in two ounces of yeast. In their moist or dry form the cells are dormant, but when added to warm water and flour they awaken and begin feeding ravenously on the sugars available in the flour. When the flour, yeast, and water are kept covered and undisturbed in a moderate and stable 75° to 80°F. environment, the cells will eat continuously and reproduce every half-hour. The simple by-products of this rapid activity are carbon dioxide and alcohol. In a properly kneaded bread dough with well-developed gluten, the carbon dioxide becomes trapped by the intricate web of glutenous strands; and under moderately warm con-

the fields were fertilized and drained.

One winter, I was turning out very high, aromatic loaves and suddenly they took a turn—the taste was dull and the breads were flat and boring to look at. I called the miller who had sold me the flour and learned that one field had suffered poor drainage. I changed flours and great taste returned.

A baker I know who lives in Paris, and who has been baking for years, so loves to talk about flour that he'll call me just to tell me about the tastes and qualities of the latest milling and the effects of the flour on his breads. Just as the French people love to debate the quality of the new beaujolais each year, my baker friend savors, applauds, or pans his latest delivery of flour. That's the fun of using organic stone-ground flours. Like him, I would rather deal with the unexpected than settle for tasteless or even ordinary bread.

You might find a mill that consistently delivers great-tasting flour, then suddenly it just doesn't taste the same. Chalk it up to a particular field and growing time. Change mills for a while. As you use organic flours, your sensitivity to the taste of different flours will become refined.

ditions, the dough rises slowly but surely. The alcohol permeates and flavors the dough. The living process is called *fermentation* and accounts for most of the time it takes to make a beautiful loaf of good-tasting bread.

Once the yeast triggers the fermentation, at least two phases follow. At first the yeast cells eat and reproduce rapidly, feeding on readily available sugars in the flour. Under moderately warm conditions (about 74° to 80°F.) this takes two to three hours. The dough rises slowly in its bowl because of the trapped carbon dioxide. The other by-product, alcohol, slowly permeates the dough with flavor. When you deflate the dough, separate it, and shape it into loaves, you invigorate the yeast cells by bringing fresh oxygen to the dough and redistributing the food in the flour. The second phase then begins. Now the still-hungry yeasts continue to feed, this time breaking down starches into sugars they can eat through the action of the enzymes present in the yeast. These two phases are called the first rising and the second rising (or proofing). They must be allowed a good measure of time because it is the slow emission of carbon dioxide and the slow permeation by the alcohol that dramatically create the varied texture, wholesome complex flavor, and crusty good look of your bread.

The yeast you use is crucial. It is the spark that ignites the fire or the gas that fuels the engine of fermentation. It must be alive and ready to work. There are three good choices:

I use *moist yeast* (cake yeast or compressed yeast), as do most bakers I know, because I can depend on it for a quick start to a predictable and steady fermentation—100 percent of the cells are usually alive and vigorous. When you sprinkle a pinch of moist yeast in a little warm water, the bubble action is immediate and unmistakably lively. You will find foil-wrapped one-ounce cubes of moist yeast in the refrigerated section of well-stocked grocery stores. If you are lucky enough to have a baker or baking supply firm nearby, buy a one-pound block of moist yeast. It is a firm little brick, light camel in color, and it is possible to cut the brick into economical one-ounce cubes. Wrap each cube tightly in plastic, freeze, and use as you need it, for up to six months.

Dry baker's yeast is sold in four- to eight-ounce airtight bags at good natural foods stores. I like this yeast, too, because it is pure and potent, providing immediate lively action with water and flour, very much like moist yeast does. It is free of preservatives and rapid-rise agents, and the cells remain dependable for up to two months if stored in an airtight container in a cool, dry place—the refrigerator is ideal. If you buy your baker's yeast at a natural foods store, don't confuse it with nutritional or brewer's yeast, which are both dietary supplements and will not leaven dough.

Active dry yeast in ¼-ounce packets that you find in grocery stores is perfectly acceptable and can make very good bread if the cells are all alive. Active dry yeast has a longer shelf life than dry baker's yeast, but it won't last forever. Check the expiration date on the packet. Old yeast cells could be dead or too lethargic to spark and sustain a good fermentation. If you have any doubts about using a packet you have on hand, sprinkle a pinch of the yeast granules in ¼ cup of 100°F. water with a pinch of sugar to proof (or "prove") that it's alive. If there is bubbling and foaming action within ten minutes, the yeast will provide good fuel for fermentation. If you use baker's or active dry yeast it may not dissolve completely in the dough's water during the first stages of the mixing process. Don't be concerned, as it will eventually dissolve. The dough's fermentation can be a little sluggish when made with dry yeast, so expect longer rising periods.

Fast-rising yeast—Don't buy it! Fast-rising yeast is treated with conditioners that accelerate the activity of the yeast and give the baker less control over the process. Even many of the imported European yeasts that you'll find in specialty food stores are fast-rising yeasts. Don't be tempted to try them. We are going to be making *slow*-rising breads. Fermentation with fast-rising yeast robs bread of good texture and flavor.

PURE SPRING WATER

Regular tap water may be treated with purifying chemicals and fluoride, which can sometimes inhibit the action of the yeast during fermentation. Use the purest water you can find. Spring water, not to be confused with distilled water, is ideal and is inexpensive when purchased by the gallon from your supermarket.

SEA SALT

Salt is an essential ingredient in bread making. It retards the yeast activity just enough so that the fermentation is moderately slow. The yeasts are searching for sugars to feed on, and the salt in the dough makes them work harder. If there weren't salt, the fermenting dough could rise above the rim of the bowl very quickly.

Use *sea salt* because it is the purest, best-tasting salt you can find. There are no preservatives added, and because it is derived from natural evaporation of seawater that has collected in shallow pits and basins, it brings a flavor to the bread that rock salt doesn't. Don't confuse it with Kosher or coarse salt, which is similar in texture but derived from rocks, not the sea.

Buy sea salt in any good natural foods store or in a well-stocked supermarket. It is available in both coarse and fine varieties. Fine sea salt will dissolve perfectly in your dough. Coarse sea salt crystals are too chunky to mix into a dough, but can be ground in a salt mill, which is like a pepper mill.

▪ EQUIPMENT ▪

Keep it simple. Most traditional professional bakers have no more equipment than the home baker: an electric mixer, a work table, a few sharp knives for dividing the dough, a thermometer, a timer, some treasured containers for the dough to rise in, and well-used cabinets, often thermostatically controlled, where the loaves proof. Professionals make bread in a kind of ritual—they place the dough in the same vats for rising in the same corner of the bakery, day in and day out. Many home bakers instinctively do the same thing. They possess only a few pieces of equipment and they use them all the time. Here's what you need:

A large (six-quart) clay, wood, or ceramic bowl for mixing the dough and for allowing it to rise. This provides a stable environment that doesn't change temperature quickly. Use this same bowl again and again. (I still use the one I bought in college.) If you simply scrape the bowl with a plastic scraper, wipe it clean with a damp cloth, and avoid detergents, it will become well seasoned: Surviving yeast cultures remain in the bowl because you can never kill off all the yeast cells. The old cells enhance the fermentation process and help build flavor in the next dough. If you develop the baking habit, your whole kitchen will be full of yeast cells eager to help your next breads develop.

I arrived on my first day of teaching at the Culinary Institute of America in Hyde Park, New York, with dough I had mixed at my bakery. I placed it to rise in their brand-new, sterilized, never-before-used containers. The fermentation that day was dull—nowhere nearly as energetic as in my own bakery. When it came time to form the loaves and set them to proof in the brand-new proofing cabinets—the same model I use at my bakery—there was not the vitality I was used to. The fermentation took a lot longer than I had anticipated. It was very slow and lethargic. I had to coax and coddle the breads, moving the cabinets closer to the ovens, then back again when I thought they might be too warm. The breads turned out well, but only because I was vigilant about watching and adjusting the temperature and time. It reminded me again of how alive bread is and how sensitive it is to its environment.

A scale is vital. I like the ultra-precise Pelouzi Balance Beam, but home bakers will do fine with a small spring scale. Bakers are incredibly precise about their ingredients. They weigh everything. It's more reliable and specific than a measuring cup, and it ensures proper absorption. If you can be content with weighing ingredients, you will find that you are much less anxious about the quantities. But remember that the exact flour weights vary from brand to brand and also with humidity.

Measuring cups and spoons are helpful. Although I encourage the use of a scale to measure dry ingredients, I realize some of you may prefer to use measuring cups. That's fine if you take the precaution to use dry metal or plastic measuring cups for dry ingredients and transparent liquid measuring cups (preferably glass) for liquids.

A board or countertop space 3 × 2 feet is essential. Any space as long as it is hard and clean will do. It must also be stable and secure enough to support you and the dough during the kneading process. A wobbly tabletop will not do. Wood, marble, Formica, and stainless-steel surfaces are all fine. Be sure your kneading area is about waist high. Sometimes a couple of inches makes all the difference in avoiding kneading fatigue. I know shorter bakers who stand on sturdy, shallow boxes in order to reach a comfortable level.

Thermometers are important for the new as well as the experienced baker. You need to know the temperature of everything—the room, the water, the flour, the finished dough, the oven—in order to make successful loaves. Buy a good *room thermometer*, an *oven thermometer*, and a *long-stemmed thermometer* that reads from 0° to 200°F. to stick deep into the flour and the dough. Mercury thermometers are generally more reliable than spring-based models, but the instant-read long-stemmed thermometers are easy to find and perfect for taking dough temperature readings.

A heavy-duty, standing electric mixer like KitchenAid with a dough hook gives you an option to kneading by hand, but is not vital. Except for some of my sweet doughs, which are too moist and sticky to work by hand, all my breads can be successfully kneaded by hand.

A timer! I use a digital cooking timer that can be set for hours. There are multiple-setting timers that allow you to time three items at once—perfect when you are preparing a number of dishes and fermenting dough, too.

An assortment of different size bread pans provide variety. Cast-iron is best because it holds the heat very well, but they are difficult to find (see mail order listings, page 322). Second-best is heavy-gauge aluminum (from ½ to ¾ cm thick) rectangular pans in large (9 by 5-inch), medium (8 by 5-inch), and small ("mini," 5 by 3-inch) sizes. If you use glass loaf pans, which are a distant third best, reduce the oven temperature by 25°F.

The most common bread-pan sizes are 9 by 5 inches (8 cups) and 8 by 4 inches (6 cups). Measurements often vary from the standard by ½ inch; don't worry about it.

Baskets are a tradition among bakers. Many line them with canvas and raise the dough in them. A soft, moist dough, such as a *levain*, needs the support of the basket until the fermentation takes over and the carbon dioxide–gluten partnership holds the bread shape on its own. In European bakeries there are beautiful *willow baskets* made especially for certain breads such as the German sourdough ryes and the French *miche*. But you can take any basket or bowl with a diameter of 8 inches and a depth of 3 to 4 inches, and lay inside a clean, lightweight linen towel dusted with flour. By letting the dough rise in a cushioned, floured container, you'll get a loaf that will take on the shape and markings of the basket, and the crust will be thicker and bolder because extra flour is embedded in the dough as it rises. This creates a rustic, earthy-looking crust.

Couche is French for "couch" or "resting place." This is a simple holding device you make yourself for proofing long loaves like logs, torpedo shapes, and *baguettes*. Using well-floured canvas or linen towels (don't use fluffy towels or you'll get lint in your dough), create folds to separate loaves while holding them securely next to each other during proofing. Use a length of fabric at least a yard long. I have a friend who uses the bottom half of a bib apron—it's the perfect size. Place 12- to 16-inch wooden blocks cut from 2-by-4s at either long end to contain the loaves. Even city dwellers can find a lumber or hardware shop to cut wooden blocks in the appropriate size. Or substitute stacks of large books to contain the loaves.

A *homemade hearth* can be created by the home baker to benefit from the advantages of a professional brick oven. It's easy to make a hearth with terra-cotta tiles. This is very important because a good clay or brick baking surface hits the breads with intense and immediate heat creating "oven spring." This boosting effect creates the high loaves and chewy crusts of successful breads. Place thick 6-inch-square terra-cotta tiles to cover the center rack of your oven. The number of tiles you use will depend on the size of the rack. The center placement is important. If you use the bottom rack, the bottom crust of the breads will tend to burn; if you use the top rack, the top crusts will tend to burn. If the tiles are brand-new, heat them once or twice at moderate temperatures as a way of seasoning them so that they don't crack or break.

Another choice is two or three refractory bricks. These are the 1½-inch-thick bricks used to build furnaces. I use them in my oven at home. And yes, if you're wondering, simple red builder's bricks will also do and the irregularities in their surface will give your breads interesting bottom crusts. Sometimes the name of the brick company becomes part of your bread.

Once you've fit your oven rack with a hearth, you can leave it there. Anything you have to bake or roast in the oven will do well on the hearth.

There are also stone hearths for sale in gourmet cookware stores for baking pizza. These are terrific, but a word of caution: when they are new, like the terra-cotta tiles, they tend to be brittle at high temperatures and they can break. They do get harder with use. I strongly recommend heating a new one once or twice at moderate temperatures as a way of seasoning it before using it at higher temperatures. Be sure to buy the largest one you can find. A good size is 15 inches square and at least ½ inch thick.

However you arrange it or whatever you choose, be sure to bake your breads on a stone or clay surface rather than on a metal baking sheet. Stone holds the heat, transfers it immediately to the ready-to-bake breads, and helps produce the large and beautiful well-risen loaves you want. When you want to clean the stone, let it cool completely, then scrub under cold water. Do not use soap, as its taste will be soaked up by the porous stone. Don't worry if the stone becomes stained. (See page 321 for sources.)

EQUIPMENT: THE NEW DEVELOPMENTS

There are home bakeries on the market: small boxlike machines that assemble, knead, ferment, and bake bread for you. My feeling is that at least they are bringing the smell of freshly made bread back into the home. So hooray for that! But using these machines is like riding a stationary bicycle. You go through some motions but get nowhere. The breads they produce have soggy, colorless crusts and are so bland-tasting that the machine quickly ends up on a shelf in the garage.

A backyard brick oven is for the zealous home baker who wants the whole brick-oven advantage. I suggest that you build your own—I did.

A spritzer bottle filled with cold water provides the steam breads need as they bake.

A very sharp thin-bladed or serrated knife is necessary for cutting the risen dough into loaf quantities or balls and for scoring the loaves. If you can find a long old-fashioned straight razor, it does a great job, as do single-edged razor blades and X-acto knives.

A dough knife, which is also called a pastry scraper or a bench knife, is a rectangular steel blade about 4 by 5 inches with a wooden handle on the long edge. I use it to lift soft or sticky doughs during the kneading. It's also great for scraping up any excess dough when cleaning the work space.

A bench brush is used to clean up excess flour in your work area and for brushing baked scorched flour off the hearth. They are available in restaurant supply shops. A wide paintbrush works well, too.

A baker's peel—the thin, flat piece of wood used for putting your loaves onto the hearth—can be found in any good cookware shop. The one I use at the bakery is on a 14-foot pole. At home the peel is considerably smaller! Buy one with a paddle that is at least 12 inches square.

If you don't want to buy a peel, you can improvise with a thin piece of Masonite or any scrap wood that can do the job. A rimless baking sheet will also do the job.

TIME AND
■ TEMPERATURE ■

These are really the most important tools of the baker. In my own experience I've gone full circle, from baking wonderful breads to lousy breads, to good breads to okay breads and back to wonderful breads for about two or three years. Along the way I wondered what it is that makes bread wonderful. When I was satisfied that the ingredients were the best I could buy, I focused on the process. I discovered that the secret was in my own hands. My precise and consistent vigilance over the process—exercising control over how long the dough fermented and at what temperatures, and manipulating the degree of heat or cold while the breads proofed—created handsome, seductive-looking loaves with full, sweet grain flavor. Wonderful bread!

Any successful baker must first be a scientist and technician in order to emerge as an artist who can create a beautiful loaf of bread. The baker who adheres to disciplines of careful awareness and manipulation of method will make consistently good bread. The paradox is, as you become more precise you also become more creative. When you control the tools of time and temperature, your breads thrive. Believe me, being careful and technically precise does not take the poetry or romance out of making bread. It enhances it.

TIME

Making good bread isn't so much work as it is wait! I just can't impress enough on new bakers that there is a great, great difference between a dough that ferments too quickly in too warm a place and one that ferments slowly at a more moderate temperature.

In the first case, the process is swift and accelerated. Boosted by high temperature, the yeast cells are much more active and vigorous than at the cooler temperature. When the dough is too warm, the fermentation is chaotic and out of control. It's like a car without a driver, gaining speed down a long hill. The dough suffers from too much of a good thing: it rises quickly and is, in fact, worn out and exhausted—what we call "old dough"—before it ever gets in the oven. Because the yeast is worn out, the loaves don't bake well; they are gassy, the flavor is unfocused, and the texture is tough. The crust becomes soft and soggy the day after baking.

On the other hand, dough that has fermented slowly will be well developed yet lively when it's ready to bake. The acids produced have had time to permeate the dough with flavor, and the gases have created a dense but light texture. Because the fermentation has been slow and even, when these breads hit the high heat of the oven there is enough vigor left in the yeast to provide a final burst of activity. This burst is called *oven spring,* and is a highly desired baking quality of dough. It creates the small irregular air holes in the crumb, the great loft, and a substantial crust that are the relished characteristics of traditional breads.

74 IS THE MAGIC
NUMBER

I use a specific temperature range (74° to 80°F.) to specify the moderately warm atmosphere that ensures your dough will rise to perfection. The magic number is 74. Below 74°, your breads will rise *too* slowly; above 80°, and the dough will rise rapidly and overferment. Use a room thermometer for your kitchen's actual temperature. The phrase "moderately warm" is accurate: the room will feel somewhat warm, but not as warm as the infamous "warm, draft-free space" of other bread cookbooks, which is more like 90°F. If you use the temperatures in the recipes, your breads should rise in the prescribed time frames. The idea is to manipulate both the dough and the kitchen temperatures. In a bakery we do this with electric thermostats in our proofing cabinets, but you can do the same without resorting to electricity. After the first couple of breads, this will become second nature.

WHAT IS YOUR REAL FRICTION FACTOR?

The *friction factor* is the number of degrees that the dough temperature will rise during the kneading process. Generally, the dough will rise 1°F. per minute of mixing or kneading. In my home and in my bakery, the friction factor is 14°F. You will have to make bread a couple of times, inserting a thermometer in the dough before and after you knead or mix it. I have seen some machines mix the dough so roughly that the temperature goes up 25°. Some

TEMPERATURE

It is the temperature of the dough and the room that determines the speed, intensity, and eventual time of fermentation. If you can manipulate this variable, you encourage a regulated and nurturing fermentation.

Generally, for most of the breads in this book the ideal temperature during fermentation is 80°F. In a perfect world, all our elements—air, flour, and water—would be 80°F. when we stir them together. But this is never the case. Your flour and spring water may have been refrigerated at 45°F., and your kitchen may be 82°F. So how can you manage the disparity? In many cases, the temperature of the water is the primary variable. Here is a scientific formula to help you exert control over the temperature of the ingredients by changing the temperature of the water or other liquid ingredients.

Temperature	of the flour
Temperature	of your kitchen
+ 10° to 14°F.	friction factor (this is the amount
Total	of heat the dough will gain simply from being mixed or kneaded) (See What Is Your Real Friction Factor? at left.)

Subtract this total from 240°F., which would be the ideal total if all ingredients were 80°F. The new number indicates what temperature to make the water you combine with the flour.
For example:

60°F.	flour temperature
80°F.	kitchen temperature
+ 14°F.	friction factor
154°F.	total

Then,

240°F.	ideal total
−154°F.	real total
86°F.	temperature to make the water

Now you know that you have to heat the water slightly before adding it to the other ingredients. Dissolve the yeast in the 86°F. water and add the 60°F. flour in a large bowl in the 80°F. kitchen. The dough should rise slowly at 80°F.—or more realistically, between 74° and 80°F.

It is important to have all your other ingredients at room temperature (*poolish,* nuts, fruits, etc.), so their temperatures will be the same as the kitchen and not throw another factor into your calculations.

When making *poolish,* the temperature of the spring water does not need to be calculated as long as it is at a room temperature of around 75°F. If your spring water is stored in the refrigerator, heat it to around 75°F. before making the *poolish.*

After the dough is kneaded, take its temperature with a long-stemmed thermometer such as an instant-read thermometer. Be sure the thermometer reads from 0°F. to about 220°F. You want the dough to be somewhere between 74°F. and 80°F.—we strive for 78°F. If the dough's temperature is higher than 78°F., place it in a cooler than 78°F. place, such as the refrigerator, a cool spot in the garage or basement, or in a cool closet. If the dough's temperature is below 78°F., place it in a warmer than 78°F. place. Warm places include a spot near a radiator or heater or even near a turned-on clothes dryer. In either scenario—warming up or cooling down—use your room thermometer!

There are exceptions to these rules, but not the goals and general principles of manipulating the time and temperature of the ingredients at hand. Some doughs in this book will get a slower and cooler fermentation.

Some doughs will involve three fermentation phases at different temperatures, instead of the usual two at the same temperature. To create a sourdough requires yet another set of times and temperatures. However, your willingness to use the thermometer and the timer will make a great old-fashioned baker out of you, and produce mouth-watering, eye-pleasing traditional breads.

bakers knead with such energy that the heat increases 20°. It will take you only a couple of loaves to know your own factor. Write it down.

INSTINCTS AND TECHNOLOGY

I asked an old baker in France how to make good bread. "You need three things," he began. We were standing in the bakery where he had worked for forty-five years and he felt the air with his fingertips. "First, you need the proper temperature of the air." Then he waved his hand over the flour. "Second, the proper temperature of the flour. When you know these you add the third—the proper temperature of water. Then you get good bread." This man had been baking so long that he could gauge temperatures with his hands. Until our instincts are as well honed we must use a little technology.

I dropped in to visit an old friend in his bakery on my last trip to Paris. He insists that his young bakers use thermometers at every step. Thermometers were everywhere: hanging from the mixers, sitting in the rising cabinets, hanging on twine around the necks of the bakers.

After years of baking I am just beginning to insist on the same discipline, paying attention to the science of baking as well as the art. At Bread Alone we have found that if we pay strict attention to temperature and time, we can manipulate the lives of our fermenting doughs and create really superb loaves—not just flukes, but consistently great-tasting, great-looking breads.

METHOD

TRADITIONAL WAYS FOR TRADITIONAL BREADS

Hearty eye-catching loaves with the rich taste of whole grain and an earthy fragrance are set apart from modern breads in more ways than appearance and flavor. From the beginning dough through the final baking, these breads have very little in common with modern breads. The difference is in their basic ingredients and traditional method.

■■ THE HANDS ■■

The traditional method requires intimate hands-on involvement of the baker in every phase of the baking: selection and handling of the freshest flour and the purest water, mixing the ingredients, attentive kneading, adjusting the temperature during fermentation, forming the loaves into a variety of shapes and sizes, and placing the loaves in the oven.

▪▪ SLOW FERMENTATION ▪▪

Fermentation of a traditional dough is slow and steady, in a stable environment. *We force a long fermentation* by keeping the temperature down. The dough itself then does the work of creating a rich flavor while it ferments in moderate—sometimes even cool—temperatures. Ironically, the struggle of the living cells in the dough to thrive in moderate conditions produces a light and complex dough, not a tough one. It's much like the struggle that forces the wheat plant to produce a good-tasting grain. When the soil is just dry enough, not too dry, the plant works harder, sending its roots deeper in search of moisture. The deeper the roots, the healthier the plant and its berry. It's the same for a dough that ferments in a not-too-hot, not-too-cold environment. It will take longer, but the final bread will have the good flavor of the grain, a dense crumb with irregular air pockets, and a wonderfully satisfying chewiness.

▪▪ THE *POOLISH* ▪▪

Every traditional baker who produces breads made with yeast saves a small hunk of yesterday's fermented dough to add to today's fresh dough. In a day's time, the piece has continued to ferment, developing a tangy nutty flavor and moisture. Adding it to the new dough creates a moist and light loaf with full-bodied flavor and a crust that is thick, chewy, and crisp. This method of baking with preconditioned dough eliminates the need for the fats, fillers, eggs, milk, and flavorings that are the identifying traits of modern breads.

Since most of you may not be baking with the regularity of a professional, and will not have a bit of yesterday's batch to count on, I will teach you how to make a *poolish*, which is the French word for a premix of fermenting dough.

The *poolish* is a combination of organic flour, water, and yeast—a small amount of soft dough, set aside in a bowl to ferment for a few hours. To the *poolish*, then, you add more flour, water, and yeast to build your final dough.

:: STONE HEARTH ::

Old World breads are traditionally baked on a stone, brick, or tile hearth. The intense and immediate heat of the hearthstone gives the dough a final burst of life that is essential to give a robust look, rich color, and texture to the loaf.

Inside a traditional bakery, the shelves and baskets are full of loaves that are ample-looking. They may be dusted with flour, and sometimes there may be circular ridges imprinted in the crust from where the dough has risen in a willow basket. They have always been formed and scored by hand, so one never looks identical to another. This uniqueness is the most obvious and eye-pleasing trait of traditional breads—and the one, I think, that makes people seek them out or bake them again and again.

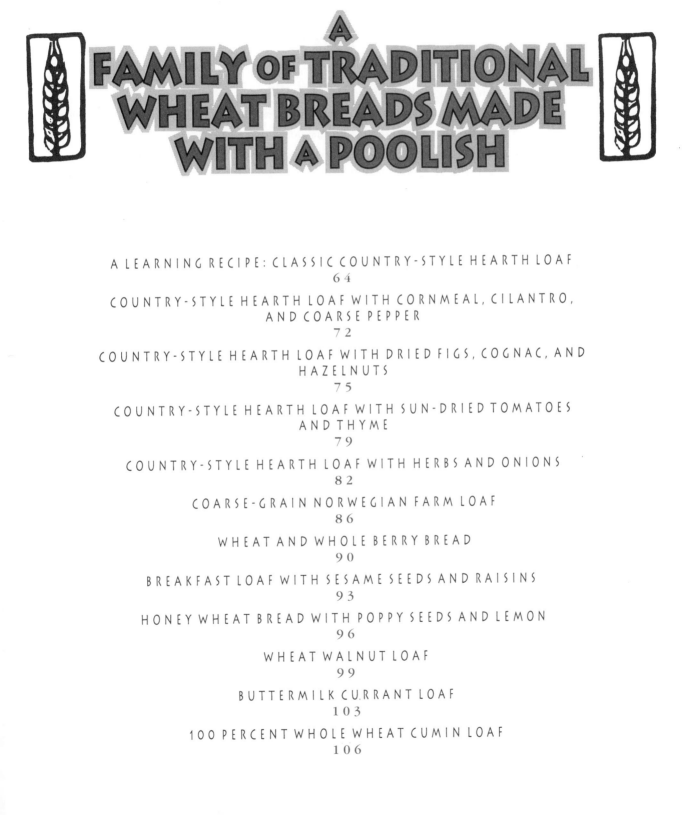

A FAMILY OF TRADITIONAL WHEAT BREADS MADE WITH A POOLISH

A LEARNING RECIPE: CLASSIC COUNTRY-STYLE HEARTH LOAF

Allow 2 to 10 hours to make and ferment the *poolish*.
Total preparation and baking time (not including the *poolish*):
6 hours, 45 minutes

You will want to bake this bread again and again. It is a large, rustic, wheaty-tasting loaf with a golden rugged crust that is both crisp and chewy. The golden crumb is airy light but full-bodied and fragrant. It is a hearty and beautiful loaf much like the peasant breads of seventeenth-century France and Italy. And it is a versatile base on which to develop your own bread repertoire. Slice it to slather with spreads for hors d'oeuvres, or to turn into toast or sandwiches, or tear off hunks of the crumb to mop up sauces, salad dressings, or the last of the stew.

Makes 2 round 10-inch loaves

POOLISH

Spring water (75°F.)	½ cup	4 fluid ounces
Moist yeast	1 teaspoon	¼ ounce
or dry yeast	½ teaspoon	⅛ ounce
20% bran wheat flour	¾ cup	4 ounces

FINAL DOUGH

Spring water	2½ cups	20 fluid ounces
Moist yeast	¼ teaspoon	1/16 ounce
or dry yeast	½ teaspoon	⅛ ounce
20% bran wheat flour*	5¼–6¼ cups	26–31 ounces
Fine sea salt	1 tablespoon	¾ ounce

---

* See Flours (pages 42–49). This is an approximate measure. You may use more or less, depending on the weight and absorbency of your flour.

This is a learning recipe. The bread develops step by step, and I guide you through each step.

1. Fermentation of the *poolish*
2. Mixing and kneading of the final dough
3. First fermentation of the final dough
4. Resting or second fermentation of the final dough
5. Dividing and shaping the dough into loaves
6. Proofing the loaves
7. Baking and cooling the loaves and storage

PREPARATION. Assemble and weigh the ingredients.   I prefer that you weigh everything. Weight is a constant, while measuring cups and cup methods vary too much to depend on. When weighing out your flour, you will find it less messy and very efficient to place a small paper bag, like a lunch bag, in the scale's measuring bowl. Scoop the flour directly into the bag.

If you are using dry measuring cups or spoons, use the dip and sweep method: dip the dry measuring cup or spoon into the flour. Using a thin metal spatula, knife, or even a ruler, sweep the excess off the top so that the flour is level with the rim of the cup or spoon. Using this method, you will come very close to my scaled measurements.

When measuring yeast with spoons, use level measurements also. For moist yeast, be sure it is packed firmly into the spoon, then leveled off. For dry yeast, use the dip and sweep method.

> *Note: All my recipes call for a certain amount of flour. You may not use all of the flour in your final dough, or you might need more; it will depend on how your flour does or doesn't absorb water.*

STEP 1. MAKE AND FERMENT THE *POOLISH* (allow 2 to 10 hours)   The water should be at room temperature, around 75°F., not ice cold from the refrigerator. Combine the water and yeast in a medium bowl. Let stand 1 minute, then stir with a wooden spoon until yeast is dissolved.

> *Note: The yeast dissolves in temperate water. I don't believe in "kick-starting" or overactivating the yeast cells with hot water, a step that many other books call for. High temperatures wake up the yeast cells with a great burst that produces rapid yeast activity, which can then create too much fermentation, too quickly. The* poolish *benefits from a long and slow fermentation, so it's best to keep temperatures moderately warm, not hot.*

Add the flour. Stir until the consistency of a thick batter. Continue stirring for about 100 strokes or until the strands of gluten come off the spoon when you press the back of the spoon against the bowl. Scrape down the sides of the bowl with a rubber spatula.

(continued)

Cover with a clean damp towel or plastic wrap, and place in a moderately warm (74°–80°F.) draft-free place until mixture is bubbly and has increased in volume.

The longer the *poolish* sits, the more time it has to become vigorous and permeated with the unmistakable aroma of wheaty fermentation. This will give your breads full body and a rich nutlike flavor. During a long fermentation, the *poolish* may rise and fall; as long as it's bubbling, don't be concerned about the volume.

A delicious alternative to a *poolish* fermented at room temperature is an even slower, cooler fermentation for 12 or 15 hours in the refrigerator. The *poolish* will bring even greater flavor and moisture to your final dough, and its yeast cells, having been retarded by the cool temperature, will bring hungry vigor to the fermentation. Allow the cold *poolish* to come to room temperature before using, about 2 hours.

STEP 2. MIX AND KNEAD THE FINAL DOUGH (about 20 minutes)

Measure out the remaining ingredients and calculate the necessary temperatures (see page 58). Bring the bowl with the *poolish* to your work space. The *poolish* should be soupy, bubbly, and puffy and it should have a wheaty aroma. Scrape the *poolish* into a large 6-quart bowl.

MIXING

Add the water and yeast. Break up the *poolish* well with a wooden spoon and stir until it loosens and the mixture foams slightly. Add 1 cup (5 ounces) of the flour and stir until well combined. Add the salt and only enough of the remaining flour to make a thick mass that is difficult to stir.

KNEADING
BY HAND

Turn out onto a well-floured 2-foot-square work surface. The dough will be quite sticky at first and difficult to work with. Dip your hands in flour to prevent them from sticking.

Knead the dough by pushing it down and forward with the heel of one hand, then pulling back from the top and folding the dough over with the other. The dough may be very sticky at first, and it will help to push the dough forward with the heel of one hand and fold it over using a dough blade. Gradually add the remaining flour as

THE ECOLOGICAL BAKER

At the bakery, we hardly ever use plastic wrap. Our rising breads are covered with canvas sheets that have been well impregnated with flour, so if the dough touches the fabric, it won't stick. At home, you may find it more convenient to use plastic wrap to cover your doughs and starters. If you use a damp kitchen towel, be sure to wet it occasionally with water so it doesn't dry out. If your towel dries out, so will your dough!

However, don't use plastic wrap like there's no tomorrow because, ecologically speaking, there *is* a tomorrow. Use the same piece of plastic wrap for all stages of rising and proofing. If it's relatively clean, set it aside to recycle for your next batch of bread.

you work the dough and knead vigorously for 15 to 17 minutes. If the dough remains wet and sticky, it may be necessary to knead in additional flour.

As the dough develops, it will become smooth, elastic, and strong. You will feel the gluten strengthening, making the dough more difficult to knead. Don't be afraid to really work the dough. Match your muscle with that of the gluten. Use your legs and knees to help you create a forward and back motion with the dough. As you work, adding more flour as you go, the dough will become smooth, satiny, slightly sticky. It is a common mistake to add too much flour to a dough, making it practically dry. Don't be afraid to end up with a slightly tacky dough. As long as the dough doesn't stick excessively to the work surface, it's not too wet.

There are three good ways to tell if the dough is well kneaded:
1. Pull a little dough from the mass and let it go. If it springs back quickly, it's ready.
2. Press your finger into the dough and remove it. If the dough springs back, it's ready.
3. Shape the dough into a ball. If it holds its shape and does not sag, it's ready.

If the dough doesn't respond in any of these ways, continue kneading for 5 minutes, adding a little more flour if you need to, until the dough is resilient and has spring.

The 15-17–minute rule is important. If the dough is under-kneaded, the gluten will not be developed enough to allow the dough to rise during fermentation. Don't skimp on kneading time. Set a timer if it helps.

IN THE MIXER

At home, I prefer to knead the dough by hand and I recommend that you knead your dough by hand. It is a good workout and it will help you tune into the life of the dough.

But if you must use a machine, a heavy-duty mixer, such as KitchenAid, comes fairly close to kneading the dough as well as a pair of hands. However, it takes attention on your part to help the machine do the job. You must use a heavy-duty model, as these heavy doughs may burn out the motor of a less powerful mixer. The KitchenAid comes equipped with a dough hook, but watch carefully and mix at low to medium speed to be sure the machine kneads the flour and doesn't beat it.

(continued)

HOT SPOTS

Ovens are notorious for their idiosyncrasies. I can almost guarantee you that your home oven has one or two areas that are much hotter than other places. These are called hot spots, and if your bread stands too long in one, it can burn.

You may want to get in the habit of checking your breads about halfway during the baking to be sure that the breads are browning evenly. The perfect time to do this in most of these recipes is when you turn the oven down, about 20 minutes into the baking period. Use the peel to move the breads around and check for signs of burning. Simply shift the breads around to compensate—move the darker bread to where the lighter one was, and vice-versa.

Perhaps you will own the rare oven that bakes evenly, and you won't have to worry about hot spots. But until you are familiar with your oven's quirks, watch out.

TAKING SHAPE

The shop windows of European traditional bakeries are visual feasts. Just seeing the abundance of golden loaves in various shapes and sizes makes me devour them all with my eyes. Traveling from region to region in France, and from town to town in Italy, I have found it delightful that each baker shapes his bread into something as basic as a *boule* or a tapered log, and it bakes up so different looking from the same shape done by another baker 100 miles away. There are only a few classic shapes, but each baker has his own techniques, sometimes placing the *boule* in a unique basket to proof or scoring his long loaves with a deeper cut, which give his breads their special look.

In addition to the basket *couche* method of shaping the loaf, which is the method I use in the Classic Country-Style Hearth Loaf (page 64), there are dozens of other shapes and methods.

I have chosen to describe the classic shapes here. As you follow these instructions, know that your breads will probably take on your and their own specialness, too.

Round. On an unfloured work surface, use slightly cupped hands to tuck the sides of the dough to meet underneath the mass, rotating the dough as you do so. After a few tucks the dough will form into a tight ball. Place the dough on a work surface that

If you want to try kneading the dough in the mixer, attach the mixer bowl with the *poolish* to your mixer fitted with a paddle blade. Add the remaining water and yeast, and mix on low speed until the *poolish* is very loose and frothy. Gradually add 5 ounces (1 cup) of the remaining flour and the salt, and mix on low speed just until a batter forms. Continue to mix on low speed, gradually adding more of the remaining flour as needed, just until a dough forms. Replace the paddle blade with a dough hook and knead until the dough is soft but not sticky, about 12 minutes. Check the dough often during this process, adding more flour as needed. If it forms a ball without sagging and springs back quickly when pulled from the mass, and the dough cleans the side of the bowl while kneading, or when removed from the bowl, then it is ready. If not, add a little more flour and continue kneading 3 to 5 minutes longer. It's a good technique to turn the dough onto a lightly floured work surface and knead briefly by hand to gauge the dough's moistness and texture, again, kneading in flour, if necessary.

> *Note: Never use any speed higher than medium or you will pummel the dough. Also, the mixer itself will quite possibly overheat, and wobble off the counter.*

STEP 3. FERMENT THE DOUGH (2 to 3 hours) Shape the dough into a ball and let it rest on a lightly floured surface while you scrape and clean and lightly oil the large bowl. Place about 1 tablespoon vegetable shortening or softened butter or 2 teaspoons of vegetable oil in the bowl. Use a pastry brush or paper towel to lightly "oil" the inside of the bowl. The solid fats are preferable, as the dough will eventually soak up the oil, but either can be used. Place the dough in the bowl and turn the dough to coat the top with oil. Take the dough's temperature: the ideal is 78°F.

> *Note: If the dough temperature is higher than 78°F., put it in a cooler than 78°F. place like the refrigerator until the dough cools to 78°F. If it is lower than 78°F., put it in a warmer than 78°F. place until the dough warms to 78°F. The point is to try to keep the dough at 78°F. during its fermentation. If you do have to move the dough, be gentle and don't jostle it, or the dough may deflate.*

Cover with a clean damp towel and place in a moderately warm

(74°–80°F.) draft-free place until doubled in volume. The dough has risen enough when a finger, pressed ½ inch into the dough leaves an indentation.

STEP 4. REST THE DOUGH (30 minutes)

Note: For some breads, this step will be called "Ferment the dough a second time" and will take 1½ to 2 hours.

Deflate the dough by pushing down in the center and pulling up on the sides. Form again into a ball, return to the bowl, and cover again with plastic wrap or a clean damp towel. Let rest in a moderate (74°–80°F.) draft-free place for 30 minutes.

STEP 5. DIVIDE AND SHAPE THE DOUGH INTO LOAVES (10 minutes)   Deflate the dough, transfer to a lightly floured work surface, and knead briefly. Cut into 2 equal pieces. Flatten each with the heel of your hand using firm direct strokes. This releases any remaining gas and invigorates the yeast in the dough. Shape each piece into a tight ball for round loaves (see Taking Shape, page 68).

STEP 6. PROOF THE LOAVES (1½ to 2 hours)   Line 2 bowls or baskets about 8 inches in diameter and 3 inches deep with well-floured lint-free towels (rub the flour right into the towels) and place the loaves smooth side down in each bowl. Dust top side with flour. Cover with a clean damp towel or plastic wrap and put in a moderately warm (74°–80°F.) draft-free place until increased in volume about 1½ times.

STEP 7. BAKE THE LOAVES (40 minutes)   Forty-five minutes to 1 hour before baking, preheat the oven and homemade hearth or baking stone (see Equipment, page 52) to 450°F.

The oven rack must be in the center of the oven. If it is in the lower third of the oven, the bottoms of the breads may burn, and if it is in the upper third, the top crusts may burn.

Gently invert the loaves from the baskets or bowls onto a floured board or peel so that they are right side up. Using a very sharp, serrated knife or a single-edged razor blade, score the loaves by making quick shallow cuts ¼ to ½ inch deep along the surface.

(continued)

---

has been dusted with cornmeal, semolina meal, or coarse wheat flour, or in a basket that has been lined with a well-floured towel. Cover with plastic wrap or a clean damp towel for proofing.

Log. On a lightly floured surface, shape the dough to form a tight ball. Cover and let it rest 10 minutes. Flatten with the heel of your hand into a disk about 1 inch thick. Fold the top edge down about one-third of the circle and seal firmly with the heel of your hand. Fold from the top a second time and seal firmly. Each fold should be uniform in width and length. Fold in half lengthwise and seal firmly, pinching the seam closed. You should have a long even log. If necessary, elongate the log by rolling the dough on the work surface. Start with your hands together at the center, and move them apart as you gently roll and stretch the dough, applying pressure as you do so. Place seam side up in a well-floured *couche* for proofing, covering with plastic wrap or a clean damp towel.

Italian (Torpedo-shaped) loaf with tapered ends. Shape dough into a ball and allow to rest 10 minutes. Flatten into a disk about 1 inch thick. Fold down from the upper right edge toward the center about 1½ inches, and seal with the heel of your hand. Beginning from the left edge, fold 1½ inches toward the center and seal. Repeat the process until all the dough has been folded and sealed.

The dough will be very thick in the center. Flatten with the heel of your hand and roll into a torpedo-shaped log. Pinch the seal firmly to close. Place seam side up in a floured *couche* and cover with plastic wrap or a clean damp towel for proofing.

Crescent. Shape the dough into a log and sculpt into a crescent. Bring ends together but do not seal. Set aside on a cornmeal-dusted surface, and cover with plastic wrap or a clean damp towel for final rising.

Pan loaves. Shape the dough into a log but keep it short enough to fit into a buttered rectangular bread pan. Cover with a clean damp towel or plastic wrap. When proofing, let the dough rise just until it barely reaches the rim of the pan. Do not let it overrise or "dome."

French-style loaf (baguette). On an *unfloured* surface, shape the dough into a log. Starting at the center and moving your hands outward, elongate it as you gently roll and stretch the dough until the log has become as long and narrow as you wish. Place seam side up, covered with a clean damp towel, or plastic wrap in a floured *couche* for final proofing.

Donut loaf. Shape dough into a log, then elongate as for a French-style loaf. Bring the ends together and seal firmly by pinching one end under the other. To proof, place seam side down on a cornmeal-dusted surface, and cover with

Using a well-floured peel, slide the loaves one at a time onto the hearth and quickly spray the inner walls and floor of the oven with cold water from a spritzer bottle. If there's an electric light bulb in the oven, avoid spraying it directly; it may burst. Spray for several seconds until steam has filled the oven. Quickly close the door to trap the steam and bake 3 minutes. Spray again in the same way, closing the door immediately so that steam doesn't escape, and bake until the loaves begin to color, about 20 minutes. Reduce heat to 400°F. and bake until the loaves are a rich caramel color and the crust is firm, another 15 to 20 minutes.

To test the loaves for doneness, remove and hold the loaves upside down. Strike the bottoms firmly with your finger. If the sound is hollow, the breads are done. If it doesn't sound hollow, bake 5 minutes longer, and test again.

STEP 8. COOLING AND STORAGE   (20 minutes)

COOLING

It is important to allow large loaves to cool at least 20 minutes because they actually finish baking as they cool. If you were to tear or cut into a large loaf too soon, you'd find the center still doughy. Cool them on a rack, so that air can circulate freely around the loaf. If you place them on a flat surface to cool, the bottom crust will become soggy.

STORAGE

Once the loaf has cooled, slice off what you want with a sharp serrated knife and leave the remaining loaf standing cut side down on a flat surface. You can do this in a bread box or on a cutting board placed on top of the refrigerator, inside a cupboard, or any out of the way spot. You needn't refrigerate it. I know of few breads that taste good when ice cold. You needn't wrap it in plastic; if the bread can breathe, the crust will remain crisp and chewy. The loaf will keep at least 3 days this way, if it lasts that long in your household.

You can also freeze freshly baked *unsliced* bread after it has cooled thoroughly. Wrap it in plastic for freezing and thaw it in the same plastic. Once thawed (it will take a few hours), place the loaf in a 350°F. oven for 10 or 15 minutes. This is important information to have, as most of my recipes make 2 loaves of bread, and you will probably want to freeze a loaf.

CLASSIC COUNTRY-STYLE HEARTH LOAF

Task	Approximate Time	Comments
Prepreparation		Ferment *poolish*.
Preparation	10 min.	Calculate temperatures. Assemble ingredients. Mix.
Knead	15 min.	Take temperature of final dough.
Ferment	3 hr.	Moderate: 74°–80°F. until doubled in volume.
Rest	30 min.	Deflate and allow to rise again. Moderate: 74°–80°F.
Divide	5 min.	Deflate and cut into 2 equal portions.
Shape	5 min.	Flatten with heel of hand. Form into balls for round loaves. Place in towel-lined and well-floured baskets or bowls.
Proof	2 hr.	Moderate: 74°–80°F. until increased 1½ × in volume.
Bake	40 min.	With steam. 450°F.–400°F.
Cool	20 min.	On rack or in baskets.

Cumulative Total Time: 7hr., 5 min.

Round

Pan

Crescent

Torpedo

Log

Fougasse

Donut

Braid

Baguette

Rolls

a clean damp towel or plastic wrap.

Fougasse. Shape dough into a log, then with a rolling pin, flatten the dough to a rectangle approximately 1½ inches thick. Proof the loaf as instructed, then with a sharp knife, make 8 slits and open them with your fingers before slipping the loaf onto the baking tiles.

Braid. Divide the dough from each loaf into thirds. On an *unfloured* surface, roll each third into a 12- to 14-inch-long log. Braid the logs, starting at the center and moving out to each end. Pinch the logs together at the ends. Place on a cornmeal- or semolina-dusted surface, cover with a clean damp towel or plastic wrap, and let proof.

Rolls. Place a small piece of dough on an *unfloured* work surface. Cup your hand slightly and cover the ball with your hand. Rotate your hand in small circles, applying a little pressure to the dough. As you rotate, the dough will eventually form into a ball. Place the ball on a cornmeal-dusted work surface, cover with a clean damp towel or plastic wrap, and proof.

In all cases, seal very carefully or the seal will pop open and your bread will take on a whole other shape. Pinch the dough closed. Always place the loaf seam side down when rising on a board and seam side up when rising in a *couche* or basket.

COUNTRY-STYLE HEARTH LOAF WITH CORNMEAL, CILANTRO, AND COARSE PEPPER

Allow 2 to 10 hours to make and ferment the *poolish*.
Total preparation and baking time (not including the *poolish*):
6 hours, 45 minutes

This is the Classic Country-Style Hearth Loaf (page 64) with a peppery taste and an airy crumb flecked with cornmeal and feisty cilantro. You'll love this with a fresh vegetable soup or a mild cheese.

Makes 2 round 10-inch loaves

POOLISH

Spring water (75°F.)	½ cup	4 fluid ounces
Moist yeast	1 teaspoon	¼ ounce
or dry yeast	½ teaspoon	⅛ ounce
20% bran wheat flour	¾ cup	4 ounces

FINAL DOUGH

Spring water	2½ cups	20 fluid ounces
Moist yeast	1 teaspoon	¼ ounce
or dry yeast	½ teaspoon	⅛ ounce
Stone-ground cornmeal	1¼ cups	6½ ounces
Fine sea salt	1 tablespoon	¾ ounce
Chopped fresh cilantro	½ cup	
Coarsely ground black pepper	2 tablespoons, or to taste	
20% bran wheat flour*	3¼–4½ cups	16–22 ounces

---

* See Flours (pages 42–49). This is a good approximate measure. You may use more or less depending on the weight and absorbency of your flour.

MAKE AND FERMENT THE *POOLISH* (allow 2 to 10 hours) Combine the water and the yeast in a medium bowl. Let stand 1 minute, then stir with a wooden spoon until yeast is dissolved. Add the flour and stir until the consistency of a thick batter. Continue stirring for about 100 strokes or until the strands of gluten come off the spoon when you press the back of the spoon against the bowl. Scrape down the sides of the bowl with a rubber spatula. Cover with a clean damp towel or plastic wrap, and put in a moderately warm (74°–80°F.) draft-free place until it is bubbly and has increased in volume.

MIX AND KNEAD THE FINAL DOUGH (25 minutes) Measure the ingredients and calculate the necessary temperatures (see page 58). The *poolish* should be soupy, bubbly, and puffy and it should have a wheaty aroma. Scrape the *poolish* into a large 6-quart bowl. Add the water and the yeast. Break up the *poolish* well with a wooden spoon and stir until the *poolish* loosens and the mixture foams slightly. Add the cornmeal and stir until well combined. Add the salt, cilantro, pepper, and only enough of the flour to make a thick mass that is difficult to stir. Turn out onto a well-floured surface. Knead, adding more of the remaining flour when necessary, until dough is soft and smooth, 15 to 17 minutes. (Or, make in a heavy-duty mixer. See page 67.) The dough is ready when a small amount pulled from the mass springs back quickly (see Kneading, page 66).

FERMENT THE DOUGH (2 to 3 hours) Shape the dough into a ball and let it rest on a lightly floured surface while you scrape, clean, and lightly oil the large bowl. Place the dough in the bowl and turn the dough to coat the top with oil. Take the dough's temperature: the ideal is 78°F. (see page 58). Cover with a clean damp towel or plastic wrap and put in a moderately warm (74°–80°F.) draft-free place until doubled in volume.

> *Note: If the dough temperature is higher than 78°F., put it in a cooler than 78°F. place like the refrigerator until the dough cools to 78°F. If it is lower than 78°F., put it in a warmer than 78°F. place until the dough warms to 78°F. The point is to try to keep the dough at 78°F. during its fermentation. If you do have to move the dough, be gentle and don't jostle it, or the dough may deflate.*

The dough has risen enough when a finger, poked ½ inch into the dough, leaves an indentation.

REST (30 minutes) Deflate the dough by pushing down in the center and pulling up on the sides. Form into a ball, return to the bowl, and cover again with a clean damp towel or plastic wrap. Let rest in a moderately warm (74°–80°F.) draft-free place for 30 minutes.

(continued)

SCORING

The marks on a loaf of bread are like a signature. Not only of the baker, but often of the bread itself. *Baguettes* usually have diagonal cuts on them. *Pains au levain* usually have one long, straight cut. Like a signature, there are rules governing the basic shapes and it takes a long time to be able to "master" them. However, it is very important to know that these cuts are not merely decorative. They serve an important function. If you were to bake the bread without the cuts, they would expand and burst the crust in a haphazard way. A few bakers prefer this for their breads. It gives the loaf a rustic and unrefined look.

The cuts act as guides for the rapidly expanding loaves and determine the final shape that the loaf will take.

If you want to cut the breads properly, you will need a *very* sharp blade. Professional bakers use a double-edge razor that they attach to a special tool; you can use a very sharp knife. (Artists' knives work great!)

When scoring a *baguette*, hold the blade almost horizontal to the loaf. Make each incision crisp, clean, and quick. Each cut should be the same length, should be straight and overlapping, and should be roughly parallel to the length of the *baguette*.

DIVIDE AND SHAPE THE DOUGH INTO LOAVES (10 minutes) Deflate the dough by pushing down in the center and pulling up on the sides. Transfer the dough to a lightly floured work surface and knead briefly. Cut into 2 equal pieces. Flatten each with the heel of your hand using firm direct strokes. Shape each piece into a tight ball for round loaves (see Taking Shape, page 68).

PROOF THE LOAVES (1½ to 2 hours) Line 2 bowls or baskets about 8 inches in diameter and 3 inches deep with well-floured towels, and place the loaves smooth side down in each bowl. Dust top sides with flour. Cover with a clean damp towel or plastic wrap. Put in a moderately warm (74°–80°F.) draft-free place until increased in volume about 1½ times.

BAKE THE LOAVES (40 minutes) Forty-five minutes to 1 hour before baking, preheat the oven and homemade hearth or baking stone on the center rack of the oven (see Equipment, page 52) to 450°F.

The oven rack must be in the center of the oven. If it is in the lower third of the oven, the bottoms of the breads may burn, and if it is in the upper third, the top crusts may burn.

Gently invert the loaves from the baskets or bowls onto a floured board or peel so that they are right side up. Using a very sharp, serrated knife or a single-edged razor blade, score the loaves by making quick shallow cuts ¼ to ½ inch deep along the surface.

Using a well-floured peel, slide the loaves one at a time onto the hearth and quickly spray the inner walls and floor of the oven with cold water from a spritzer bottle. If there's an electric light bulb in the oven, avoid spraying it directly—it may burst. Spray for several seconds until steam has filled the oven. Quickly close the door to trap the steam and bake 3 minutes. Spray again in the same way, closing the door immediately so that steam doesn't escape, and bake until loaves begin to color, about 20 minutes. Reduce heat to 400°F. and bake until loaves are a rich caramel color and the crust is firm, another 15 to 20 minutes. To test the loaves for doneness, remove and hold the loaves upside down. Strike the bottoms firmly with your finger. If the sound is hollow, the breads are done. If it doesn't sound hollow, bake 5 minutes longer. Cool completely on a wire rack.

COUNTRY-STYLE HEARTH LOAF WITH DRIED FIGS, COGNAC, AND HAZELNUTS

Allow 8 hours to soak the figs.
Allow 2 to 10 hours to make and ferment the *poolish*.
Total preparation and baking time (not including the *poolish*):
6 hours, 45 minutes

This is a rich aromatic bread with a fruity-dense crumb, lightly perfumed by the cognac. It's delicious toasted, slathered with cream cheese or sweet butter, and served with hot steamy coffee.

Makes 2 round 10-inch loaves

POOLISH

Spring water (75°F.)	½ cup	4 fluid ounces
Moist yeast	1 teaspoon	¼ ounce
or dry yeast	½ teaspoon	⅛ ounce
20% bran wheat flour	¾ cup	4 ounces

FINAL DOUGH

Dried figs, cut in ¼-inch pieces	1 cup	6 ounces
Cognac	2 tablespoons	1 fluid ounce
Hazelnuts	1 cup	5 ounces
Spring water	2½ cups	20 fluid ounces
Moist yeast	1 teaspoon	¼ ounce
or dry yeast	½ teaspoon	⅛ ounce
20% bran wheat flour*	5¼–6¼ cups	26–31 ounces
Cracked rye or wheat	¼ cup	1⅓ ounces
Fine sea salt	1 tablespoon	¾ ounce

* See Flours (pages 42–49). This is a good approximate measure. You may use more or less depending on the weight and absorbency of your flour.

MAKE AND FERMENT THE *POOLISH* (allow 2 to 10 hours) Combine the water and yeast in a medium bowl. Let stand 1 minute, then stir with a wooden spoon until yeast is dissolved. Add the flour and stir until the consistency of a thick batter. Continue stirring for about 100 strokes or until the strands of gluten come off the spoon when you press the back of the spoon against the bowl. Scrape down the sides of the bowl with a rubber spatula. Cover with a clean damp towel or plastic wrap, and put in a moderately warm (74°–80°F.) draft-free place until it is bubbly and has increased in volume.

(continued)

If the *baguette* is the proper length, there will be seven cuts on the loaf. Don't be afraid if you can only fit four or five. It takes practice to be able to get the *baguette* cut right.

When scoring a loaf or a roll, simply decide what pattern to use, based on my ideas or your own, hold the blade firmly, and swiftly slice into the loaf. Make your cuts about ¼ inch deep and straight into the dough.

KNEADING IN

Many recipes call for kneading ingredients into the dough. Be sure you have kneaded the dough first for at least 10 minutes to develop a strong gluten structure before incorporating any nuts, dried fruits, herbs, or fresh vegetables. If added too early, the incorporated ingredients will weaken the dough.

Flatten the partly kneaded dough with the heel of your hand into a thin disk. Sprinkle with ¼ to ½ cup of the additional ingredients. Fold a portion of the dough over the ingredients and knead. When incorporated, repeat the process until gradually all the ingredients are kneaded into the dough. This will take about 5 minutes.

If the added ingredients are excessively moist, the dough could change texture and you may have to add extra flour to return the dough to a proper texture.

If you are using an electric mixer, the same caveats apply: knead the dough, gradually adding the ingredients during the last 5 minutes of kneading, and adjusting the moistness of the dough with additional flour, if needed. Finish the kneading by hand on a work surface to ensure the ingredients are evenly distributed and the dough isn't too moist.

PREPARE THE FIGS (8 hours or overnight) Combine the figs and the cognac in a small bowl. Soak 8 hours or overnight. The cognac should be almost completely absorbed. Drain if necessary.

PREPARE THE HAZELNUTS (30 minutes) Place the hazelnuts on a baking sheet and bake in a preheated 350°F. oven until the skins are peeling, about 12 minutes. Place the nuts in a clean kitchen towel and let stand 10 minutes. Use the towel to rub off as much of the skins as possible. Cool completely, then coarsely chop.

MIX AND KNEAD THE FINAL DOUGH (25 minutes) Measure the remaining ingredients and calculate the necessary temperatures (see page 58). Scrape the *poolish* into a 6-quart bowl. Add the water and the yeast. Break up the *poolish* well with a wooden spoon and stir until it loosens and the mixture foams slightly. Add 1 cup (5 ounces) of the flour and the cracked rye, and stir until well combined. Add the salt and only enough of the remaining flour to make a thick mass that is difficult to stir. Turn out onto a well-floured work surface. The dough will be quite sticky at first and difficult to work with. Knead, adding more flour as necessary, for 10 minutes. Gradually add the hazelnuts as you continue kneading 3 minutes longer. Then knead in the figs. Since the moist figs will change the moisture of the dough, you may have to knead in more flour after adding them. Continue kneading 2 minutes longer or until the dough is soft and smooth, 15 to 17 minutes total, (or make in a heavy-duty mixer; see page 67). The dough is ready when a small amount pulled from the mass springs back quickly (see Kneading, page 66, and Kneading In, at left).

FERMENT THE DOUGH (2 to 3 hours) Shape the dough into a ball and let it rest on a lightly floured surface while you scrape, clean, and lightly oil the large bowl. Place the dough in the bowl and turn the dough to coat the top with oil. Take the dough's temperature: the ideal is 78°F. (see page 58). Cover with a clean damp towel or plastic wrap and put in a moderately warm (74°–80°F.) draft-free place until doubled in volume.

Note: If the dough temperature is higher than 78°F., put it in a cooler than 78°F. place like the refrigerator until the dough cools to 78°F. If it is lower than 78°F., put it in a warmer than 78°F. place until the dough warms to 78°F. The point is to try to keep the dough at 78°F. during its fermentation. If you do have to move the dough, be gentle and don't jostle it, or the dough may deflate.

The dough has risen enough when a finger, poked ½ inch into the dough leaves an indentation.

REST (30 minutes)   Deflate the dough by pushing down in the center and pulling up on the sides. Form into a ball, return to the bowl, and cover again with a clean damp towel or plastic wrap. Let rest in a moderately warm (74°–80°F.) draft-free place for 30 minutes.

DIVIDE AND SHAPE THE DOUGH INTO LOAVES (10 minutes)   Deflate the dough by pushing down in the center and pulling up on the sides. Transfer the dough to a lightly floured work surface and knead briefly. Cut into 2 equal pieces. Flatten each with the heel of your hand using firm direct strokes. Shape each piece into a tight ball for round loaves (see Taking Shape, page 68).

PROOF THE LOAVES (1½ to 2 hours)   Line 2 bowls or baskets about 8 inches in diameter and 3 inches deep with well-floured towels, and place the loaves smooth side down in each bowl. Dust top sides with flour. Cover with a clean damp towel or plastic wrap. Put in a moderately warm (74°–80°F.) draft-free place until increased in volume about 1½ times.

BAKE THE LOAVES (40 minutes)   Forty-five minutes to 1 hour before baking, preheat the oven and homemade hearth or baking stone on the center rack of the oven (see Equipment page 52) to 450°F.

The oven rack must be in the center of the oven. If it is in the lower third of the oven, the bottoms of the breads may burn, and if it is in the upper third, the top crusts may burn.

Gently flip the loaves from the baskets or bowls onto a floured board or peel so that they are right side up. Using a very sharp, serrated knife or a single-edged razor blade, score the loaves by making quick shallow cuts ¼ to ½ inch deep along the surface.

(continued)

Using a well-floured peel, slide the loaves one at a time onto the hearth and quickly spray the inner walls and floor of the oven with cold water from a spritzer bottle. If there's an electric light bulb in the oven, avoid spraying it directly—it may burst. Spray for several seconds until steam has filled the oven. Quickly close the door to trap the steam and bake 3 minutes. Spray again in the same way, closing the door immediately so that steam doesn't escape, and bake until loaves begin to color, 15 to 20 minutes. Reduce heat to 400°F. and bake until loaves are a rich caramel color and the crusts are firm, another 15 to 20 minutes.

To test the loaves for doneness, remove and hold the loaves upside down. Strike the bottoms firmly with your finger. If the sound is hollow, the breads are done. If it doesn't sound hollow, bake 5 minutes longer. Cool completely on a wire rack.

COUNTRY-STYLE HEARTH LOAF WITH SUN-DRIED TOMATOES AND THYME

Allow 2 to 10 hours to make and ferment the *poolish.*
Total preparation and baking time (not including the *poolish*):
6 hours, 45 minutes

This is a favorite of mine because I love sun-dried tomatoes, any time of year, any way I can get them; and the flavor of this bread is full of all the tomato I want. I like this with soups, salads, or toasted all by itself.

Makes 2 round 10-inch loaves

POOLISH

Spring water (75°F.)	½ cup	4 fluid ounces
Moist yeast	1 teaspoon	¼ ounce
or dry yeast	½ teaspoon	⅛ ounce
20% bran wheat flour	¾ cup	4 ounces

FINAL DOUGH

Spring water	2½ cups	20 fluid ounces
Moist yeast	1 teaspoon	¼ ounce
or dry yeast	½ teaspoon	⅛ ounce
20% bran wheat flour*	5¼–6¼ cups	26–31 ounces
Fine sea salt	1 tablespoon	¾ ounce
7-ounce jar sun-dried tomatoes packed in oil, drained, patted dry on paper towels, and chopped	1 cup	4 ounces
Chopped fresh thyme leaves	¼ cup	¼ ounce

---

* See Flours (pages 42–49). This is a good approximate measure. You may use more or less depending on the weight and absorbency of your flour.

MAKE AND FERMENT THE *POOLISH* (allow 2 to 10 hours) Combine the water and yeast in a medium bowl. Let stand 1 minute, then stir with a wooden spoon until yeast is dissolved. Add the flour and stir until the consistency of a thick batter. Continue stirring for about 100 strokes or until the strands of gluten come off the spoon when you press the back of the spoon against the bowl. Scrape down the sides of the bowl with a rubber spatula. Cover with a clean damp towel or plastic wrap, and put in a moderately warm (74°–80°F.) draft-free place until it is bubbly and has increased in volume.

(continued)

MIX AND KNEAD THE FINAL DOUGH (25 minutes)   Measure
the ingredients and calculate the necessary temperatures (see page
58). Bring the bowl with the *poolish* to your work space. The *poolish*
should be soupy, bubbly, and puffy and it should have a wheaty
aroma. Scrape the *poolish* into a 6-quart bowl. Add the water and
yeast. Break up the *poolish* well with a wooden spoon and stir until
it loosens and the mixture foams slightly. Add 1 cup (5 ounces) of
the flour and stir until well combined. Add the salt and only enough
of the remaining flour to make a thick mass that is difficult to stir.
Turn out onto a well-floured surface. Knead, adding more flour as
necessary, for 10 minutes. Gradually knead in the tomatoes and the
thyme and continue kneading longer until the dough is soft and
smooth, 15 to 17 minutes total (or make in a heavy-duty mixer; see
page 67). The dough is ready when a small amount pulled from the
mass springs back quickly (see Kneading, page 66).

FERMENT THE DOUGH (2 to 3 hours)   Shape the dough into a
ball and let it rest on a lightly floured surface while you scrape, clean,
and lightly oil the large bowl. Place the dough in the bowl and turn
the dough to coat the top with oil. Take the dough's temperature:
the ideal is 78°F. (see page 58). Cover with a clean damp towel or
plastic wrap and put in a moderate (74°–80°F.) draft-free place until
doubled in volume.

> *Note: If the dough temperature is higher than 78 F., put it
> in a cooler than 78°F. place like the refrigerator until the
> dough cools to 78°F. If it is lower than 78°F., put it in a
> warmer than 78°F. place until the dough warms to 78°F.
> The point is to try to keep the dough at 78°F. during its
> fermentation. If you do have to move the dough, be gentle
> and don't jostle it, or the dough may deflate.*

The dough has risen enough when a finger poked ½ inch into
the dough leaves an indentation.

REST (30 minutes)   Deflate the dough by pushing down in the center and pulling up on the sides. Form again into a ball, return to the
bowl, and cover again with a clean damp towel or plastic wrap. Let
rest in a moderately warm (74°–80°F.) draft-free place for 30 minutes.

DIVIDE AND SHAPE THE DOUGH INTO LOAVES (10 minutes) Deflate the dough by pushing down in the center and pulling up on the sides. Transfer the dough to a lightly floured work surface and knead briefly. Cut into 2 equal pieces. Flatten each with the heel of your hand using firm direct strokes. Shape each piece into a tight ball for round loaves (see Taking Shape, page 68).

PROOF THE LOAVES (1½ to 2 hours) Line 2 bowls or baskets about 8 inches in diameter and 3 inches deep with well-floured towels, and place the loaves smooth side down in each bowl. Dust top sides with flour. Cover with a clean damp towel or plastic wrap. Put in a moderately warm (74°–80°F.) draft-free place until increased in volume about 1½ times.

BAKE THE LOAVES (40 minutes) Forty-five minutes to 1 hour before baking, preheat the oven and homemade hearth or baking stone on the center rack of the oven (see Equipment, page 52) to 450°F.

The oven rack must be in the center of the oven. If it is in the lower third of the oven, the bottoms of the breads may burn, and if it is in the upper third, the top crusts may burn.

Gently invert the loaves from the baskets or bowls onto a floured board or peel so that they are right side up. Using a very sharp serrated knife or a single-edged razor blade, score the loaves by making quick shallow cuts ¼ to ½ inch deep along the surface.

Using a well-floured peel, slide the loaves one at a time onto the hearth and quickly spray the inner walls and floor of the oven with cold water from a spritzer bottle. If there's an electric light bulb in the oven, avoid spraying it directly—it may burst. Spray for several seconds until steam has filled the oven. Quickly close the door to trap the steam and bake 3 minutes. Spray again in the same way, closing the door immediately so that steam doesn't escape, and bake until loaves begin to color, 15 to 20 minutes. Reduce heat to 400°F. and bake until loaves are a rich caramel color and the crusts are firm, another 15 to 20 minutes.

To test the loaves for doneness, remove and hold the loaves upside down. Strike the bottoms firmly with your finger. If the sound is hollow, the breads are done. If it doesn't sound hollow, bake 5 minutes longer. Cool completely on a wire rack.

COUNTRY-STYLE HEARTH LOAF WITH HERBS AND ONIONS

Allow 2 to 10 hours to make and ferment the *poolish*.
Total preparation and baking time (not including the *poolish*):
6 hours, 45 minutes

In summer I love harvesting fresh herbs from my garden and kneading them into dough. This is a golden bread ripe with wild garden fragrances and the tantalizing flavors of onions and herbs. I serve it with summer soups, but it's great any time.

Makes 2 round 10-inch loaves

POOLISH

Spring water (75°F.)	½ cup	4 fluid ounces
Moist yeast	1 teaspoon	¼ ounce
or dry yeast	½ teaspoon	⅛ ounce
20% bran wheat flour	¾ cup	4 ounces

FINAL DOUGH

Olive oil	1 tablespoon	
2 small onions, finely chopped	1 cup	5 ounces
Spring water	2½ cups	20 fluid ounces
Moist yeast	¼ teaspoon	¹⁄₁₆ ounce
or dry yeast	½ teaspoon	⅛ ounce
20% bran wheat flour*	6–7 cups	30–35 ounces
Fine sea salt	1 tablespoon	¾ ounce
Chopped fresh chives	¼ cup	½ ounce
Chopped fresh scallions	¼ cup	½ ounce
Chopped fresh dill	½ cup	1 ounce
8 garlic cloves, minced	⅓ cup	1½ ounces

---

* See Flours (pages 42–49). This is a good approximate measure. You may use more or less depending on the weight and absorbency of your flour.

MAKE AND FERMENT THE *POOLISH* (allow 2 to 10 hours)
Combine the water and yeast in a medium bowl. Let stand 1 minute, then stir with a wooden spoon until yeast is dissolved. Add the flour and stir until the consistency of a thick batter. Continue stirring for

about 100 strokes or until the strands of gluten come off the spoon when you press the back of the spoon against the bowl. Scrape down the sides of the bowl with a rubber spatula. Cover with a clean damp towel or plastic wrap, and put in a moderately warm (74°–80°F.) draft-free place until it is bubbly and has increased in volume.

ROAST THE ONIONS (1 hour, including cooling) Preheat the oven to 400°F. Combine the oil and onions in a medium bowl; toss until well combined. Spread the onions on a baking sheet. Bake, stirring occasionally, until onions are golden brown, about 15 to 20 minutes. Cool completely.

MIX AND KNEAD THE FINAL DOUGH (25 minutes) Measure the remaining ingredients and calculate the necessary temperatures (see page 58). Bring the bowl with the *poolish* to your work space. The *poolish* should be soupy, bubbly, and puffy and it should have a wheaty aroma. Scrape the *poolish* into a 6-quart bowl. Add the water and yeast. Break up the *poolish* well and stir with a wooden spoon until it loosens and the mixture foams slightly. Add 1 cup (5 ounces) of the flour and stir until well combined. Add the salt and only enough of the remaining flour to make a thick mass that is difficult to stir. Turn out onto a well-floured surface. Knead, adding more of the remaining flour when needed for 10 minutes. Gradually knead in the cooled onions, chives, scallions, dill, and garlic. Since the addition of the onions and herbs will change the moisture of the dough, you may have to knead in more flour after adding them. Continue kneading until the dough is soft and smooth, 15 to 17 minutes total. (Or knead in a heavy-duty mixer; see page 67.) The dough is ready when a small amount pulled from the mass springs back quickly (see Kneading and Kneading In, pages 66 and 76).

FERMENT THE DOUGH (2 to 3 hours) Shape the dough into a ball and let it rest on a lightly floured surface while you scrape, clean, and lightly oil the large bowl. Place the dough in the bowl and turn to coat the top with oil. Take the dough's temperature: the ideal is 78°F. (see page 58). Cover with a clean damp towel or plastic wrap and put in a moderately warm (74°–80°F.) draft-free place until doubled in volume.

(continued)

Note: If the dough temperature is higher than 78°F., put it in a cooler than 78°F. place like the refrigerator until the dough cools to 78°F. If it is lower than 78°F., put it in a warmer than 78°F. place until the dough warms to 78°F. The point is to try to keep the dough at 78°F. during its fermentation. If you do have to move the dough, be gentle and don't jostle it, or the dough may deflate.

The dough has risen enough when a finger poked ½ inch into the dough leaves an indentation.

REST (30 minutes)　Deflate the dough by pushing down in the center and pulling up on the sides. Form into a ball, return to the bowl, and cover again with a clean damp towel or plastic wrap. Let rest in a moderately warm (74°–80°F.) draft-free place for 30 minutes.

DIVIDE AND SHAPE THE DOUGH INTO LOAVES (10 minutes)　Deflate the dough by pushing down in the center and pulling up on the sides. Transfer the dough to a lightly floured work surface and knead briefly. Cut into 2 equal pieces. Flatten each with the heel of your hand using firm direct strokes. Shape each piece into a tight ball for round loaves (see Taking Shape, page 68).

PROOF THE LOAVES (1½ to 2 hours)　Line 2 bowls or baskets about 8 inches in diameter and 3 inches deep with well-floured towels, and place the loaves smooth side down in each bowl. Dust top sides with flour. Cover with a clean damp towel or plastic wrap. Put in a moderately warm (74°–80°F.) draft-free place until increased in volume about 1½ times.

BAKE THE LOAVES (40 minutes)　Forty-five minutes to 1 hour before baking, preheat the oven and homemade hearth or baking stone in the center rack of the oven (see Equipment, page 52) to 450°F.

The oven rack must be in the center of the oven. If it is in the lower third of the oven, the bottoms of the breads may burn, and if it is in the upper third, the top crusts may burn.

Gently invert the loaves from the baskets or bowls onto a floured board or peel so that they are right side up. Using a very sharp, serrated knife or a single-edged razor blade, score the loaves by making quick shallow cuts ¼ to ½ inch deep along the surface.

Using a well-floured peel, slide the loaves one at a time onto the hearth and quickly spray the inner walls and floor of the oven with cold water from a spritzer bottle. If there's an electric light bulb in the oven, avoid spraying it directly—it may burst. Spray for several seconds until steam has filled the oven. Quickly close the door to trap the steam and bake 3 minutes. Spray again in the same way, closing the door immediately so that steam doesn't escape, and bake until loaves begin to color, about 20 minutes. Reduce heat to 400°F. and bake until loaves are a rich caramel color and the crusts are firm, another 15 to 20 minutes.

To test the loaves for doneness, remove and hold the loaves upside down. Strike the bottoms firmly with your finger. If the sound is hollow, the breads are done. If it doesn't sound hollow, bake 5 minutes longer. Cool completely on a wire rack.

COARSE-GRAIN NORWEGIAN FARM LOAF

> Allow 2 to 10 hours to make and ferment the *poolish*.
> Total preparation and baking time (not including the *poolish*):
> 6 hours, 25 minutes

This deep caramel-colored loaf was inspired by a farm bread that I first tasted in Norway. The cracked wheat and rye give the golden crumb a tangy nutlike flavor and the crust an irresistible crunch.

Makes 2 round 12-inch loaves

POOLISH

Spring water	¾ cup	6 fluid ounces
Moist yeast	1 teaspoon	¼ ounce
or dry yeast	½ teaspoon	⅛ ounce
20% bran wheat flour	¾ cup	4 ounces
Whole wheat flour, preferably coarse ground	½ cup	2½ ounces

FINAL DOUGH

Spring water	2¼ cups	18 fluid ounces
Moist yeast	1 teaspoon	¼ ounce
or dry yeast	½ teaspoon	⅛ ounce
Whole wheat flour, preferably coarse ground*	1¾ cups	8 ounces
Fine sea salt	1 tablespoon	¾ ounce
Cracked wheat	¼ cup	2 ounces
Cracked rye	¼ cup	1½ ounces
20% bran wheat flour*	3¾–4¾ cups	18–23 ounces

---

* See Flours (pages 42–49). These are good approximate measures. You may use more or less depending on the weight and absorbency of your flours.

MAKE AND FERMENT THE *POOLISH* (allow 2 to 10 hours) Combine the water and yeast in a medium bowl. Let stand 1 minute, then stir with a wooden spoon until yeast is dissolved. Add the flours and stir until the consistency of a thick batter. Continue stirring for about 100 strokes or until the strands of gluten come off the spoon when you press the back of the spoon against the bowl, 2 to 4 minutes. There will be lively bubbles on the surface. Cover with a clean damp towel or plastic wrap, and put in a moderately warm (74°–80°F.) draft-free place until it is bubbly and has increased in volume.

MIX AND KNEAD THE FINAL DOUGH (25 minutes) Measure the ingredients and calculate the necessary temperatures (see page 58). Bring the bowl with the *poolish* to your work space. The *poolish* should be soupy, bubbly, and puffy and it should have a wheaty aroma. Scrape the *poolish* into a 6-quart bowl. Add the water and yeast. Break up the *poolish* with a wooden spoon and stir until it loosens and the mixture foams slightly. Add the whole wheat flour and stir until well combined. Add the salt, half each of the cracked wheat and cracked rye, and enough bran flour to make a thick mass that is difficult to stir. Turn out onto a well-floured surface. Knead, adding more of the remaining bran flour when needed, until dough is soft and smooth, 15 to 17 minutes. (Or make the dough in a heavy-duty mixer; see page 67.) The dough is ready when a small amount pulled from the mass springs back quickly (see Kneading, page 66).

FERMENT THE DOUGH (2 to 3 hours) Shape the dough into a ball and let it rest on a lightly floured surface while you scrape, clean, and lightly oil the large bowl. Place the dough in the bowl and turn the dough to coat the top with oil. Take the dough's temperature: the ideal is 78°F. (see page 58). Cover with a clean damp towel or plastic wrap and put in a moderately warm (74°–80°F.) draft-free place until doubled in volume.

> *Note: If the dough temperature is higher than 78°F., put it in a cooler than 78°F. place like the refrigerator until the dough cools to 78°F. If it is lower than 78°F., put it in a warmer than 78°F. place until the dough warms to 78°F. The point is to try to keep the dough at 78°F. during its fermentation. If you do have to move the dough, be gentle and don't jostle it, or the dough may deflate.*

The dough has risen enough when a finger poked ½ inch into the dough leaves an indentation.

DIVIDE AND SHAPE THE DOUGH INTO LOAVES (10 minutes) Deflate the dough by pushing down in the center and pulling up on the sides. Transfer the dough to a lightly floured work surface and knead briefly. Cut into 2 equal pieces. Flatten each with the heel of your hand using firm direct strokes. Shape each piece into

(continued)

a tight ball for round loaves (see Taking Shape, page 68). Combine the *remaining* 2 tablespoons each cracked wheat and rye, and sprinkle them over a small area of the work surface. Roll each ball in the cracked grains, pressing the grains into the tops of the balls.

PROOF THE LOAVES (1½ to 2 hours)　Line 2 bowls or baskets about 8 inches in diameter and 3 inches deep with well-floured towels, and place the loaves smooth side down in each bowl. Dust top sides with flour. Cover with a clean damp towel or plastic wrap. Put in a moderately warm (74°–80°F.) draft-free place until increased in volume about 1½ times.

BAKE THE LOAVES (40 minutes)　Forty-five minutes to 1 hour before baking, preheat the oven and homemade hearth or baking stone placed on the center rack of the oven (see Equipment, page 52) to 450°F.

The oven rack must be in the center of the oven. If it is in the lower third of the oven, the bottoms of the breads may burn, and if it is in the upper third, the top crusts may burn.

Gently invert the loaves from the baskets or bowls onto a floured board or peel so that they are right side up. Using a very sharp, serrated knife or a single-edged razor blade, score the loaves by making quick shallow cuts ¼ to ½ inch deep along the surface.

Using a peel, slide the loaves one at a time onto the hearth and quickly spray the inner walls and floor of the oven with cold water from a spritzer bottle. If there's an electric light bulb in the oven, avoid spraying it directly—it may burst. Spray for several seconds until steam has filled the oven. Quickly close the door to trap the steam and bake 3 minutes. Spray again in the same way, closing the door immediately so that steam doesn't escape, and bake until loaves begin to color, about 20 minutes. Reduce heat to 400°F. and bake until loaves are a rich caramel color and the crusts are firm, another 15 to 20 minutes.

To test the loaves for doneness, remove and hold the loaves upside down. Strike the bottoms firmly with your finger. If the sound is hollow, the breads are done. If it doesn't sound hollow, bake 5 minutes longer. Cool completely on a wire rack.

COARSE-GRAIN NORWEGIAN FARM LOAF*

Task	Approximate Time	Comments
Prepreparation		Ferment *poolish*.
Preparation	10 min.	Calculate temperatures. Assemble ingredients. Mix.
Knead	15 min.	Take temperature of final dough.
Ferment	3 hr.	Moderate: 74°–80°F. until doubled in volume.
Divide	5 min.	Deflate and cut into 2 equal portions.
Shape	5 min.	Flatten with heel of hand. Form balls for round loaves. Place on floured board.
Proof	2 hr.	Moderate: 74°–80°F. until increased 1½ × in volume.
Bake	40 min.	With steam. 450°–400°F.
Cool	20 min.	On rack or in baskets.

Cumulative Total Time: 6 hr., 45 min.

*This chart also applies to Wheat and Whole Berry Bread (page 90),
Breakfast Loaf with Sesame Seeds and Raisins (page 93),
Honey Wheat Bread with Poppy Seeds and Lemon (page 96),
Wheat Walnut Loaf (page 99), Buttermilk Currant Loaf (page 103),
and 100 Percent Whole Wheat Cumin Loaf (page 106).

WHEAT AND WHOLE BERRY BREAD

> Allow 8 hours to soak the wheat berries.
> Allow 2 to 10 hours to make and ferment the *poolish*.
> Total preparation and baking time (not including the *poolish*):
> 6 hours, 25 minutes

Here is the classic integration of fresh whole grain from the fields into a loaf of bread. The round wheat berry in the crumb makes this bread alive with wild nutlike flavor. It is rich, dense, and hearty. Slice it for sandwiches or toast it if you want to bring alive all the intense wheat flavor.

Makes 2 round 10-inch loaves

Whole wheat berries	1 cup	7 ounces

POOLISH

Spring water (75°F.)	¾ cup	6 fluid ounces
Moist yeast	1 teaspoon	¼ ounce
or dry yeast	½ teaspoon	⅛ ounce
20% bran wheat flour	¾ cup	4 ounces
Whole wheat flour, preferably coarse ground*	½ cup	3 ounces

FINAL DOUGH

Spring water	2¼ cups	18 fluid ounces
Moist yeast	1 teaspoon	¼ ounce
or dry yeast	½ teaspoon	⅛ ounce
Whole wheat flour, preferably coarse ground*	2¾ cups	14 ounces
Fine sea salt	1 tablespoon	¾ ounce
20% bran wheat flour*	3¼–4¼ cups	16–21 ounces
Cornmeal, for dusting		

* See Flours (pages 42–49). These are good approximate measures. You may use more or less depending on the weight and absorbency of your flours.

PREPARE THE WHEAT BERRIES (8 hours or overnight) Place the wheat berries in a medium bowl; add enough hot water to cover (preferably spring water, but tap will do). Let stand at least 8 hours or overnight.

MAKE AND FERMENT THE *POOLISH* (allow 2 to 10 hours) Combine the water and yeast in a medium bowl. Let stand 1 minute, then stir with a wooden spoon until yeast is dissolved. Add flours and stir until the consistency of a thick batter. Continue stirring for about 100 strokes or until the strands of gluten come off the spoon when you press the back of the spoon against the bowl. Scrape down the sides of the bowl with a rubber spatula. Cover with a clean damp towel or plastic wrap, and put in a moderately warm (74°–80°F.) draft-free place until it is bubbly and has increased in volume.

MIX AND KNEAD THE FINAL DOUGH (25 minutes) Measure the ingredients and calculate the necessary temperatures (see page 58). Drain the wheat berries. Bring the bowl with the *poolish* to your work space. The *poolish* should be soupy, bubbly, and puffy and it should have a wheaty aroma. Transfer the *poolish* to a 6-quart bowl. Add the water and yeast. Break up the *poolish* with a wooden spoon and stir until it loosens and the mixture foams slightly. Add the whole wheat flour and the drained whole wheat berries; stir until well combined. Add the salt and enough of the bran flour to make a thick mass that is difficult to stir. Turn out onto a well-floured surface. Knead, adding more of the remaining flour when needed, until dough is soft, 15 to 17 minutes. (Or knead in a heavy-duty mixer. See page 67). The dough is ready when a small amount pulled from the mass springs back quickly (see Kneading, page 66).

FERMENT THE DOUGH (2 to 3 hours) Shape the dough into a ball and let it rest on a lightly floured surface while you scrape, clean, and lightly oil the large bowl. Place the dough in the bowl and turn the dough to coat the top with oil. Take the dough's temperature: the ideal is 78°F. (see page 58). Cover with a clean damp towel or plastic wrap and put in a moderately warm (74°–80°F.) draft-free place until doubled in volume.

> *Note: If the dough temperature is higher than 78°F., put it in a cooler than 78°F. place like the refrigerator until the dough cools to 78°F. If it is lower than 78°F., put it in a warmer than 78°F. place until the dough warms to 78°F. The point is to try to keep the dough at 78°F. during its fermentation. If you do have to move the dough, be gentle and don't jostle it, or the dough may deflate.*

(continued)

The dough has risen enough when a finger poked ½ inch into the dough leaves an indentation.

DIVIDE AND SHAPE THE DOUGH INTO LOAVES (10 minutes) Deflate the dough by pushing down in the center and pulling up on the sides. Transfer the dough to a lightly floured work surface and knead briefly. Cut into 2 equal pieces. Flatten each with the heel of your hand using firm direct strokes. Shape each piece into a tight ball for round loaves (see Taking Shape, page 68).

PROOF THE LOAVES (1½ to 2 hours) Place the loaves on a board that has been lightly dusted with cornmeal. Cover with a clean damp towel and put in a moderately warm (74°–80°F.) draft-free place until increased in volume about 1½ times.

BAKE THE LOAVES (40 minutes) Forty-five minutes to 1 hour before baking, preheat the oven and homemade hearth or baking stone on the center rack of the oven (see Equipment, page 52) to 450°F.

The oven rack must be in the center of the oven. If it is in the lower third of the oven, the bottoms of the breads may burn, and if it is in the upper third, the top crusts may burn.

Gently invert the loaves onto a floured board or peel so that they are right side up. Using a very sharp, serrated knife or a single-edged razor blade, score the loaves by making quick shallow cuts ¼ to ½ inch deep along the surface.

Using a well-floured peel, slide the loaves one at a time onto the hearth and quickly spray the inner walls and floor of the oven with cold water from a spritzer bottle. If there's an electric light bulb in the oven, avoid spraying it directly—it may burst. Spray for several seconds until steam has filled the oven. Quickly close the door to trap the steam and bake 3 minutes. Spray again in the same way, closing the door immediately so that steam doesn't escape, and bake until loaves begin to color, 15 to 20 minutes. Reduce heat to 400°F. and bake until loaves are a rich caramel color and the crusts are firm, another 15 to 20 minutes.

To test the loaves for doneness, remove and hold the loaves upside down. Strike the bottoms firmly with your finger. If the sound is hollow, the breads are done. If it doesn't sound hollow, bake 5 minutes longer. Cool completely on a wire rack.

See chart on page 89.

BREAKFAST LOAF WITH SESAME SEEDS AND RAISINS

Allow 2 to 10 hours to make and ferment the *poolish*.
Total preparation and baking time (not including the *poolish*):
6 hours, 25 minutes

I got hooked on raisin bran cereal as a kid; now I want raisins in my bread at breakfast. This bread is deep golden, sweet, nutty, crunchy, and delightfully scented by the toasted sesame seeds. Bake these in rectangular loaf pans. You'll want the easy shape for toaster-size slices.

Makes two 9 by 5-inch loaves

POOLISH

Spring water (75°F.)	¾ cup	6 fluid ounces
Moist yeast	1 teaspoon	¼ ounce
or dry yeast	½ teaspoon	⅛ ounce
20% bran wheat flour	¾ cup	4 ounces
Whole wheat flour, preferably coarse ground*	½ cup	2½ ounces

FINAL DOUGH

Sesame seeds	½ cup	2½ ounces
Spring water	2¼ cups	18 fluid ounces
Moist yeast	1 teaspoon	¼ ounce
or dry yeast	½ teaspoon	⅛ ounce
Whole wheat flour, preferably coarse ground*	1¾ cups	9 ounces
Fine sea salt	1 tablespoon	¾ ounce
20% bran wheat flour*	3¼–4¼ cups	16–21 ounces
Golden seedless raisins	3 cups	1 pound

* See Flours (pages 42–49). These are good approximate measures. You may use more or less depending on the weight and absorbency of your flours.

MAKE AND FERMENT THE *POOLISH* (allow 2 to 10 hours)
Combine the water and yeast in a medium bowl. Let stand 1 minute, then stir with a wooden spoon until yeast is dissolved. Add flours and stir until the consistency of a thick batter. Continue stirring for

(*continued*)

about 100 strokes or until the strands of gluten come off the spoon when you press the back of the spoon against the bowl. There will be lively bubbles on the surface. Cover with a clean damp towel or plastic wrap and put in a moderately warm (74°–80°F.) draft-free place until it is bubbly and has increased in volume.

PREPARE THE SESAME SEEDS (20 minutes; includes cooling)   Place the sesame seeds in a small dry skillet. Cook over medium heat, stirring constantly, until lightly toasted, 2 to 3 minutes. Transfer immediately to a plate, place in the refrigerator, and cool completely.

MIX AND KNEAD THE FINAL DOUGH (25 minutes)   Measure the remaining ingredients and calculate the necessary temperatures (see page 58). Bring the bowl with the *poolish* to your work space. The *poolish* should be soupy, bubbly, and puffy and it should have a wheaty aroma. Scrape the *poolish* into a 6-quart bowl. Add the water and yeast. Break the *poolish* up well with a wooden spoon and stir until it loosens and the mixture foams slightly. Add the whole wheat flour and cooled sesame seeds; stir until well combined. Add the salt and enough bran flour to make a thick mass that is difficult to stir. Turn out onto a well-floured surface. Knead, adding more of the remaining flour as needed, for 10 minutes. Gradually knead in the raisins and continue kneading until the dough is soft and smooth, 15 to 17 minutes total. The dough is ready when a small amount pulled from the mass springs back quickly (see Kneading, page 66).

FERMENT THE DOUGH (2 to 3 hours)   Shape the dough into a ball and let it rest on a lightly floured surface while you scrape, clean, and lightly oil the large bowl. Place the dough in the bowl and turn the dough to coat the top with oil. Take the dough's temperature: the ideal is 78°F. (see page 58). Cover with a clean damp towel or plastic wrap and put in a moderately warm (74°–80°F.) draft-free place until doubled in volume.

> <u>Note:</u> *If the dough temperature is higher than 78°F., put it in a cooler than 78°F. place like the refrigerator until the dough cools to 78°F. If it is lower than 78°F., put it in a warmer than 78°F. place until the dough warms to 78°F. The point is to try to keep the dough at 78°F. during its*

*fermentation. If you do have to move the dough, be gentle
and don't jostle it, or the dough may deflate.*

The dough has risen enough when a finger poked ½ inch into
the dough leaves an indentation.

DIVIDE AND SHAPE THE DOUGH INTO LOAVES (10
minutes) Deflate the dough by pushing down in the center and
pulling up on the sides. Transfer the dough to a lightly floured work
surface and knead briefly. Cut into 2 equal pieces. Flatten each with
the heel of your hand, using firm direct strokes. Shape each piece
into a 9-inch-long log (see Taking Shape, page 68), sealing firmly and
pinching closed.

PROOF THE LOAVES (1½ to 2 hours) Place the loaves seam side
down in lightly buttered 9 × 5 × 3-inch baking pans. Cover with a
clean damp towel or plastic wrap and put in a moderately warm (74°–
80°F.) draft-free place until dough rises just to the rim of the pan.

BAKE THE LOAVES (40 minutes) Forty-five minutes to 1 hour before baking, preheat the oven and homemade hearth or baking stone
on the center rack of the oven (see Equipment, page 52) to 450°F.

The oven rack must be in the center of the oven. If it is in the
lower third of the oven, the bottoms of the breads may burn, and if
it is in the upper third, the top crusts may burn.

Using a sharp serrated knife or single-edged razor, score the
loaves by making quick shallow cuts ¼ to ½ inch deep on the top
of the loaf. Place the pans on the hearth and bake 15 to 20 minutes.
Reduce heat to 400°F. and bake until loaves are a rich caramel color
and the crusts are firm, another 15 to 20 minutes.

To test the loaves for doneness, remove from the pans and hold
upside down. Strike the bottoms firmly with your finger. If the sound
is hollow, the breads are done. If it doesn't sound hollow, return
breads to the pans and bake 5 minutes longer. Cool completely on
a wire rack.

*Note: If you prefer a soft top crust, brush the warm loaves
with melted butter after removing them from the oven.*

See chart on page 89.

HONEY WHEAT BREAD WITH POPPY SEEDS AND LEMON

Allow 2 to 10 hours to make and ferment the *poolish*.
Total preparation and baking time (not including the *poolish*):
6 hours, 25 minutes

Although I consider myself a purist, I do on occasion add a sweetener to my breads. Honey and lemon combine to form a sweet zest in this loaf and poppy seeds add the pleasure of crunch. The light crumb is flecked with lemon and tiny seeds. This bread complements a sharp cheese splendidly. It also makes great breakfast toast.

Makes two 9 by 5-inch loaves

POOLISH

Spring water (75°F.)	¾ cup	6 fluid ounces
Moist yeast	1 teaspoon	¼ ounce
or dry yeast	½ teaspoon	⅛ ounce
20% bran wheat flour*	¾ cup	4 ounces
Whole wheat flour, preferably coarse ground*	½ cup	2½ ounces

FINAL DOUGH

Spring water	2¼ cups	18 fluid ounces
Moist yeast	1 teaspoon	¼ ounce
or dry yeast	½ teaspoon	⅛ ounce
Whole wheat flour, preferably coarse ground*	1½ cups	8¾ ounces
Grated zest of 1 large lemon	2 teaspoons	
Honey, preferably wildflower	¼ cup	1 ounce
Poppy seeds	3 tablespoons	¾ ounce
Fine sea salt	1 tablespoon	¾ ounce
20% bran wheat flour*	3¼–4¼ cups	16–21 ounces

---

* See Flours (pages 42–49). These are good approximate measures. You may use more or less depending on the weight and absorbency of your flours.

MAKE AND FERMENT THE *POOLISH* (allow 2 to 10 hours) Combine the water and yeast in a medium bowl. Let stand 1 minute, then stir with a wooden spoon until yeast is dissolved. Add flours and stir until the consistency of a thick batter. Continue stirring for about 100 strokes or until the strands of gluten come off the spoon when you press the back of the spoon against the bowl. Scrape down the sides of the bowl with a rubber spatula. Cover with a clean damp towel or plastic wrap, and put in a moderately warm (74°–80°F.) draft-free place until it is bubbly and increased in volume.

MIX AND KNEAD THE FINAL DOUGH (25 minutes) Measure the ingredients and calculate the necessary temperatures (see page 58). Bring the bowl with the *poolish* to your work space. The *poolish* should be soupy, bubbly, and puffy and it should have a wheaty aroma. Scrape the *poolish* into a 6-quart bowl. Add the water and yeast. Break up the *poolish* well with a wooden spoon and stir until it loosens and the mixture foams slightly. Add the whole wheat flour, lemon, honey, and poppy seeds; stir until well combined. Add the salt and enough of the bran flour to make a thick mass that is difficult to stir. Turn out onto a well-floured surface. Knead, adding more of the remaining flour as needed for 10 minutes. Gradually knead in the raisins and continue kneading until dough is soft and smooth, 15 to 17 minutes total. (Or make in a heavy-duty mixer; see page 67.) The dough is ready when a small amount, pulled from the mass, springs back quickly. (See Kneading and Kneading In pages 66 and 76).

FERMENT THE DOUGH (2 to 3 hours) Shape the dough into a ball and let it rest on a lightly floured surface while you scrape, clean, and lightly oil the large bowl. Place the dough in the bowl and turn the dough to coat the top with oil. Take the dough's temperature: the ideal is 78°F. (see page 58). Cover with a clean damp towel or plastic wrap and put in a moderately warm (74°–80°F.) draft-free place until doubled in volume.

> *Note: If the dough temperature is higher than 78°F., put it in a cooler than 78°F. place like the refrigerator until the dough cools to 78°F. If it is lower than 78°F., put it in a warmer than 78°F. place until the dough warms to 78°F.*

(continued)

The point is to try to keep the dough at 78°F. during its fermentation. If you do have to move the dough, be gentle and don't jostle it, or the dough may deflate.

The dough has risen enough when a finger poked ½ inch into the dough leaves an indentation.

DIVIDE AND SHAPE THE DOUGH INTO LOAVES (10 minutes) Deflate the dough by pushing down in the center and pulling up on the sides. Transfer the dough to a lightly floured work surface and knead briefly. Cut into 2 equal pieces. Flatten each with the heel of your hand using firm direct strokes. Shape each piece into a log (see Taking Shape, page 68), sealing firmly and pinching closed.

PROOF THE LOAVES (1½ to 2 hours) Place the loaves seam side down in lightly buttered 9 x 5 x 3-inch baking pans. Cover with a clean damp towel or plastic wrap and put in a moderately warm (74°–80°F.) draft-free place until dough rises just to the rim of the pan.

BAKE THE LOAVES (40 minutes) Forty-five minutes to 1 hour before baking, preheat the oven and homemade hearth or baking stone on the center rack of the oven (see Equipment, page 52) to 450°F.

The oven rack must be in the center of the oven. If it is in the lower third of the oven, the bottoms of the breads may burn, and if it is in the upper third, the top crusts may burn.

Using a sharp serrated knife or single-edged razor, score the loaves by making quick shallow cuts ¼ to ½ inch deep on the top of the loaf. Place the pans on the hearth and bake 15 to 20 minutes. Reduce heat to 400°F. and bake until loaves are a rich caramel color and the crusts are firm, another 15 to 20 minutes.

To test the loaves for doneness, remove the loaves from the pans and hold them upside down. Strike the bottoms firmly with your finger. If the sound is hollow, the breads are done. If it doesn't sound hollow, return breads to the pans and bake 5 minutes longer. Cool completely on a wire rack.

See chart on page 89.

WHEAT WALNUT LOAF

Allow 2 to 10 hours to make and ferment the *poolish*.
Allow 1 hour to prepare the walnuts.
Total preparation and baking time (not including the *poolish*):
6 hours, 25 minutes

This is a favorite with my customers, my family, and me. It's a dark, rich loaf packed with walnuts. Full of earthy flavor and sweet nut crunch, I love this bread toasted and spread with butter and preserves or served with a mild cheese.

Makes 2 round 7½-inch loaves, or 2 long 11-inch torpedo-shaped loaves

POOLISH

Spring water (75°F.)	¾ cup	6 fluid ounces
Moist yeast	1 teaspoon	¼ ounce
or dry yeast	½ teaspoon	⅛ ounce
20% bran wheat flour*	¾ cup	4 ounces
Whole wheat flour, preferably coarse ground*	½ cup	3 ounces

FINAL DOUGH

Walnut halves and pieces	4 cups	16 ounces
Spring water	2¼ cups	18 fluid ounces
Moist yeast	1 teaspoon	¼ ounce
or dry yeast	½ teaspoon	⅛ ounce
Whole wheat flour, preferably coarse ground*	1½ cups	8¾ ounces
Cracked wheat	½ cup	3¼ ounces
Cracked rye	½ cup	2½ ounces
Fine sea salt	1 tablespoon	¾ ounce
20% bran wheat flour*	3¼–4¼ cups	16–21 ounces
Cornmeal, for dusting		

---

* See Flours (pages 42–49). These are good approximate measures. You may use more or less depending on the weight and absorbency of your flours.

MAKE AND FERMENT THE *POOLISH* (allow 2 to 10 hours)

Combine the water and yeast in a medium bowl. Let stand 1 minute,

(continued)

then stir with a wooden spoon until yeast is dissolved. Add the flours and stir until the consistency of a thick batter. Continue stirring for about 100 strokes or until the strands of gluten come off the spoon when you press the back of the spoon against the bowl. Scrape down the sides of the bowl with a rubber spatula. Cover with a clean damp towel or plastic wrap, and put in a moderately warm (74°–80°F.) draft-free place until it is bubbly and increased in volume.

PREPARE THE WALNUTS (1 hour including cooling time) Preheat the oven to 350°F. Place the walnuts on a baking sheet and bake, stirring once or twice, until the walnuts are lightly toasted, 8 to 12 minutes. Transfer to a platter and place in the refrigerator to cool completely.

Transfer 1 cup of the cooled walnuts to the container of a food processor fitted with the steel chopping blade. Pulse the machine until the nuts are finely chopped. Set aside the finely chopped nuts and the remaining 3 cups toasted walnuts.

MIX AND KNEAD THE FINAL DOUGH (25 minutes) Measure the remaining ingredients and calculate the necessary temperatures (see page 58). Bring the bowl with the *poolish* to your work space. The *poolish* should be soupy, bubbly, and puffy and it should have a wheaty aroma. Scrape the *poolish* into a 6-quart bowl. Add the water and yeast. Break up the *poolish* well with a wooden spoon and stir until it loosens and the mixture foams slightly. Add the whole wheat flour, cracked wheat, cracked rye, and finely chopped walnuts; stir until well combined. Add the salt and enough of the bran flour to make a thick mass that is difficult to stir. Turn out onto a well-floured surface. Knead, adding more of the remaining flour, for 10 minutes. Gradually knead in the walnut halves and continue kneading until the dough is soft and smooth, 15 to 17 minutes total. (Or make in a heavy-duty mixer; see page 67.) The dough is ready when a small amount, pulled from the mass, springs back quickly (see Kneading, page 66).

FERMENT THE DOUGH (2 to 3 hours) Shape the dough into a ball and let it rest on a lightly floured surface while you scrape, clean, and lightly oil the large bowl. Place the dough in the bowl and turn the dough to coat the top with oil. Take the dough's temperature:

the ideal is 78°F. (see page 58). Cover with a clean damp towel or plastic wrap and put in a moderately warm (74°–80°F.) draft-free place until doubled in volume.

> *Note: If the dough temperature is higher than 78°F., put it in a cooler than 78°F. place like the refrigerator until the dough cools to 78°F. If it is lower than 78°F., put it in a warmer than 78°F. place until the dough warms to 78°F. The point is to try to keep the dough at 78°F. during its fermentation. If you do have to move the dough, be gentle and don't jostle it, or the dough may deflate.*

The dough has risen enough when a finger poked ½ inch into the dough leaves an indentation.

DIVIDE AND SHAPE THE DOUGH INTO LOAVES (10 minutes) Deflate the dough by pushing down in the center and pulling up on the sides. Transfer the dough to a lightly floured work surface; knead briefly and cut into 2 equal pieces. Flatten each with the heel of your hand using firm direct strokes. Shape each piece into a tight ball for round loaves or torpedo-shaped loaves (see Taking Shape, page 68).

PROOF THE LOAVES (1½ to 2 hours) Place the loaves on a board that has been lightly dusted with cornmeal. Cover with a clean damp towel or plastic wrap and put in a moderately warm (74°–80°F.) draft-free place until increased in volume about 1½ times.

BAKE THE LOAVES (40 minutes) Forty-five minutes to 1 hour before baking, preheat the oven and homemade hearth or baking stone on the center rack of the oven (see Equipment, page 52) to 450°F.

The oven rack must be in the center of the oven. If it is in the lower third of the oven, the bottoms of the breads may burn, and if it is in the upper third, the top crusts may burn.

Gently slip the loaves onto a floured board or peel so that they are right side up. Using a very sharp, serrated knife or a single-edged razor blade, score the loaves by making quick shallow cuts ¼ to ½ inch deep along the surface.

Using a well-floured peel, slip the loaves one at a time onto the hearth and quickly spray the inner walls and floor of the oven with

(continued)

cold water from a spritzer bottle. If there's an electric light bulb in the oven, avoid spraying it directly—it may burst. Spray for several seconds until steam has filled the oven. Quickly close the door to trap the steam and bake 3 minutes. Spray again in the same way, closing the door immediately so that steam doesn't escape, and bake until loaves begin to color, about 20 minutes. Reduce heat to 400°F. and bake until loaves are a rich caramel color and the crusts are firm, another 15 to 20 minutes.

To test the loaves for doneness, remove and hold the loaves upside down. Strike the bottoms firmly with your finger. If the sound is hollow, the breads are done. If it doesn't sound hollow, bake 5 minutes longer. Cool completely on a wire rack.

See chart on page 89.

BUTTERMILK CURRANT LOAF

Allow 2 to 10 hours to make and ferment the *poolish*.
Total preparation and baking time (not including the *poolish*):
6 hours, 25 minutes

The tang of buttermilk and the sweet currants make this the kind of bread I eat all by itself. The dark currants are packed tightly through the dense golden crumb. I eat it warm as soon as I can after baking.

Makes two round 10-inch loaves

POOLISH

Spring water (75°F.)	¾ cup	6 fluid ounces
Moist yeast	1 teaspoon	¼ ounce
or dry yeast	½ teaspoon	⅛ ounce
20% bran wheat flour*	¾ cup	4 ounces
Whole wheat flour, preferably coarse ground*	½ cup	2½ ounces

FINAL DOUGH

Spring water	1½ cups	12 fluid ounces
Moist yeast	1 teaspoon	¼ ounce
or dry yeast	½ teaspoon	⅛ ounce
Whole wheat flour, preferably coarse ground*	1½ cups	8¾ ounces
Buttermilk	1½ cups	12 ounces
Honey	2 tablespoons	½ ounce
Fine sea salt	1 tablespoon	¾ ounce
20% bran wheat flour*	3¼–4¼ cups	16–21 ounces
Dried currants	3 cups	16 ounces
Cornmeal, for dusting		

---

* See Flours (pages 42–49). These are good approximate measures. You may use more or less depending on the weight and absorbency of your flours.

MAKE AND FERMENT THE *POOLISH* (allow 2 to 10 hours) Combine the water and yeast in a medium bowl. Let stand 1 minute, then stir with a wooden spoon until yeast is dissolved. Add the flours and stir until the consistency of a thick batter. Continue stirring for

(continued)

about 100 strokes or until the strands of gluten come off the spoon when you press the back of the spoon against the bowl. Scrape down the sides of the bowl with a rubber spatula. Cover with a clean damp towel or plastic wrap, and put in a moderately warm (74°–80°F.) draft-free place until it is bubbly and increased in volume.

MIX AND KNEAD THE FINAL DOUGH (25 minutes) Measure the ingredients and calculate the necessary temperatures (see page 58). Bring the bowl with the *poolish* to your work space. The *poolish* should be soupy, bubbly, and puffy and it should have a wheaty aroma. Scrape the *poolish* into a 6-quart bowl. Add the water and yeast. Break up the *poolish* with a wooden spoon and stir until it loosens and the mixture foams slightly. Add the whole wheat flour, buttermilk, and honey; stir until well combined. Add the salt and enough of the bran flour to make a thick mass that is difficult to stir. Turn out onto a well-floured surface. Knead, adding more of the remaining flour, for 10 minutes. Gradually knead in the currants and continue kneading until the dough is soft and smooth, 15 to 17 minutes total. (Or make in a heavy-duty mixer; see page 67.) The dough is ready when a small amount pulled from the mass springs back quickly (see Kneading and Kneading In, pages 66 and 76).

FERMENT THE DOUGH (2 to 3 hours) Shape the dough into a ball and let it rest on a lightly floured surface while you scrape, clean, and lightly oil the large bowl. Place the dough in the bowl and turn the dough to coat the top with oil. Take the dough's temperature: the ideal is 78°F. (see page 58). Cover with a clean damp towel or plastic wrap and put in a moderately warm (74°–80°F.) draft-free place until doubled in volume.

> *Note: If the dough temperature is higher than 78°F., put it in a cooler than 78°F. place like the refrigerator until the dough cools to 78°F. If it is lower than 78°F., put it in a warmer than 78°F. place until the dough warms to 78°F. The point is to try to keep the dough at 78°F. during its fermentation. If you do have to move the dough, be gentle and don't jostle it, or the dough may deflate.*

The dough has risen enough when a finger poked ½ inch into the dough leaves an indentation.

DIVIDE AND SHAPE THE DOUGH INTO LOAVES (10 minutes) Deflate the dough by pushing down in the center and pulling up on the sides. Transfer the dough to a lightly floured work surface; knead briefly and cut into 2 equal pieces. Flatten each with the heel of your hand using firm direct strokes. Scrape away excess flour from the work surface. Shape each piece into a tight ball for round loaves (see Taking Shape, page 68).

PROOF THE LOAVES (1½ to 2 hours) Place the loaves on a board that has been sprinkled lightly with cornmeal. Cover with a clean damp towel or plastic wrap and put in a moderately warm (74°–80°F.) draft-free place until increased in volume about 1½ times.

BAKE THE LOAVES (40 minutes) Forty-five minutes to 1 hour before baking, preheat the oven and homemade hearth or baking stone on the center rack of the oven (see Equipment, page 52) to 450°F.

The oven rack must be in the center of the oven. If it is in the lower third of the oven, the bottoms of the breads may burn, and if it is in the upper third, the top crusts may burn.

Using a well-floured peel, slip the loaves one at a time onto the hearth and quickly spray the inner walls and floor of the oven with cold water from a spritzer bottle. If there's an electric light bulb in the oven, avoid spraying it directly—it may burst. Spray for several seconds until steam has filled the oven. Quickly close the door to trap the steam and bake 3 minutes. Spray again in the same way, closing the door immediately so that steam doesn't escape, and bake until loaves begin to color, about 20 minutes. Reduce heat to 400°F. and bake until loaves are a rich caramel color and the crusts are firm, another 15 to 20 minutes.

To test the loaves for doneness, remove and hold the loaves upside down. Strike the bottoms firmly with your finger. If the sound is hollow, the breads are done. If it doesn't sound hollow, bake 5 minutes longer. Cool completely on a wire rack.

See chart on page 89.

100 PERCENT WHOLE WHEAT CUMIN LOAF

Allow 2 to 10 hours to make and ferment the *poolish*.
Total preparation and baking time (not including the *poolish*):
6 hours, 25 minutes

Here is a dense spicy bread, perfect for savory appetizers or to serve with highly seasoned dishes like chili or curry.

Makes 2 round 10-inch loaves

POOLISH

Spring water (75°F.)	¾ cup	6 fluid ounces
Moist yeast	1 teaspoon	¼ ounce
or dry yeast	½ teaspoon	⅛ ounce
20% bran wheat flour*	¾ cup	4 ounces
Whole wheat flour, preferably coarse ground*	½ cup	2½ ounces

FINAL DOUGH

Unsalted butter	2 tablespoons	1 ounce
1 large red onion, thinly sliced	1 cup	5 ounces
Spring water	2¼ cups	18 fluid ounces
Moist yeast	1 teaspoon	¼ ounce
or dry yeast	½ teaspoon	⅛ ounce
Fine sea salt	1 tablespoon	¾ ounce
Whole wheat flour, preferably medium ground*	4¼–5¼ cups	24–29 ounces
Cumin seeds, freshly crushed in a mortar or spice mill	3 tablespoons	¼ ounce
Cornmeal, for dusting		

---

* See Flours (pages 42–49). These are good approximate measures. You may use more or less depending on the absorbency of your flours.

MAKE AND FERMENT THE *POOLISH* (allow 2 to 10 hours)
Combine the water and yeast in a medium bowl. Let stand 1 minute, then stir with a wooden spoon until yeast is dissolved. Add the flour and stir until the consistency of a thick batter. Continue stirring for

about 100 strokes or until the strands of gluten come off the spoon when you press the back of the spoon against the bowl. There will be lively bubbles on the surface. Cover with a clean damp towel or plastic wrap, and put in a moderately warm (74°–80°F.) draft-free place until it is bubbly and increased in volume.

PREPARE THE ONIONS (20 minutes includes cooling time) Melt the butter in a skillet over medium heat. Add the onion and cook until softened, about 5 minutes. Transfer to a plate, and place in the refrigerator to cool completely.

MIX AND KNEAD THE FINAL DOUGH (25 minutes) Measure the remaining ingredients and calculate the necessary temperatures (see page 58). Bring the bowl with the *poolish* to your work space. The *poolish* should be soupy, bubbly, and puffy and it should have a wheaty aroma. Scrape the *poolish* into a 6-quart bowl. Add the water and yeast. Break up the *poolish* with a wooden spoon and stir until it loosens and the mixture foams slightly. Add the salt, cooled onions, cumin, and enough of the flour to make a thick mass that is difficult to stir. Turn out onto a well-floured surface. Knead, adding more of the remaining flour, until the dough is soft and smooth, 15 to 17 minutes. (Or make in a heavy-duty mixer; see page 67.) The dough is ready when a small amount, pulled from the mass springs back quickly (see Kneading, page 66).

FERMENT THE DOUGH (2 to 3 hours) Shape the dough into a ball and let it rest on a lightly floured surface while you scrape, clean, and lightly oil the large bowl. Place the dough in the bowl and turn the dough to coat the top with oil. Take the dough's temperature: the ideal is 78°F. (see page 58). Cover with a clean damp towel or plastic wrap and put in a moderately warm (74°–80°F.) draft-free place until doubled in volume.

> *Note: If the dough temperature is higher than 78°F., put it in a cooler than 78°F. place like the refrigerator until the dough cools to 78°F. If it is lower than 78°F., put it in a warmer than 78°F. place until the dough warms to 78°F. The point is to try to keep the dough at 78°F. during its*

(continued)

*fermentation. If you do have to move the dough, be gentle
and don't jostle it, or the dough may deflate.*

The dough has risen enough when a finger poked ½ inch into
the dough leaves an indentation.

DIVIDE AND SHAPE THE DOUGH INTO LOAVES (10 minutes) Deflate the dough by pushing down in the center and pulling up on
the sides. Transfer the dough to a lightly floured work surface; knead
briefly and cut into 2 equal pieces. Flatten each with the heel of your
hand using firm direct strokes. Shape each piece into a tight ball.

PROOF THE LOAVES (1½ to 2 hours) Place the loaves on a board
that has been lightly dusted with cornmeal. Cover with a clean damp
towel or plastic wrap and put in a moderately warm (74°–80°F.) draft-
free place until increased in volume about 1½ times.

BAKE THE LOAVES (40 minutes) Forty-five minutes to 1 hour before baking, preheat the oven and homemade hearth or baking stone
on the center rack of the oven (see Equipment, page 52) to 450°F.

The oven rack must be in the center of the oven. If it is in the
lower third of the oven, the bottoms of the breads may burn, and if
it is in the upper third, the top crusts may burn.

Using a very sharp, serrated knife or a single-edged razor blade,
score the loaves by making quick shallow cuts ¼ to ½ inch deep
along the surface.

Using a well-floured peel, slip the loaves one at a time onto the
hearth and quickly spray the inner walls and floor of the oven with
cold water from a spritzer bottle. If there's an electric light bulb in
the oven, avoid spraying it directly—it may burst. Spray for several
seconds until steam has filled the oven. Quickly close the door to
trap the steam and bake 3 minutes. Spray again in the same way,
closing the door immediately so that steam doesn't escape, and bake
until loaves begin to color, about 20 minutes. Reduce heat to 400°F.
and bake until loaves are a rich caramel color and the crusts are firm,
another 15 to 20 minutes.

To test the loaves for doneness, remove and hold the loaves
upside down. Strike the bottoms firmly with your finger. If the sound
is hollow, the breads are done. If it doesn't sound hollow, bake 5
minutes longer. Cool completely on a wire rack.

See chart on page 89.

STRAIGHT-DOUGH BREADS

TRADITIONAL BREADS FOR A
MODERN LIFE-STYLE

Bread made from a straight dough has no *poolish* to begin with. Simply line up the ingredients (water, yeast, flour, salt), combine, and knead. The straight-dough method allows for spontaneity in the kitchen, and probably sounds the most familiar because it's how many of us learned to make bread. Most bread books, however, will have you play it straight with a classic straight-dough recipe: knead, let the dough rise at room temperature, deflate, proof in pans or free-form loaves, and bake.

Those breads are honest, homemade loaves, but the flavor, texture, and look are often disappointing—flat and characterless. As a new home baker once asked me, "Why do I like the smell of the baking better than the taste of the bread?" The reason is that in order to get a quality loaf with complex taste, good crust, and moist texture from a straight dough, the baker must do something a little extraordinary with it. Using your tools, apply a little technique, vary the development of the dough slightly, increase the time and life of the fermentation. In other words, add some curves to straight-dough breads. In this chapter, we make some great breads from straight doughs because we add a lot of curves to them.

For example, because yeast cells have a lifespan of six to seven hours at a very warm (85°F.) temperature, decrease the temperature to a moderately warm 74°F. and increase the fermentation time by

DOUGH, IT'S ALIVE

Dough is a living thing, but it's not a monster. And bread making is simple—simple problems, simple solutions.

If your dough is too cool to work with, warm it up in the oven until it reaches 75°F. If it's too warm (above 80°F.), cool it in the refrigerator.

A dough made with high-quality flour will behave well and have life for twenty-four to thirty hours.

giving the dough two complete risings, deflating after each rise to invigorate the yeast with new oxygen. Give a final rising of 20 minutes to an hour in loaves. When the loaves reach the oven, the yeast is still lively, vigorous enough to provide another burst of activity in the sudden heat. This produces the lofty look and fine texture that you want in your breads. What might have been an ordinary bread is now one of more complex character and flavor because you made a five-hour bread rather than a three-hour bread.

Another way to create a rich and vital bread from a straight dough is to greatly increase the time and decrease the temperature during fermentation. This is a common practice among professional bakers who will do anything to get the best taste and texture from a simple dough. At Bread Alone we mix a straight dough for our popular Peasant Bread (see Classic Country-Style Hearth Loaf, page 64) at 9:30 P.M. It ferments for seven hours in a retarder, a refrigeratorlike box that cools the dough so the yeast activates slowly. By the time the morning baker comes on at 4:00 A.M., the dough has fermented and grown in volume, all the while building flavor. He deflates it, invigorates it with new oxygen, and lets it rise again at room temperature another 2 hours. Again he deflates it, shapes it, gives it a final rise, and bakes. By 9:30 A.M., twelve hours later, we have beautiful Peasant Bread loaves from a simple straight dough. If we had developed the dough according to a standard bread recipe, we would not have a bread with such taste, texture, and beauty.

My friend Steve Sullivan of Acme Bakery in Berkeley, California, manipulates the time and temperature of such fermentations. He builds a dough slowly, often mixing one-third of his dough at a time over a three-day period. Each day he adds fresh flour and water to the dough begun the day before.

The techniques are as unique to a professional baker as his or her breads, and they are usually developed to suit the baker's own tastes. The point is that you can create great bread from a straight dough—not from a recipe, but from combining the best available ingredients with your very own conscious and enthusiastic manipulations!

BREADS FROM
▪▪ STRAIGHT DOUGH ▪▪

All of the recipes in Chapter 7 will work as straight-dough breads. Here's how to make them in five hours.

FIVE-HOUR STRAIGHT-DOUGH BREAD

Task	Approximate Time	Comments
Preparation	10 min.	Calculate temperatures. Assemble ingredients. Mix.
Knead	15 min.	Take temperature of final dough.
Ferment	90 min.	Moderate: 74°–80°F. until doubled in volume.
Ferment	60 min.	Until doubled.
Divide	5 min.	Deflate and cut into 2 equal portions.
Shape	10 min.	Flatten with heel of hand. Form balls for round loaves. Place on floured board.
Proof	50 min.	Moderate: 74°–80°F. until increased 1½ × in volume.
Bake	30–35 min.	With steam. 450°F.– 400°F.
Cool	20 min.	On rack or in baskets.

Cumulative Total Time: 5 hr., 5 min.

MORNING-TO-NIGHT STRAIGHT DOUGH

Task	Approximate Time	Comments
Preparation	10 min.	Calculate temperatures. Assemble ingredients. Mix.
Knead	15 min.	Take temperature of final dough.
Ferment	8 hr.	Cool: 50F. until doubled in volume.
Come to room temp.	2 hr.	Moderate: 74°–80°F.
Ferment	45 min.	Moderate: 74°–80°F. until doubled in volume.
Divide	5 min.	Deflate and cut into 2 equal portions.
Shape	10 min.	Flatten with heel of hand. Form balls for round loaves. Place on floured board.
Proof	45 min.	Moderate: 74°–80°F. until increased 1½ × in volume.
Bake	45–50 min.	With steam. 450°F–400°F.
Cool	20 min.	On rack or in baskets.

Cumulative Total Time: 13 hr., 25 min.

This dough ferments for twenty-four hours at a very low temperature. As a result, it has a moist texture, dense crumb, and full-bodied taste of the grain. Let it come to room temperature, then treat it as you would the morning-to-night bread. Since it ferments for so long, use only half the amount of yeast called for.

NIGHT-TO-NIGHT STRAIGHT-DOUGH BREAD

Task	Approximate Time	Comments
Preparation	10 min.	Calculate temperatures. Assemble ingredients. Use half the amount of yeast. Mix.
Knead	15 min.	Take temperature of final dough.
Ferment	24 hrs.	Cold: 50°–60°F. until doubled in volume.
Come to room temperature	2 hr.	Moderate: 74°–80°F.
Ferment	45 min.	Moderate: 74°–80°F.
Divide	5 min.	Deflate and cut into 2 equal portions.
Shape	10 min.	Flatten with heel of hand. Form balls for round loaves. Place on floured board.
Proof	1 hr.	Moderate: 74°–80°F. until increased 1½ × in volume.
Bake	45 min.	With steam. 450°F.–400°F.
Cool	20 min.	On rack or in baskets.

Cumulative Total Time: 29 hr., 30 min.

THE BAKERS

THE STORY OF A BAKER'S LUNCH

During my first career as a chef, I was serious about developing my skills and spent several weeks every year in France, visiting and studying with renowned chefs. The experiences were always enriching as well as much too rich. I spent every night out, eating highly decorated food in restaurants, touring intensely busy kitchens, and returning to my hotel feeling overstimulated and overstuffed.

In the late mornings, craving substantial food in simple surroundings, I would wander into my neighborhood *boulangerie*. Inside was the comforting sight of the baker and his wife, the soothing smells of breads baking, the faces of the neighborhood customers, and the bounty of husky and delicate traditional loaves piled in baskets and arranged on shelves and in the window. The simplicity of it all was an elixir. Breaking open a warm and crackling *baguette*, I felt grounded once again.

Each morning I found a safe place to recoup my energy, and in the process I became ever more attracted to the warm and stable qualities of the bakery and less attracted to what I was in France to do. I began to talk to bakers, and I discovered they were very obvious characters—passionate, open, giving, excitable. They had an enthusiastic steadiness that I liked.

Seven years later I opened my bakery. But even then I had

worked in only one other. I had absorbed the trade only secondhand while devouring lots of good bread, and I needed to visit and do serious work with other bakers. I went back to Europe again, this time as a baker.

I landed in Paris with a *New York Times* article as my guide. Patricia Wells, the author of *The Food Lover's Guide to Paris* (Workman, 1984) had written a piece about searching out traditional *boulangeries* and the perfect *baguette*. In her story she mentioned the shops of ten prominent artisans in Paris where one could find good *baguettes*. I made it my task to find and visit all of them, among them Bernard Ganauchaud, known for his inventive and expert hand with decorative breads; Jean-Luc Poujauran, who at that time was one of the young bakers returning to traditional artisan breads made only with *blé biologique* (French organically grown wheat); Bernard Lebon, whose breads were baked in historic oak wood-fired brick ovens built in 1700; Lionel Poilâne, then the most acclaimed baker in Paris, famous for his moist sourdough loaves; and Michel Perruche, whose oven was slate-floored, rotating, wood-fired, and of great interest to me.

Each day I chose another baker. I arrived in the morning and ate warm bread as I watched the bakers pull the last loaves from the oven and the customers come and go. Eventually I asked to speak to the owner. Each baker was receptive. Each one took me in, showed me around, and talked about the breads he chose to make and the flours he used. And each was excited to introduce me to other bakers.

I had hundreds of questions about flour and wood fires, about slate and brick ovens, about machine and hand kneading. But each baker had a different answer—his own opinion. Flour and water in the hands of traditional bakers were like clay in the hands of different sculptors. The loaves I devoured during that trip were as unique as the bakers I visited. Each was particular in size, shape, and color; distinct in flavor and texture; and as singular as the baker's own signature.

This was the big, big lesson of that trip: the baker, like any artist, emerges in his work. His or her personal involvement and special craft within the craft create the great variety of fine tastes and appearances of the traditional breads. One baker kneaded his dough a special way, another had a unique method of shaping and scoring his loaves, another focused on the proofing process, and another demanded a particularly unusual time and temperature for fermentation. One baker tended to underbake certain breads and overbake others. Another chose only special wood from a certain forest for the fire. This is at the heart of traditional bread making: the precision and craft of the baker along with all his or her idiosyncrasies and flair.

On my next trip to France I had lunch with Patricia Wells. We talked about the traditional bakeries in Paris and the quiet revival going on—the few bakers making traditional bread as it was baked before World War II brought modernization to the corner bakery. She was interested in the bakers who were making bread simply for the love of traditional bread. She was attracted to the kind of bakers I was attracted to—those whose work was personal, who became attached to their bowls, their ovens, their customers. These were bakers who were artists taking time, not looking for the fast way to hot bread.

We both knew there were and are very few bakers like that around. Even some of the bakeries we spoke about that day no longer exist. Under the best circumstances, with New Age equipment and all, the baker's hours are still long, the work is hard, and the baker must literally put his face in the oven! It is hot, hard, long, tedious, lonely work. In all of France and America there may be but a few handfuls of old-fashioned bakeries where there is one baker and one oven, and where the personality of the baker is present in the bread and bakery.

After that visit I traveled to Paris as often as I could because I craved being around these other bakers. On one trip, a *boulanger* had arranged a morning tour for me, which included visits to a few bakeries and then lunch with all the bakers. We began at a bakery on the Right Bank. The baker was a large, gregarious man who happily showed me around his shop. When it was time to go, the *boulanger,* still heavily dusted with flour, accompanied us. On our way, we stopped at a café to have a drink. The three of us then went on to the next bakery, where I met the new baker, toured his bakery, and when it was time to go, that *boulanger,* also heavily dusted with flour, accompanied us. The four of us then stopped at a café for a drink. On the way to the next bakery, my friend the *boulanger* Basil Kamir joined us and by lunchtime there were six bakers, four of whom were still white-haired from flour and five of whom were pretty well plied from the stops we had been making along the way. We tumbled into the local *brasserie.*

When the waiter poured wine for us all, one thick-chested baker whose name I've forgotten, raised his glass and proposed a toast, *"Pain chaud, tout la journée."* Basil groaned and mumbled, refusing to lift his glass. The big baker slapped the table, sending puffs of flour flying from his hand. "Parisians care only for hot bread," he said staring at Basil. "It's our responsibility as *boulangers* to provide it—*pain chaud, tout la journée*—all day long."

Basil, who is known by the others as the one who stubbornly makes no modern compromises at his bakery, who fusses with "old-fashioned" brick ovens, and who spends hours developing a *levain* when shorter methods will do, looked at the big baker with a cool eye. "What good is hot bread if it is *pain dégoûtant.* Disgusting bread! Parisians are tired of bread without a soul, hot but limp-crusted loaves full of air instead of flavor. We must return to making breads that take time to grow and we must bake them until the crust is thick and tough. We have to bake breads that we can feel with our teeth." Basil raised his glass. "To slow breads—for the soul . . . for the teeth!"

The big baker sat back in his chair and grinned at Basil. "While you are chewing your bread, we will be selling ours." The others laughed.

Basil grew red-faced. *"Pain industriel,"* he growled. The insult snatched the laughter from their throats. "You're so busy," he steamed on, "with your *hot bread, hot bread, hot bread* all day long that I am certain you have forgotten how to make a good *levain*! Or worse, you've forgotten what it is!"

The table was shaking from Basil's adamant gestures and the eyes of the other patrons were fixed on us. I was sure a fistfight was seconds away. But instead there was silence while the waiter placed food in front of us, then more silence as our glances roamed and bounced from one to another around the table. Finally another baker raised his glass of wine, *"Tout les boulanger.* To all bakers!" Each man raised his glass and lunch began.

"The discussions are always heated," Basil told me later. "We don't agree sometimes more vehemently than others. Once I didn't speak to one of the others, nor he to me, for six months. We speak now. But we still fight all the time. I think it's better for the bread this way. Yes, I really think that it's better for the bread if we fight about it every once in a while."

SOURDOUGH

A GENTLE INTRODUCTION

Sourdough, or *levain* as French bakers call it, is an intensely alive mass of fermenting yeast, flour, and water that leavens and flavors a larger amount of dough. It is cultivated by combining water with organic whole-grain flour and allowing the natural yeasts present in the flour to grow and multiply over a period of days. In a professional bakery there are plenty of yeast cells present in the environment to spontaneously react with flour and water to ferment. In the home kitchen, however, I suggest adding a pinch of commercial yeast to ensure good fermentation. (See Stalking the Wild Yeast, page 186.) In time, the culture becomes tangy-sour, musty smelling, and strong enough to raise a larger mass of dough. The unique flavor and texture that sourdough gives a bread is unmatched by any other process.

Sourdough is the oldest leavener known. Years ago, before packets of active dry yeast were invented, if the family baker didn't have a sourdough, he or she couldn't make leavened bread. A good sourdough was treasured, maintained, and passed on within families.

We go to the trouble to make sourdough breads today because they possess qualities that breads made from packaged yeast don't have. The loaves baked with commercial yeast tend to be light and gassy, and generally stale faster than sourdough breads. A vigorous sourdough culture instead of a packet of commercial yeast accounts for as much as 30 percent of the final dough mass of your bread and supplies tremendous flavor, density, and moisture to the developing dough and final bread. Sourdough breads also undergo a much slower fermentation than do other yeast breads. This builds flavor and creates a chewy, tender, and often irregular texture that is never gassy.

Making a sourdough to use in baking your breads is a very simple and natural process that is, however, the most misunderstood procedure in all of bread making.

"Sourdough is so difficult," I've heard people say. "You must be in the right climate in the right place . . . in a two-hundred-year-old bakery . . . in a cellar . . . in an attic . . . in a dark place . . . in a light place."

A man I know recently returned from Europe and spoke reverently about eating the bread of a baker who has maintained the sourdough culture he got from his mother, who got it from her father. And the culture has been maintained for 150 years! These attitudes surround the making of a simple sourdough, giving it an intimidating mystery and off-putting fussiness. There is excessive value placed on sourdough from old, well-guarded cultures, as if these features imparted greater authenticity to a sourdough.

The truth is that many of us, professional and amateur bakers alike, perpetuate this myth. It inhibits the home baker from attempting sourdough and participating in the romance of bread making.

In this book you will learn to make a sourdough starter that will have tremendous vitality, and you will create delicious sourdough breads that will equal or surpass the bread made from a culture supposedly maintained for years in the family crock in the cellar or guarded by a baker in a vault somewhere. The whole process, from beginning the culture to pulling a loaf from the oven, takes four days, depending on weather, humidity, and air temperature.

All you need is fresh, stone-ground organic whole-grain flour, water, a pinch of yeast, and a safe and secure spot in the kitchen. Most important, you need patient awareness and attention.

Use fresh organic flour because it contains more wild yeast. Like the almost translucent white film of the yeast culture you can see on fresh grapes, there is a thin film of wild yeast on whole grain berries. The plentitude of these wild yeast cells in the flour will generate good fermentation. A lesser quality flour that has been de-braned, bromated, enriched, and stripped of its original goodness will take a long, long time to produce the same results because the amount of wild yeast is much less. A fresh whole-grain flour also provides an

THE POLISH BAKER

When I opened Bread Alone, one of my first customers was an older Polish woman. When she walked in she was immediately ecstatic because the bakery looked so much like the one in her hometown in Poland. She had been baking her own bread for years because she hadn't found good bread since arriving in the United States. She asked me to sell her some coarse rye flour, and she promised to bring me a loaf of her own sourdough rye bread the next week.

True to her promise, she came in a week or so later with a loaf of bread in one hand and a wooden bowl in the other. She was thrilled about being able to bake such good bread. She said the flour she bought from us was so much better than the flat-tasting flours she had been using. I tasted the bread.

"This is delicious," I said, "Tell me how you made it."

"The first thing I do is I take the rye flour and mix it with a little water and leave it overnight in this bowl," she said, offering the bowl for me to examine.

"So?" I asked, looking blankly at the bowl.

"I've been baking with this bowl for so long," she said, "that the sourdough culture is strong in the wood." She said she wiped the bowl each time but never scrubbed it. I could smell the sourness in the wood.

This woman shared a trait with all traditional bakers I've met. She learned her routine from her mother or father or grandmother and successfully maintains the sourdough culture in her timeless wooden bowl. I had never seen or heard of such a thing, but her way of doing things certainly produced a fragrant, hearty sourdough rye.

I will teach you a more conventional way of creating and maintaining a rye sourdough culture. Once you get into your own routine of keeping the culture alive and baking breads with it, your breads will taste and look as good as my Polish baker friend's.

abundance of instant-ready sugars and starches for the yeast to feed upon, guaranteeing that fermentation will be steady and robust.

The key to making sourdough is providing the best environment for this fermentation to take place. In my bakery, there are yeast cells everywhere. The moment I step inside the door, the intense perfume of developing sourdough hits me. The constant presence of wild yeasts makes for a fertile sourdough-making environment.

Create a microbakery by using a plastic container with a tight-fitting lid. All yeast cells are not the same. Some will develop a more sour flavor; some will grow quickly producing a lot of gas, some will become bitter. To get the best-tasting results, place the container in a not-too warm, stable environment (a draft-free corner of the kitchen) of 68° to 72°F. The yeast cells that thrive in this particular environment produce a sourdough that is acidic but not bitter, fragrant but not too pungent, with enough leavening power to raise the dough.

Allow three to four days to make your sourdough. During this time, your most important baker's tools are patience and your power of observation. Every sourdough process is unique. I think this is where the mystique surrounding sourdough enters into the picture. The culture and its activity are never completely predictable. There are always surprises depending on the flour and the yeast cells present, the weather, and the environment you provide. When you begin a sourdough you must be willing to watch, observe, and discover as you and the culture progress. What some call mystery I think is simply the baker developing greater skills of awareness by learning what happens during fermentation.

The point is don't be afraid to watch and learn from your own culture. In Chapter 10 I guide you, telling you what generally happens when a culture becomes sourdough. Become an astute observer; each day you will smell, touch, and taste the sourdough. The musty smell will become more alcoholic and the taste will be much more acidic with a tangy aftertaste. Note the changes in volume, cellular structure, and color. Write down in a notebook what you see on each day; this can only make you a better baker. Professional bakers have such good luck with sourdough breads because they deal with sourdough cultures every day, developing a keen sensitivity to its growth and changes. This is the ideal you the home baker can work toward as you shepherd the growth of a culture.

SOURDOUGH RYE

MAKING THE RYE *CHEF* AND
THE RYE SOURDOUGH STARTER

▦ THE RYE *CHEF* ▦

Making a rye sourdough starter is a two-step process. First you create a rye *chef*, the seed from which your sourdough starter will grow. Like any seed, it needs time to grow and a bit of attention, although the actual labor is minimal. The healthier and more vital your *chef*, the more vigorous the sourdough starter and the livelier your rising dough.

Use organic stone-ground rye flour and spring water. Rye flour is highly responsive to the fermentation process. The tiny amount of yeast in the recipe may seem like an error, but it isn't. I use just the tiniest bit of commercial yeast as a magnet to attract the wild yeasts in the air. (See Stalking the Wild Yeast, page 186.) Too much yeast and you will get an acidic, overly active culture that will taste aggressively sour and inhibit the rising of the dough. But with a pinch of yeast, a lively fermentation takes over, producing a sourdough starter with a distinctive tangy flavor and the rich aroma of moist autumn leaves.

DAY 1

Spring water	½ cup	4 fluid ounces
Organic stone-ground rye flour, preferably medium ground	⅔ cup	3 ounces
Moist yeast or dry yeast		a pinch—less than ¹⁄₁₆ teaspoon

In a tall 2- to 3-quart clear plastic container with a tight-fitting lid, stir together the water, flour, and yeast. Scrape down the sides of the container with a rubber spatula. Cover tightly and put in a moderate (74°–80°F.) place for 24 hours.

DAY 2

Spring water	½ cup	4 fluid ounces
Organic stone-ground rye flour, preferably medium ground	⅔ cup	3 ounces

Open the container. The young *chef* will probably show few signs of activity; the mixture will look like cardboard pulp. Don't worry! It's still a young *chef*. It will, however, have a sweet and musty smell and the beginnings of a tangy taste. Continue building the *chef* by adding the water and rye flour. Stir vigorously to bring fresh oxygen into the *chef* and distribute the fresh flour and water. Scrape down the sides, cover tightly and put in a moderate (74°–80°F.) place for another 24 hours.

DAY 3

Spring water	½ cup	4 fluid ounces
Organic stone-ground rye flour, preferably medium ground	⅔ cup	3 ounces

The *chef* should have expanded noticeably. There should be bubbles on the surface. Taste it—it will have a pronounced sour taste and smell. Hold the container up and observe the large and small holes formed beneath the surface. Stir it with a wooden spoon; you should hear the faint crackle of gas bubbles popping. The *chef* is very much alive and maturing. Insert the spoon again and lift it up slowly.

Short glutenous strands will stick to the spoon. Once again, nourish the *chef* by vigorously stirring in another addition of the spring water and rye flour. Scrape down the sides, cover tightly again, and return to its moderate-temperature place. Let stand for another 24 hours.

DAY 4

Spring water	½ cup	4 fluid ounces
Organic stone-ground rye flour, preferably medium ground	⅔ cup	3 ounces

The *chef* is almost mature and ripe. It has expanded a great deal—maybe almost doubled in volume from Day 3, and it is very lively with bubbles and a well-developed cellular structure. You will see a honeycomb of large and small holes through the clear plastic container. Taste and smell the *chef*—it is pungent and unmistakably tangy, sour but not bitter. Nourish again with the last addition of spring water and rye flour, stirring vigorously. Using a black marker pen, mark the level of the *chef* on the side of the clear plastic container. Scrape down the sides, cover tightly, and let stand again in the same place for only 8 hours.

If your *chef* was ripe, the mixture should almost double in volume. You can check its growth by comparing the height of the risen chef against the mark you made on the side of the container before the last rising.

The *chef* is now ready to use to create your sourdough starter. If you are not going to make the starter immediately, refrigerate the *chef* in its tightly covered container for up to three days. If you haven't used any of the *chef* within the three-day period, maintain the *chef* according to Maintaining the Rye *Chef,* page 125.

THE RYE
:: SOURDOUGH ::

Once the *chef* is ripe and lively enough to double in volume in eight hours, you're ready for the next step: putting the *chef* to work. Each of the rye bread recipes in this chapter calls for a certain amount of sourdough starter, usually 18 ounces. You combine a portion of the *chef* (usually 9 ounces) with rye flour and water to grow the starter. This is another process that takes time, but not effort. Also, it is only a matter of hours, not days.

There are three ways to measure out the *chef:*

1. Place the fermenting container on a scale, and note its weight. (For example, suppose the container weighs 5 ounces.) Spoon out 9 ounces of the *chef* directly into the container. With the weight of the bowl (5 ounces) and the weight of the chef (9 ounces), you now have 14 ounces total.

2. If you have a small scale that only measures 1 pound, measure the *chef* in batches directly into the scale's container, rinsing out the container with water before spooning in the *chef* (this helps avoid sticking). Use a rubber spatula to scrape out the *chef* into your mixing bowl.

3. Measure out the rye *chef* into a rinsed metal measuring cup. Stir the *chef* well before measuring to expel any gas bubbles, and use a level measure of the *chef.*

SOURDOUGH RYE STARTER

Allow 3 to 4 days to make the *chef.*
Total preparation time (not including *chef*): 8 to 10 hours

Ripe rye *chef,* at room temperature	1 cup	9 ounces
Rye flour, preferably medium ground	1 cup	5 ounces
Spring water	½ cup	4 fluid ounces

Place the *chef* in a tall 2- to 3-quart flat-bottomed, round, clear plastic container with a tight-fitting lid. Reserve the remaining *chef* (see Maintaining the Rye *Chef*, below). Add the rye flour and spring water, and stir vigorously with a wooden spoon until the mixture becomes thick and pasty. Mark the level of the mixture on the side of the container with a black marking pen. Scrape down, cover tightly, and let stand in a moderately warm (74°–80°F.) draft-free place until almost doubled in volume, 8 to 10 hours. The mixture will look light and spongy. You can observe the level of the sourdough by using the black mark on the side of the container as an indicator. Do not let the sourdough ferment for longer than 10 hours, or the yeast may exhaust itself and the dough not raise properly.

The ripe *chef* has now produced 18 ounces of ripe sourdough, which you can use in any rye sourdough recipe.

MAINTAINING THE ▪▪ RYE *CHEF* ▪▪

After you make your first batch of sourdough starter, you will have a small amount of leftover ripe *chef.* By adding fresh spring water and rye flour to the remaining *chef,* you can create a perpetual batch of *chef* for your next sourdough, and not have to start from scratch.

Rye flour, preferably medium ground	¾ cup	4 ounces
Spring water	½ cup plus 2 tablespoons	5 fluid ounces
Chef		9 ounces

Add the water and flour to the remaining *chef* in the plastic container, and stir well to make a thick paste. Remember that each flour is slightly different, so if you feel that you need a little more water or flour to create this texture, add it at this time. Scrape down the sides, cover tightly, and let stand in a moderately warm (74°–80°F.) place for 8 to 10 hours. If all is well, the *chef* will expand, and you will see the network of large and small gas bubbles through the container. Refrigerate and make sourdough starter within 7 days or renourish the *chef.*

NOURISHING THE
▦ *CHEF* ▦

Keeping an alive, fermenting, and active ripe *chef* in the refrigerator will allow you to bake sourdough rye breads often with some degree of spontaneity. Whether freshly made or extended, the *chef* can be stored in the refrigerator for up to one week. During that time, the cool temperature will slow the fermentation but not stop it, and the yeast will continue to consume the sugars in the flour. Eventually, the sugars will be completely consumed, the yeast will not have food, and the *chef* will die. To keep your *chef* alive, you must feed or "nourish" it every seven days.

To nourish the *chef,* use or discard 1 cup (9 ounces) of the *chef* from the container. Stir in ½ cup plus 2 tablespoons (5 ounces) spring water and ¾ cup (4 ounces) rye flour to make a thick paste. Scrape down the sides with a rubber spatula, cover tightly, and return the covered container to the refrigerator, where it will slowly ferment, for up to seven days.

The *chef* must be nourished once a week in order to stay alive. If you go away on vacation, leave instructions for feeding with the person who feeds your pet or waters your plants. Some healthy *chefs* can last longer without nourishment; while I don't recommend it, you can give it a shot. Other bakers tell me that they have had success freezing the starter for up to two months. Again, I have never done it.

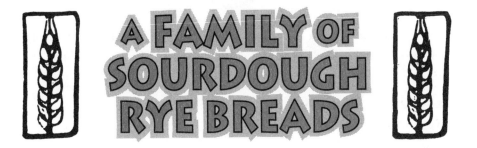

A FAMILY OF SOURDOUGH RYE BREADS

SOURDOUGH RYE WITH CARAWAY SEEDS

Allow 8 to 10 hours to make the starter.
Total preparation and baking time (not including the starter):
6 hours, 50 minutes

This is a classic Eastern European robust rye with pungent caraway flavor. It has much more flavor and color than the light rye you'd get in a deli.

Makes 2 long 12-inch loaves

Rye sourdough starter (page 124)	2 cups	18 ounces
Spring water	3 cups	24 fluid ounces
Rye flour,* preferably medium ground	1¾ cups	9 ounces
Whole wheat flour,* preferably coarse ground	1¾ cups	9 ounces
Fine sea salt	1 tablespoon	¾ ounce
Caraway seeds	¼ cup	1 ounce
20% bran wheat flour*	4–5 cups	20–25 ounces

---

* See Flours (pages 42–49). These are good approximate measures. You may use more or less depending on the weight and absorbency of your flour.

MIX AND KNEAD THE FINAL DOUGH (20 minutes) Measure the ingredients and calculate the temperatures (see page 58). Combine the starter and water in a 6-quart bowl. Break up the starter well with a wooden spoon and stir until it loosens and the mixture is slightly frothy. Add the rye flour and stir until well combined. Add the whole wheat flour, salt, caraway seeds, and just enough of the bran flour to make a thick mass that is difficult to stir. Turn out onto a well-floured surface and knead, adding remaining flour when needed, until dough is soft and smooth, 15 to 17 minutes. (Or make in a heavy-duty mixer; see page 67.) All finished rye doughs will remain slightly sticky. Be cautious about adding too much flour when kneading. The dough is ready when a little pulled from the mass springs back quickly (see Kneading, page 66).

FERMENT THE DOUGH (2½ to 3 hours) Shape the dough into a ball and let it rest on a lightly floured surface while you scrape, clean, and lightly oil the large bowl. Place the dough in the bowl and turn once to coat with oil. Take the dough's temperature (see page 58). The ideal is 78°F. Cover with a clean damp towel or plastic wrap and place in a moderately warm (74°–80°F.) draft-free place until doubled in volume.

> *Note: If the dough temperature is higher than 78°F., put it in a cooler than (78°F.) place like the refrigerator, until the dough cools to 78°F. If it is lower than 78°F., put it in a warmer than 78°F. place until the dough warms to 78°F. The point is to try to keep the dough at 78°F. during its fermentation. If you do have to move the dough, be gentle and don't jostle it, or the dough may deflate.*

DIVIDE THE DOUGH AND SHAPE THE LOAVES (10 minutes) Deflate the dough by pushing down in the center and pulling up on the sides. Transfer the dough to a lightly floured work surface and knead briefly. Cut into 2 equal pieces. Flatten each with the heel of your hand. Shape each piece into a 12-inch log for long loaves (see Taking Shape, page 68).

PROOF THE LOAVES (1½ to 2 hours) Using 2 well-floured towels and wood blocks, make a *couche* in a moderately warm (74°–80°F.) draft-free place. (See Equipment, page 52.) Place the loaves seam side up in the *couche.* Cover with a clean damp towel or plastic wrap and let proof until almost doubled in volume, or until a slight indentation remains when the dough is pressed with the fingertip.

BAKE THE LOAVES (35 to 40 minutes) Forty-five minutes to 1 hour before baking, preheat the oven and homemade hearth or baking stone on the center rack of the oven (see Equipment, page 52) to 450°F.

The oven rack must be in the center of the oven. If it is in the lower third of the oven, the bottoms of the breads may burn, and if it is in the upper third, the top crusts may burn.

Gently slip the loaves from the *couche* onto a well-floured peel so that they are right side up. Using a very sharp, serrated knife or a single-edged razor blade, score the loaves by making quick shallow cuts ¼ to ½ inch deep along the surface.

(*continued*)

Using the peel, slide the loaves onto the hearth. Quickly spray the inner walls and floor of the oven with cold water from a spritzer bottle. If there's an electric light bulb in the oven, avoid spraying it directly—it may burst. Spray for several seconds until steam has filled the oven. Quickly close the door to trap the steam and bake 3 minutes. Spray again in the same way, closing the door immediately so that steam doesn't escape. Bake until loaves begin to color, about 20 minutes. Reduce heat to 375°F. and bake until loaves are a rich caramel color and the crusts are firm, another 15 to 20 minutes.

To test the loaves for doneness, remove and hold the loaves upside down. Strike the bottoms firmly with your finger. If the sound is hollow, the breads are done. If it doesn't sound hollow, bake 5 minutes longer. Cool completely on wire racks.

SOURDOUGH RYE WITH CARAWAY SEEDS

Task	Approximate Time	Comments
Prepreparation		Ferment sourdough.
Preparation	5 min.	Calculate temperatures. Assemble ingredients. Mix.
Knead	15 min.	Take temperature of final dough.
Ferment	3 hr.	Moderate: 74°–80°F. until doubled.
Divide	5 min.	Deflate and cut into 2 equal portions.
Shape	5 min.	Form into logs for long loaves (see page 68). On lightly floured board.
Proof	2 hr.	Moderate: 74°–80°F. Cover with a clean damp towel or plastic wrap.
Bake	40 min.	With steam. 450°–375°F.
Cool	20 min.	On rack or in basket.

Cumulative Total Time: 7 hr., 10 min.

COARSE-GRAINED RYE WITH CRACKED RYE BERRIES

Allow 8 hours to make the starter.
Total fermentation and baking time (not including starter):
6 hours, 10 minutes

This is a hearty sandwich bread, well crusted with crunchy cracked rye berries. Its deep amber crumb has a mildly sour tone that even my kids love.

Makes 2 round 10-inch loaves

Rye sourdough starter (page 124)	2 cups	18 ounces
Spring water	3 cups	24 fluid ounces
Cracked rye	1½ cups	8 ounces
20% bran wheat flour*	4½–5 cups	22–26 ounces
Fine sea salt	1 tablespoon	¾ ounce
Whole wheat flour	2½ cups	13 ounces

---

* See Flours (pages 42–49). This is a good approximate measure. You may use more or less depending on the weight and absorbency of your flour.

MIX AND KNEAD THE FINAL DOUGH (20 minutes) Measure the ingredients and calculate the temperatures (see page 58). Combine the starter and water in a 6-quart bowl. Break up the starter well and stir with a wooden spoon until it loosens and the mixture is slightly frothy. Add 1⅓ cups (7 ounces) of the cracked rye and 1 cup (5 ounces) of the bran flour; stir until well combined. Add the salt, whole wheat flour and just enough of the remaining bran flour to make a thick mass that is difficult to stir. Turn onto a well-floured surface and knead, adding remaining flour when needed, until dough is soft and smooth, 15 to 17 minutes. (Or make in a heavy-duty mixer; see page 67.) All finished rye doughs will remain slightly sticky. Be cautious about adding too much flour when kneading. The dough is ready when a little pulled from the mass springs back quickly (see Kneading, page 66).

FERMENT THE DOUGH (2 to 3 hours) Shape the dough into a ball and let it rest on a lightly floured surface while you scrape, clean, and lightly oil the large bowl. Place the dough in the bowl and turn

(continued)

once to coat with oil. Take the dough's temperature: the ideal is 78°F. (see page 58). Cover with a clean damp towel or plastic wrap and put in a moderately warm (74°–80°F.) draft-free place until doubled in volume.

> *Note: If the dough temperature is higher than 78°F., put it in a cooler than 78°F. place like the refrigerator until the dough cools to 78°F. If it is lower than 78°F., put it in a warmer than 78°F. place until the dough warms to 78°F. The point is to try to keep the dough at 78°F. during its fermentation. If you do have to move the dough, be gentle and don't jostle it, or the dough may deflate.*

DIVIDE THE DOUGH AND SHAPE THE LOAVES (10 minutes) Deflate the dough by pushing down in the center and pulling up on the sides. Transfer to a lightly floured work surface and cut into 2 equal pieces. Knead briefly, then flatten each with the heel of your hand. Shape each piece into a tight ball for round loaves (see Taking Shape, page 68). Sprinkle the tops of each with the remaining cracked rye and gently pat the rye into the dough.

PROOF THE LOAVES (1½ to 2 hours) Line 2 bowls or baskets about 8 inches in diameter and 3 inches deep with well-floured towels. Place the loaves seam side up in the prepared bowls or baskets. Cover with a clean damp towel or plastic wrap and put in a moderately warm (74°–80°F.) draft-free place until almost doubled in volume, or until a slight indentation remains when the dough is pressed with the fingertip.

BAKE THE LOAVES (30 to 35 minutes) Forty-five minutes to 1 hour before baking, preheat the oven and homemade hearth or baking stone on the center rack of the oven (see Equipment, page 52) to 450°F.

The oven rack must be in the center of the oven. If it is in the lower third of the oven, the bottoms of the breads may burn, and if it is in the upper third, the top crusts may burn.

Gently invert the loaves from the baskets or bowls onto a floured peel so that they are right side up. Using a very sharp, serrated knife or a single-edged razor blade, score the loaves by making quick shallow cuts ¼ to ½ inch deep along the surface. Using the peel, slide the loaves onto the hearth. Quickly spray the inner walls and floor of the oven with cold water from a spritzer bottle. If there's an electric light bulb in the oven, avoid spraying it directly—it may burst. Spray for several seconds until steam has filled the oven. Quickly close the door to trap the steam and bake 3 minutes. Spray again in the same way, closing the door immediately so that steam doesn't escape. Bake until the loaves begin to color, about 20 minutes. Reduce the heat to 400°F., and bake until loaves are a rich caramel color and the crust is firm, 15 to 20 minutes longer.

To test the loaves for doneness, remove and hold the loaves upside down. Strike the bottoms firmly with your finger. If the sound is hollow, the breads are done. If it doesn't sound hollow, bake 5 minutes longer. Cool completely on a wire rack.

COARSE-GRAINED RYE WITH CRACKED RYE BERRIES

Task	Approximate Time	Comments
Prepreparation		Ferment sourdough.
Preparation	5 min.	Calculate temperatures. Assemble ingredients. Mix.
Knead	15 min.	Take temperature of final dough.
Ferment	2–3 hrs.	Moderate: 74°–80°F. until doubled in volume.
Shape	10 min.	Deflate: Form into balls for round loaves (see page 68). Place in well-floured basket.
Proof	2 hr.	Moderate: 74°–80°F. until doubled in volume.
Bake	40 min.	With steam. 450°F-400°F.
Cool	20 min.	On rack or in baskets.

Cumulative Total Time: 6 hr., 30 min.

DANISH LIGHT RYE

Allow 8 to 10 hours to make the starter.
Total preparation and baking time (not including the starter):
7 hours, 15 minutes

When it comes to bread, the Danes like the best of both worlds—the sophistication of a southern European wheat bread and the flavor and heartiness of their traditional sour rye breads. This bread has a mild rye flavor with a light texture and appealing color. It makes wonderful sandwiches, and tastes great with almost any cheese.

Makes 2 round 10-inch loaves

Rye sourdough starter (page 124)	2 cups	18 ounces
Spring water	3 cups	24 fluid ounces
Cracked rye	½ cup	2½ ounces
20% bran wheat flour*	7–8 cups	35–40 ounces
Fine sea salt	1 tablespoon	¾ ounce

* See Flours (pages 42–49). This is a good approximate measure. You may use more or less depending on the weight and absorbency of your flour.

MIX AND KNEAD THE FINAL DOUGH (20 minutes) Measure the ingredients and calculate the temperatures (see page 78). Combine the starter and water in a 6-quart bowl. Break up the starter with a wooden spoon and stir until it loosens and the mixture is slightly frothy. Add half the cracked rye and 1 cup (5 ounces) of the flour and stir until well combined. Add the salt and just enough of the remaining flour to make a thick mass that is difficult to stir. Turn onto a lightly floured surface and knead, adding remaining flour when needed, until dough is soft and smooth, 15 to 17 minutes. (Or make in a heavy-duty mixer; see page 67.) All finished rye doughs will remain slightly sticky. This also tends to be a very soft dough. So be cautious about adding too much flour when kneading. The dough is ready when a little pulled from the mass springs back quickly (see Kneading, page 66).

FERMENT THE DOUGH (4 hours) Shape the dough into a ball and let it rest on a lightly floured surface while you scrape, clean, and lightly oil the large bowl. Place the dough in the bowl and turn once to coat with oil. Take the dough's temperature. The ideal is 78°F. (see page 58). Cover with a clean damp towel or plastic wrap and put in a moderately warm (74°–80°F.) draft-free place until doubled in volume.

> *Note: If the dough temperature is higher than 78°F., put it in a cooler than 78°F. place like the refrigerator until the dough cools to 78°F. If it is lower than 78°F., put it in a warmer than 78°F. place until the dough warms to 78°F. The point is to try to keep the dough at 78°F. during its fermentation. If you do have to move the dough, be gentle and don't jostle it, or the dough may deflate.*

DIVIDE THE DOUGH AND SHAPE THE LOAVES (10 minutes) Deflate the dough by pushing down in the center and pulling up on the sides. Transfer to a lightly floured work surface and knead briefly. Cut into 2 equal pieces. Flatten each with the heel of your hand. Shape each piece into a tight ball for round loaves (see Taking Shape, page 68). Sprinkle the work space with the remaining cracked rye and gently roll the loaves in the cracked rye so that the tops are covered and the grain adheres to the dough.

PROOF THE LOAVES (1½ to 2 hours) Line 2 bowls or baskets about 8 inches in diameter and 3 inches deep with well-floured towels. (Since this tends to be a very soft dough, be sure the towels are well floured.) Place the loaves seam side up in the prepared bowls or baskets. Cover with a clean damp towel or plastic wrap and put in a moderately warm (74°–80°F.) draft-free place until almost doubled in volume, or until a slight indentation remains when the dough is pressed with the fingertip.

BAKE THE LOAVES (35 to 40 minutes) Forty-five minutes to 1 hour before baking, preheat the oven and homemade hearth or baking stone on the center rack of the oven (see Equipment, page 52) to 450°F.

The oven rack must be in the center of the oven. If it is in the lower third of the oven, the bottoms of the breads may burn, and if it is in the upper third, the top crusts may burn.

(continued)

Gently invert the loaves from the baskets or bowls onto a floured board so that they are right side up. Using a very sharp, serrated knife or a single-edged razor blade, score the loaves by making quick shallow cuts ¼ to ½ inch deep along the surface.

Using a well-floured peel, slide the loaves one at a time onto the hearth. Quickly spray the inner walls and floor of the oven with cold water from a spritzer bottle. If there's an electric light bulb in the oven, avoid spraying it directly—it may burst. Spray for several seconds until steam has filled the oven. Quickly close the door to trap the steam and bake 3 minutes. Spray again in the same way, closing the door immediately so that steam doesn't escape, and bake until loaves begin to color, about 20 minutes. Reduce heat to 400°F. and bake until loaves are a rich caramel color and the crusts are firm, another 15 to 20 minutes.

To test the loaves for doneness, remove and hold the loaves upside down. Strike the bottoms firmly with your finger. If the sound is hollow, the breads are done. If it doesn't sound hollow, bake 5 minutes longer. Cool completely on a wire rack.

DANISH LIGHT RYE

Task	Approximate Time	Comments
Prepreparation		Ferment sourdough.
Preparation	5 min.	Calculate temperatures. Assemble ingredients. Mix.
Knead	15 min.	Take temperature of final dough.
Ferment	4 hr.	Moderate 74°–80°F. until doubled in volume.
Divide	5 min.	Deflate. Cut into 2 equal portions.
Shape	5 min.	In balls for round loaves. Top with cracked rye.
Proof	2 hr.	Moderate: 74°–80°F. In floured towel–lined basket or bowl.
Bake	40 min.	With steam. 450°F.–400°F.
Cool	20 min.	On rack or in basket.

Cumulative Total Time: 7 hr., 35 min.

DARK PUMPERNICKEL WITH RAISINS

Allow 8 to 10 hours to make the starter.
Total preparation and baking time (not including the starter):
9 hours, 30 minutes

This is a strong, pungent black bread. The coffee, cocoa, and molasses create a slightly bitter taste that contrasts wonderfully with the sweetness of the raisins. I like this bread toasted and served with hot creamy coffee. It's also good with a strong cheese.

Makes 2 round 10-inch loaves

Raisins	2 cups	10 ounces
Spring water, heated to boiling	1½ cups, approximately	12 fluid ounces, approximately
Rye sourdough starter (page 124)	2 cups	18 ounces
Brewed espresso, or strong coffee, at room temperature	1 cup	8 fluid ounces
Rye flour,* preferably coarse ground and dark shade	½ cup	2½ ounces
Whole wheat flour,* preferably medium ground	3½ cups	19 ounces
Unsweetened cocoa powder	½ cup	1½ ounces
Unsulphured molasses	1 cup	8 fluid ounces
Fine sea salt	1 tablespoon	¾ ounce
20% bran wheat flour*	3–4 cups	15–20 ounces
Cornmeal, for dusting		

---

* See Flours (pages 42–49). These are good approximate measures. You may use more or less depending on the weight and absorbency of your flours.

PREPARE THE RAISINS   (allow 8 hours or overnight) Soak the raisins in enough of the hot spring water to cover by 1 inch. Let stand 8 hours or overnight; drain and reserve liquid. Add enough fresh spring water at room temperature to the reserved soaking liquid to measure 1 cup (8 fluid ounces). Reserve.

(continued)

MIX AND KNEAD FINAL DOUGH (20 minutes) Measure remaining ingredients and calculate the temperatures (see page 58). Combine the starter, reserved raisin-soaking liquid, and coffee in a 6-quart bowl. Break up the starter well with a wooden spoon and stir until it loosens and the mixture becomes slightly frothy. Add the rye and whole wheat flours, cocoa, molasses, drained raisins, and salt; stir until well combined. Gradually add enough of the bran flour to make a thick mass that is difficult to stir. Turn out onto a lightly floured surface and knead, adding remaining flour when needed, until dough is soft and smooth, 15 to 17 minutes. (Or make in a heavy-duty mixer; see page 67.) All finished rye doughs will remain slightly sticky. Be cautious about adding too much flour when kneading. The dough is ready when a little pulled from the mass springs back quickly (see Kneading, page 66).

FERMENT THE DOUGH (3 to 4 hours) Shape the dough into a ball and let it rest on a lightly floured surface while you scrape, clean, and lightly oil the large bowl. Place the dough in the bowl and turn once to coat with oil. Take the dough's temperature (see page 58). The ideal is 78°F. Cover with a clean damp towel or plastic wrap and put in a moderately warm (74°–80°F.) draft-free place until increased in volume by one-third.

> *Note: If the dough temperature is higher than 78°F., put it in a cooler than 78°F. place like the refrigerator until the dough cools to 78°F. If it is lower than 78°F., put it in a warmer than 78°F. place until the dough warms to 78°F. The point is to try to keep the dough at 78°F. during its fermentation. If you do have to move the dough, be gentle and don't jostle it, or the dough may deflate.*

FERMENT THE DOUGH A SECOND TIME (about 2 hours) Deflate the dough by pulling up on the sides and pushing down in the center. Form into a ball, return to the bowl, and cover. Allow to rise again by one-third.

DIVIDE AND SHAPE THE DOUGH INTO LOAVES (10 minutes) Deflate the dough by pushing down in the center and pulling up on the sides. Transfer the dough to a lightly floured work surface and knead briefly. Cut into 2 equal pieces. Flatten each with the heel of your hand using firm direct strokes. Shape each piece into a tight ball for round loaves (see Taking Shape, page 68).

PROOF THE LOAVES (1½ to 2 hours) Place the loaves on a board that has been lightly dusted with cornmeal. Cover with a clean damp towel or plastic wrap and put in a moderately warm (74°–80°F.) draft-free place until increased in volume by one-third.

BAKE THE LOAVES (1½ hours) Forty-five minutes to 1 hour before baking, preheat the oven and homemade hearth or baking stone on the center rack of the oven (see Equipment, page 52) to 375°F.

The oven rack must be in the center of the oven. If it is in the lower third of the oven, the bottoms of the breads may burn, and if it is in the upper third, the top crusts may burn.

Using a sifter, spinkle loaves with extra rye flour, giving them a light dusting. Using a very sharp, serrated knife or a single-edged razor blade, score the loaves by making quick shallow cuts ¼ to ½ inch deep along the surface.

Using a well-floured peel, slide the loaves one at a time onto the hearth and quickly spray the inner walls and floor of the oven with cold water from a spritzer bottle. If there's an electric light bulb in the oven, avoid spraying it directly—it may burst. Spray for several seconds until steam has filled the oven. Quickly close the door to trap the steam and bake 3 minutes. Spray again in the same way, closing the door immediately so that steam doesn't escape, and bake 1½ hours.

To test the loaves for doneness, remove and hold the loaves upside down. Strike the bottoms firmly with your finger. If the sound is hollow, the breads are done. If it doesn't sound hollow, bake 5 minutes longer. Cool completely on a wire rack.

DARK PUMPERNICKEL WITH RAISINS

Task	Approximate Time	Comments
Prepreparation		Ferment sourdough and soak raisins.
Preparation	5 min.	Calculate temperatures. Assemble ingredients. Mix.
Knead	15 min.	Take temperature of final dough.
Ferment I	4 hr.	Moderate: 74°–80°F. until increased 30%.
Ferment II	2 hr.	Until increased 20%.
Divide	5 min.	Deflate. Cut into 2 equal portions.
Shape	5 min.	Form balls for round loaves. On lightly floured board.
Proof	1 hr., 30 min.	Moderate: 74°–80°F.
Bake	1 hr., 30 min.	With steam. 375°F.
Cool	20 min.	On rack or in basket.

Cumulative Total Time: 9 hr., 50 min.

SOURDOUGH RYE BUNS WITH CURRANTS

Allow 8 to 10 hours to make the starter.
Total preparation and baking time (not including the starter):
6 hours, 55 minutes

Small, dense, fruity, and intensely habit-forming, these are big sellers at my bakery. My customers' only complaint is that the buns never make it home. This recipe makes a huge batch—halve it if you want less. I suggest making the full amount and freezing any leftovers.

Makes about 40 buns

Rye sourdough starter (page 124)	2 cups	18 ounces
Spring water	3 cups	24 fluid ounces
20% bran wheat flour*	6–7 cups	30–35 ounces
Fine sea salt	1 tablespoon	¾ ounce
Currants	1 cup	8 ounces
Cornmeal or fine semolina for dusting		

* See Flours (pages 42–49). This is a good approximate measure. You may use more or less depending on the weight and absorbency of your flour.

MIX AND KNEAD THE FINAL DOUGH (20 minutes) Measure the ingredients and calculate the temperatures (see page 58). Combine the starter and water in a 6-quart bowl. Break up the starter well, and stir with a wooden spoon until it loosens and the mixture is slightly frothy. Add 1 cup (5 ounces) of the flour and stir until well combined. Add the salt and just enough of the remaining flour to make a thick mass that is difficult to stir. Turn out onto a lightly floured surface and knead, adding remaining flour when needed, 12 minutes. Gradually knead in the currants and continue kneading until dough is soft and smooth. Be cautious about adding too much flour during kneading—the final dough should be slightly sticky. The dough is ready when a small amount pulled from the mass springs back quickly, 15 to 17 minutes total. (Or make the dough in a heavy-duty mixer; see page 67.) (See Kneading and Kneading In, pages 66 and 76.)

(continued)

FERMENT THE DOUGH (3 to 4 hours) Shape the dough into a ball and let it rest on a lightly floured surface while you scrape, clean, and lightly oil the large bowl. Place the dough in the bowl and turn the dough to coat the top with oil. Take the dough's temperature: the ideal is 78°F. (see page 58). Cover with a clean damp towel or plastic wrap and put in a moderately warm (74°–80°F.) draft-free place until doubled in volume.

> *Note: If the dough temperature is higher than 78°F., put it in a cooler than 78°F. place like the refrigerator until the dough cools to 78°F. If it is lower than 78°F., put it in a warmer than 78°F. place until the dough warms to 78°F. The point is to try to keep the dough at 78°F. during its fermentation. If you do have to move the dough, be gentle and don't jostle it, or the dough may deflate.*

DIVIDE AND SHAPE THE DOUGH INTO BUNS (10 minutes) Deflate the dough by pushing down in the center and pulling up on the sides. Transfer the dough to a lightly floured work surface and knead briefly. Cut into forty 2½-inch (2½-ounce) pieces. Flatten each with the heel of your hand. Scrape the work surface clean of excess flour. Shape each piece into a tight ball (see Taking Shape, page 68).

PROOF THE BUNS (1½ to 2 hours) Place the buns on a board that has been dusted lightly with cornmeal or semolina. Cover with a clean damp towel or plastic wrap and put in a moderately warm (74°–80°F.) draft-free place until almost doubled in volume or until a slight indentation remains when pressed with the fingertip.

BAKE THE BUNS (20 minutes) Forty-five minutes to 1 hour before baking, preheat the oven and homemade hearth or baking stone on the center rack of the oven (see Equipment, page 52) to 450°F.

The oven rack must be in the center of the oven. If it is in the lower third of the oven, the bottoms of the breads may burn, and if it is in the upper third, the top crusts may burn.

Gently place a few buns onto a floured peel so that they are right side up. Using the peel, slide the buns a few at a time onto the hearth. Quickly spray the inner walls and floor of the oven with cold water from a spritzer bottle. If there's an electric light bulb in the oven, avoid spraying it directly—it may burst. Spray for several seconds until steam has filled the oven. Quickly close the door to trap the steam and bake 3 minutes. Spray again in the same way, closing the door immediately so that steam doesn't escape, and bake until the buns are golden brown, 12 to 15 minutes.

To test for doneness, remove one bun and hold upside down. Strike the bottom firmly with your finger. If the sound is hollow, the buns are done. If it doesn't sound hollow, bake 3 to 5 minutes longer. Cool the buns completely on a wire rack.

SOURDOUGH RYE BUNS WITH CURRANTS

Task	Approximate Time	Comments
Prepreparation		Ferment sourdough.
Preparation	5 min.	Calculate temperatures. Assemble ingredients. Mix.
Knead	15 min.	Take temperature of final dough.
Ferment	4 hr.	Moderate: 74°–80°F. until doubled.
Divide	5 min.	Deflate and cut into 40 2½-ounce portions.
Shape	10 min.	Form into balls for round loaves on lightly floured board.
Proof	2 hr.	Moderate: 74°–80°F.
Bake	20 min.	With steam. 450°F.
Cool	10 min.	On rack or in baskets.

Cumulative Total Time: 7 hr., 5 min.

SOURDOUGH RYE WITH ONION

Allow 40 minutes to prepare the onions.
Allow 8 hours to make the starter.
Total fermentation and baking time (not including starter):
5 hours, 35 minutes

The flavor of the rye blends beautifully with the aromatic sweetness of the onions. This is a robust bread that tastes great all by itself or with cheese that has a lot of character, such as Stilton or a sharp cheddar.

Makes 2 round 9-inch loaves

2 large onions, peeled and finely chopped	2 cups	1 pound
Vegetable oil	1 tablespoon	
Rye sourdough starter (page 124)	2 cups	18 ounces
Spring water	3 cups	24 fluid ounces
Whole wheat flour,* preferably coarse ground	1 cup	5 ounces
Fine sea salt	1 tablespoon	¾ ounce
20% bran wheat flour*	5–6 cups	30–35 ounces
Cornmeal, for dusting		

* See Flours (pages 42–49). These are good approximate measures. You may use more or less depending on the weight and absorbency of your flour.

ROAST THE ONIONS (40 minutes) Preheat the oven to 400°F. Combine the onions and vegetable oil in a bowl and toss well. Spread the onions on a baking sheet and bake, stirring occasionally, until the onions are golden and tinged with dark brown, 20 to 25 minutes. Transfer to a platter and place in the refrigerator to cool completely, about 20 minutes.

MIX AND KNEAD THE FINAL DOUGH (20 minutes) Measure the remaining ingredients and calculate the temperatures (see page 58). Combine the starter and water in a 6-quart bowl. Break up the starter well with a wooden spoon and stir until it loosens and the mixture is slightly frothy. Add the whole wheat flour and all except ¼ cup (2 ounces) of the onions; stir until well combined. Add the salt and just enough of the bran flour to make a thick mass that is difficult to stir. Turn out onto a lightly floured surface and knead, adding remaining flour when needed, until dough is soft and smooth, 15 to 17 minutes.

(Or make in a heavy-duty mixer; see page 67.) All finished rye doughs will remain slightly sticky. Be cautious about adding too much flour when kneading. The dough is ready when a little pulled from the mass springs back quickly (see Kneading, page 66).

FERMENT THE DOUGH (2 to 2½ hours) Shape the dough into a ball and let it rest on a lightly floured surface while you scrape, clean, and lightly oil the large bowl. Place the dough in the bowl and turn once to coat with oil. Take the dough's temperature: the ideal is 78°F. (see page 58). Cover with a clean damp towel or plastic wrap and put in a moderately warm (74°–80°F.) draft-free place until doubled in volume.

> *Note: If the dough temperature is higher than 78°F., put it in a cooler than 78°F. place like the refrigerator, until the dough cools to 78°F. If it is lower than 78°F., put it in a warmer than 78°F. place until the dough warms to 78°F. The point is to try to keep the dough at 78°F. during its fermentation. If you do have to move the dough, be gentle and don't jostle it, or the dough may deflate.*

DIVIDE THE DOUGH AND SHAPE THE LOAVES (10 minutes) Deflate the dough by pushing down in the center and pulling up on the sides. Transfer to a lightly floured work surface and knead briefly. Cut into 2 equal pieces. Flatten each with the heel of your hand. Shape each piece into a tight ball for round loaves (see Taking Shape, page 68).

PROOF THE LOAVES (1½ to 2 hours) Place the loaves seam side down on a cornmeal-dusted board. Cover with a clean damp towel or plastic wrap and put in a moderately warm (74°–80°F.) draft-free place until almost doubled in volume or until a slight indentation remains when the dough is pressed with a fingertip.

BAKE THE LOAVES (35 to 40 minutes) Forty-five minutes to 1 hour before baking, preheat the oven and homemade hearth or baking stone on the center rack of the oven (see Equipment, page 52) to 450°F.

The oven rack must be in the center of the oven. If it is in the lower third of the oven, the bottoms of the breads may burn, and

(*continued*)

if it is in the upper third, the top crusts may burn.

Using a very sharp, serrated knife or a single-edged razor blade, score the loaves by making quick shallow cuts ¼ to ½ inch deep along the surface. Sprinkle the tops evenly with the reserved onions. Using a well-floured peel, slide the loaves one at a time onto the hearth. Quickly spray the inner walls and floor of the oven with cold water from a spritzer bottle. If there's an electric light bulb in the oven, avoid spraying it directly—it may burst. Spray for several seconds until steam has filled the oven. Quickly close the door to trap the steam and bake 3 minutes. Spray again in the same way, closing the door immediately so that steam doesn't escape. Reduce heat to 400°F. and bake until loaves are a rich caramel color and the crust is firm, 30 to 35 minutes.

To test the loaves for doneness, remove and hold the loaves upside down. Strike the bottoms firmly with your finger. If the sound is hollow, the breads are done. If it doesn't sound hollow, bake 5 minutes longer. Cool completely on a wire rack.

SOURDOUGH RYE WITH ONION

Task	Approximate Time	Comments
Prepreparation		Ferment sourdough. Roast onion.
Preparation	5 min.	Calculate temperatures. Assemble ingredients. Mix.
Knead	15 min.	Take temperature of final dough.
Ferment	2 hr., 30 min.	Moderate: 74°–80°F. until doubled.
Divide	5 min.	Deflate. Cut into 2 equal portions.
Shape	5 min.	Form into balls for round loaves on lightly floured board.
Proof	2 hr.	Moderate: 74°–80°F. Cover with a clean damp towel or plastic wrap.
Bake	35 min.	With steam. 450°F-400°F.
Cool	20 min.	On rack or in basket.

Cumulative Total Time: 5 hr., 55 min.

SOURDOUGH RYE WITH POTATO

> Allow 8 hours to make the starter.
> Total fermentation and baking time (not including starter):
> 6 hours, 35 minutes

This is a very moist bread with a pâtélike texture and light potato flecks.

Makes 2 round 10-inch loaves

2 large Russet potatoes, peeled		1 pound
Spring water	4 cups	32 fluid ounces
Fine sea salt	1 tablespoon	¾ ounce
Rye sourdough starter (page 124)	2 cups	18 ounces
Rye flour,* preferably coarse ground	2 cups	11 ounces
Whole wheat flour,* preferably medium ground	2 cups	11 ounces
20% bran wheat flour*	5–5½ cups	26–28 ounces
Cornmeal, for dusting		

---

* See Flours (pages 42–49). These are good approximate measures. You may use more or less depending on the weight and absorbency of your flours.

PREPARE THE POTATOES (1¼ hours, including cooling time) In a medium saucepan, combine the potatoes and spring water. Add ½ teaspoon of the salt. Cook the potatoes until just tender when pierced with the tip of a knife, 20 to 30 minutes. Remove the potatoes with a slotted spoon. Cool potatoes and cooking water in the refrigerator. (Don't worry if the cooking water has bits of potato in it.) Cut cooled potatoes into ½-inch cubes. Reserve 3 cups of cooking water.

MIX AND KNEAD THE FINAL DOUGH (20 minutes) Measure the remaining ingredients and calculate the temperatures (see page 58). Combine the starter, ½ cup of the potato cubes, and spring water in a 6-quart bowl. Break up the starter well with a wooden spoon and stir until it loosens and the mixture is slightly frothy. Add the rye flour, whole wheat flour, remaining salt, and just enough of the bran flour to make a thick mass that is difficult to stir. Turn out onto

(continued)

a well-floured surface and knead, adding remaining flour when needed, until dough is fairly soft and smooth, 12 minutes. Gradually knead in remaining potato cubes and continue kneading, adding flour when needed until potatoes are evenly distributed through the dough, 15 to 17 minutes total. (Or make the dough in a heavy-duty mixer; see page 67.) This dough will need extra flour during the last 5 minutes of kneading because of the added moisture of the potatoes. Be cautious, however, about adding too much flour during kneading, as the final dough should be slightly sticky. The dough is ready when a little dough pulled from the mass springs back quickly (see Kneading and Kneading In, pages 66 and 76).

FERMENT THE DOUGH (2½ to 3 hours) Shape the dough into a ball and let it rest on a lightly floured surface while you scrape, clean, and lightly oil the large bowl. Place the dough in the bowl and turn once to coat with oil. Take the dough's temperature: the ideal is 78°F. (see page 58). Cover with a clean damp towel or plastic wrap and put in a cool moderately warm (74°–80°F.) draft-free place until doubled in volume.

> *Note: If the dough temperature is higher than 78°F., put it in a cooler than 78°F. place like the refrigerator, until the dough cools to 78°F. If it is lower than 78°F., put it in a warmer than 78°F. place until the dough warms to 78°F. The point is to try to keep the dough at 78°F. during its fermentation. If you do have to move the dough, be gentle and don't jostle it, or the dough may deflate.*

DIVIDE THE DOUGH AND SHAPE THE LOAVES (10 minutes) Deflate the dough by pushing down in the center and pulling up on the sides. Transfer to a lightly floured work surface and knead briefly. Cut into 2 equal pieces and flatten each piece with the heel of your hand. Shape each piece into tight balls for round loaves (see Taking Shape, page 68).

PROOF THE LOAVES (1½ to 2 hours) Place the loaves smooth side up on a board dusted with cornmeal. Cover with a clean damp towel or plastic wrap and put in a moderately warm (74°–80°F.) draft-free place until almost doubled in volume, or until a slight indentation remains when the dough is pressed with a fingertip.

BAKE THE LOAVES (about 1 hour) Forty-five minutes to 1 hour before baking, preheat the oven and homemade hearth or baking stone on the center rack of the oven (see Equipment, page 52) to 400°F.

The oven rack must be in the center of the oven. If it is in the lower third of the oven, the bottoms of the breads may burn, and if it is in the upper third, the top crusts may burn.

Using a very sharp, serrated knife or a single-edged razor blade, score the loaves by making quick shallow cuts ¼ to ½ inch deep along the surface. Using a well-floured peel, slide the loaves one at a time onto the hearth. Quickly spray the inner walls and floor of the oven with cold water from a spritzer bottle. If there's an electric light bulb in the oven, avoid spraying it directly—it may burst. Spray for several seconds until steam has filled the oven. Quickly close the door to trap the steam and bake 3 minutes. Spray again in the same way, closing the door immediately so that steam doesn't escape. Bake until loaves are a rich caramel color and the crust is firm, about 50 to 60 minutes.

To test the loaves for doneness, remove and hold the loaves upside down. Strike the bottoms firmly with your finger. If the sound is hollow, the breads are done. If it doesn't sound hollow, bake 5 minutes longer. Cool completely on a wire rack.

SOURDOUGH RYE WITH POTATO

Task	Approximate Time	Comments
Prepreparation		Ferment sourdough. Cook and cube potato.
Preparation	5 min.	Calculate temperatures. Assemble ingredients. Mix.
Knead	15 min.	Take temperature of final dough.
Ferment	3 hr.	Moderate: 74°–80°F. until doubled.
Divide	5 min.	Deflate. Cut into 2 equal portions.
Shape	10 min.	Form into balls for round loaves on lightly floured board.
Proof	2 hr.	Moderate: 74°–80°F. until doubled in volume.
Bake	1 hr.	With steam. 400°F.
Cool	20 min.	On rack or in baskets.

Cumulative Total Time: 6 hr., 55 min.

SUMMER HERB RYE

Allow 8 hours to make the starter.
Total preparation and baking time (not including starter):
7 hours, 35 minutes

When your garden is wild with herbs and exploding with the many aromas and flavors of summer, harvest your favorites and bake them into this bread. You can use any combination—the herbs in this recipe happen to be my personal favorites and they were in vast supply on the day I made this bread.

Makes 2 round 10-inch loaves

Rye sourdough starter (page 124)	2 cups	18 ounces
Spring water	3 cups	24 fluid ounces
Rye flour,* preferably medium ground	2 cups	11 ounces
4 cloves garlic, minced	1 tablespoon	
Freshly chopped chives, thyme, basil, rosemary, parsley	½ cup	
Fine sea salt	1 tablespoon	¾ ounce
20% bran wheat flour*	4¾–6 cups	25–30 ounces
Cornmeal, for dusting		

* See Flours (pages 42–49). These are good approximate measures. You may use a little more or less depending on the weight and absorbency of your flours.

MIX AND KNEAD THE FINAL DOUGH (20 minutes) Measure the ingredients and calculate the temperatures (see page 58). Combine the starter and water in a 6-quart bowl. Break up the starter well with a wooden spoon and stir until it loosens and the mixture is slightly frothy. Add the rye flour and stir until well combined. Add the garlic, fresh herbs, salt, and just enough of the bran flour to make a thick mass that is difficult to stir. Turn out onto a well-floured surface and knead, adding remaining flour until dough is soft and smooth, 15 to 17 minutes total. (Or make in a heavy-duty mixer; see page 67.) All finished rye doughs will remain slightly sticky. Be cautious about adding too much flour when kneading. The dough is ready when a little pulled from the mass springs back quickly (see Kneading, page 66).

FERMENT THE DOUGH (3 to 4 hours) Shape the dough into a ball and let it rest on a lightly floured surface while you scrape, clean, and lightly oil the large bowl. Place the dough in the bowl and turn once to coat with oil. Take the dough's temperature: the ideal is 78°F. (see page 58). Cover with a clean damp towel or plastic wrap and put in a moderately warm (74°–80°F.) draft-free place until almost doubled in volume.

> *Note:* *If the dough temperature is higher than 78°F., put it in a cooler than 78°F. place like the refrigerator until the dough cools to 78°F. If it is lower than 78°F., put it in a warmer than 78°F. place until the dough warms to 78°F. The point is to try to keep the dough at 78°F. during its fermentation. If you do have to move the dough, be gentle and don't jostle it, or the dough may deflate.*

DIVIDE THE DOUGH AND SHAPE THE LOAVES (10 minutes) Deflate the dough by pushing down in the center and pulling up on the sides. Transfer the dough to a lightly floured work surface and cut into 2 equal pieces. Knead the dough briefly and flatten each piece with the heel of your hand. Shape each piece into a tight ball for round loaves (see Taking Shape, page 68).

PROOF THE LOAVES (2 to 2 ½ hours) Place the loaves seam side down on a board dusted with cornmeal. Cover with a clean damp towel or plastic wrap and put in a moderately warm (74°–80°F.) draft-free place until almost doubled in volume, or until a slight indentation remains when the dough is pressed with a fingertip.

BAKE THE LOAVES (35 to 40 minutes) Forty-five minutes to 1 hour before baking, preheat the oven and homemade hearth or baking stone on the center rack of the oven (see Equipment, page 52) to 450°F.

The oven rack must be in the center of the oven. If it is in the lower third of the oven, the bottoms of the breads may burn, and if it is in the upper third, the top crusts may burn.

(continued)

Using a very sharp, serrated knife or a single-edged razor blade, score the loaves by making quick shallow cuts ¼ to ½ inch deep along the surface. Using a well-floured peel, slide the loaves onto the hearth. Quickly spray the inner walls and floor of the oven with cold water from a spritzer bottle. If there's an electric light bulb in the oven, avoid spraying it directly—it may burst. Spray for several seconds until steam has filled the oven. Quickly close the door to trap the steam and bake 3 minutes. Spray again in the same way, closing the door immediately so that steam doesn't escape. Reduce the heat to 425°F. and bake until the loaves are a rich caramel color and the crust is firm, 30 to 35 minutes.

To test the loaves for doneness, remove and hold the loaves upside down. Strike the bottoms firmly with your finger. If the sound is hollow, the breads are done. If it doesn't sound hollow, bake 5 minutes longer. Cool completely on wire racks.

SUMMER HERB RYE

Task	Approximate Time	Comments
Prepreparation		Ferment sourdough. Prepare herbs and spices.
Preparation	5 min.	Calculate temperatures. Assemble ingredients. Mix.
Knead	15 min.	Take temperature of final dough.
Ferment	4 hr.	Moderate 74°–80°F. until doubled in volume.
Divide	5 min.	Deflate and cut into 2 equal portions.
Shape	5 min.	Deflate: Form into balls for round loaves. Place on floured board.
Proof	2 hr., 30 min.	Moderate: 74°–80°F. until doubled in volume.
Bake	35 min.	With steam. 450°F.–425°F.
Cool	20 min.	On rack or in baskets.

Cumulative Total Time: 7 hr., 55 min.

LIMPA RYE

Allow 12 hours to prepare candied peel.
Allow 8 hours to make the starter.
Total preparation and baking time (not including starter):
7 hours, 45 minutes

A classic Swedish rye sourdough bread, Limpa is flavored with citrus and cardamom. Here is a twist on the classic with stout ale giving a slightly bitter edge that contrasts perfectly with the sweet candied orange and lemon peels. You will get the best flavor if you use freshly crushed cardamom seeds; remove them from the pods and grind them in a mortar.

Makes 2 round 9-inch loaves

2 medium oranges		
2 medium lemons		
Granulated sugar	1 cup	7 ounces
Spring water	½ cup	4 fluid ounces
Dark ale such as Guinness	3 cups	24 ounces
Rye sourdough starter (page 124)	2 cups	18 ounces
Rye flour,* preferably coarse ground	2 cups	11 ounces
Whole wheat flour,* preferably medium ground	2 cups	10 ounces
Fine sea salt	1 tablespoon	¾ ounce
Freshly ground cardamom seeds	2 teaspoons	
Honey, preferably wildflower	1 tablespoon	
20% bran wheat flour*	3½–4½ cups	16–22 ounces
Cornmeal, for dusting		

* See Flours (pages 42–49). These are good approximate measures. You may use a little more or less depending on the weight and absorbency of your flour.

PREPARE THE CANDIED CITRUS PEELS (40 minutes plus 12 hours drying time) Using a sharp or serrated knife, cut the colored (zest) and the white pith off the oranges and lemons in wide slices. (Don't worry if a little of the fruit remains on the pith.) Cut the peels

(continued)

into ¼-inch-wide slivers. Place the peels in a medium saucepan and add enough tap water to cover by 1 inch. Heat to boiling over high heat; cook 4 minutes, then drain well. Repeat the procedure with fresh water, drain again, and do a third time. (This removes any bitterness from the peels.)

In the same saucepan, combine the sugar, water, and drained peels. Heat to a simmer over medium heat, stirring to help dissolve the sugar. When the syrup comes to a boil, stop stirring. Do not stir with a spoon from this point on, or the syrup may crystallize. Reduce the heat to medium-low and cook, swirling the pan by the handle occasionally to avoid scorching, until the peels have absorbed the syrup and they are tender and translucent, about 20 minutes.

Using 2 forks, transfer the peels to a lightly oiled wire cake rack set over waxed paper. Use the forks to separate the peels. Allow the peels to dry at room temperature at least 12 hours. With a sharp knife rinsed with hot water, chop the peels into ¼-inch pieces. Use the peels within 24 hours of making.

MIX AND KNEAD THE FINAL DOUGH (20 minutes) Measure out the remaining ingredients and calculate the temperatures (see page 68.) Heat the ale to the calculated temperature. Combine the starter and ale in a 6-quart bowl. Break up the starter well with a wooden spoon and stir until it loosens and the mixture is slightly frothy. Add the rye flour and whole wheat flour; stir until well combined. Add the salt, cardamom, honey, and just enough of the bran flour to make a thick mass that is difficult to stir. Turn out onto a well-floured surface and knead, adding remaining flour when needed, 10 minutes. Gradually knead in the candied citrus peels and continue kneading until dough is soft and smooth, 15 to 17 minutes total. (Or make in a heavy-duty mixer; see page 67.) All finished rye doughs will remain slightly sticky. Be cautious about adding too much flour when kneading. The dough is ready when a little pulled from the mass springs back quickly (see Kneading and Kneading In, pages 66 and 76).

FERMENT THE DOUGH (3 to 4 hours) Shape the dough into a ball and let it rest on a lightly floured surface while you scrape, clean, and lightly oil the large bowl. Place the dough in the bowl and turn once to coat with oil. Take the dough's temperature: the ideal is 78°F. (see page 58). Cover with a clean damp towel and put in a moderately warm (74°–80°F.) draft-free place until almost doubled.

<u>Note:</u> If the dough temperature is higher than 78°F., put it in a cooler than 78°F. place like the refrigerator until the dough cools to 78°F. If it is lower than 78°F., put it in a warmer than 78°F. place until the dough warms to 78°F. The point is to try to keep the dough at 78°F. during its fermentation. If you do have to move the dough, be gentle and don't jostle it, or the dough may deflate.

DIVIDE THE DOUGH AND SHAPE THE LOAVES (10 minutes) Deflate the dough by pushing down in the center and pulling up on the sides. Transfer the dough to a lightly floured work surface and knead briefly. Cut into 2 equal pieces and flatten each piece with the heel of your hand. Shape each piece into a tight ball for round loaves (see Taking Shape, page 68).

PROOF THE LOAVES (2 to 2½ hours) Place the loaves seam side down on a board dusted with cornmeal. Cover with a clean damp towel or plastic wrap and put in a moderately warm (74°–80°F.) draft-free place until almost doubled in volume, or until a slight indentation remains when the dough is pressed with a fingertip.

BAKE THE LOAVES (35 to 40 minutes) Forty-five minutes to 1 hour before baking, preheat the oven and homemade hearth or baking stone on the center rack of the oven (see Equipment, page 52) to 450°F.

The oven rack must be in the center of the oven. If it is in the lower third of the oven, the bottoms of the breads may burn, and if it is in the upper third, the top crusts may burn.

Using a very sharp, serrated knife or a single-edged razor blade, score the loaves by making quick shallow cuts ¼ to ½ inch deep along the surface. Using a well-floured peel, slide the loaves onto the hearth. Quickly spray the inner walls and floor of the oven with cold water from a spritzer bottle. If there's an electric light bulb in the oven, avoid spraying it directly—it may burst. Spray for several seconds until steam has filled the oven. Quickly close the door to trap the steam and bake 3 minutes. Spray again in the same way, closing the door immediately so that steam doesn't escape and bake until

(continued)

loaves are golden brown, about 20 minutes. Reduce the heat to 400°F. and bake until the loaves are a rich caramel color and the crust is firm, 15 to 20 minutes.

To test the loaves for doneness, remove and hold the loaves upside down. Strike the bottoms firmly with your finger. If the sound is hollow, the breads are done. If it doesn't sound hollow, bake 5 minutes longer. Cool completely on a wire rack.

LIMPA RYE

Task	Approximate Time	Comments
Prepreparation		Ferment sourdough. Candy the fruit.
Preparation	5 min.	Calculate temperatures. Assemble ingredients. Mix.
Knead	15 min.	Take temperature of final dough.
Ferment	4 hr.	Moderate: 74°–80°F. until doubled in volume.
Divide	5 min.	Deflate and cut into 2 equal portions.
Shape	5 min.	Deflate: Form into balls for round loaves. Place on floured board.
Proof	2 hr., 30 min.	Moderate: 74°–80°F. until doubled in volume.
Bake	45 min.	With steam. 450°F.–400°F.
Cool	20 min.	On rack or in baskets.

Cumulative Total Time: 8 hr., 5 min.

RYE WITH HAVARTI CHEESE

Allow 8 hours to make the starter.
Total preparation and baking time (not including starter):
6 hours, 30 minutes

If you love Havarti cheese, you'll love this bread. It is rich with the creamy taste of the cheese and accented by a good sour tang. If you like, use dill-flavored Havarti for a twist.

Makes 2 round 10-inch loaves

Rye sourdough starter (page 124)	2 cups	18 ounces
Spring water	3 cups	24 fluid ounces
Rye flour,* preferably medium ground	1½ cups	8¼ ounces
Whole wheat flour,* preferably coarse ground	1½ cups	8¼ ounces
Fine sea salt	1 tablespoon	¾ ounce
20% bran wheat flour*	4½–5½ cups	18–20 ounces
Havarti cheese, grated	2¼ cups	9 ounces
Cornmeal, for dusting		

* See Flours (pages 42–49). These are good approximate measures. You may use more or less depending on the weight and absorbency of your flour.

MIX AND KNEAD THE FINAL DOUGH (20 minutes) Measure the ingredients and calculate the temperatures (see page 58). Combine the starter and water in a 6-quart bowl. Break up the starter well with a wooden spoon and stir until it loosens and the mixture is slightly frothy. Add the rye and whole wheat flours; stir until well combined. Add the salt and just enough of the bran flour to make a thick mass that is difficult to stir. Turn out onto a well-floured surface and knead until fairly soft, 12 minutes. Gradually knead in the cheese and continue kneading, adding remaining flour when needed, until dough is soft and smooth, 15 to 17 minutes total. (Or make in a heavy-duty mixer; see page 67.) This dough will need extra flour during the last few minutes of kneading because of the added moisture given off by the cheese. Be cautious, however, about adding too much flour during kneading, as the final dough should be slightly

(continued)

sticky. The dough is ready when a little pulled from the mass, springs back quickly (see Kneading and Kneading In, pages 66 and 76).

FERMENT THE DOUGH (2 to 2½ hours) Shape the dough into a ball and let it rest on a lightly floured surface while you scrape, clean, and lightly oil the large bowl. Place the dough in the bowl and turn once to coat with oil. Take the dough's temperature: the ideal is 78°F. (see page 58). Cover with a clean damp towel or plastic wrap and put in a moderately warm (74°–80°F.) draft-free place until almost doubled in volume.

> *Note: If the dough temperature is higher than 78°F., put it in a cooler than 78°F. place like the refrigerator until the dough cools to 78°F. If it is lower than 78°F., put it in a warmer than 78°F. place until the dough warms to 78°F. The point is to try to keep the dough at 78°F. during its fermentation. If you do have to move the dough, be gentle and don't jostle it, or the dough may deflate.*

DIVIDE THE DOUGH AND SHAPE THE LOAVES (10 minutes) Deflate the dough by pushing down in the center and pulling up on the sides. Transfer to a lightly floured work surface and cut into 2 equal pieces. Flatten each with the heel of your hand. Shape into tight balls for round loaves (see Taking Shape, page 68).

PROOF THE LOAVES (1½ to 2 hours) Place the loaves seam side down on a board dusted with cornmeal. Cover with a clean damp towel or plastic wrap and put in a moderately warm (74°–80°F.) draft-free place until almost doubled in volume, or until a slight indentation remains when the dough is pressed with a fingertip.

BAKE THE LOAVES (35 to 40 minutes) Forty-five minutes to 1 hour before baking, preheat the oven and homemade hearth or baking stone on the center rack of the oven (see Equipment, page 52) to 450°F.

The oven rack must be in the center of the oven. If it is in the lower third of the oven, the bottoms of the breads may burn, and if it is in the upper third, the top crusts may burn.

Using a very sharp, serrated knife or a single-edged razor blade, score the loaves by making quick shallow cuts ¼ to ½ inch deep along the surface. Using a well-floured peel, slide the loaves onto the hearth. Quickly spray the inner walls and floor of the oven with cold water from a spritzer bottle. If there's an electric light bulb in the oven, avoid spraying it directly—it may burst. Spray for several seconds until steam has filled the oven. Quickly close the door to trap the steam and bake 3 minutes. Spray again in the same way, closing the door immediately so that steam doesn't escape. Bake until the loaves turn golden, about 20 minutes. Reduce heat to 400°F. and bake until loaves are a rich caramel color and the crust is firm, 15 to 20 minutes.

To test the loaves for doneness, remove and hold the loaves upside down. Strike the bottoms firmly with your finger. If the sound is hollow, the breads are done. If it doesn't sound hollow, bake 5 minutes longer. Cool completely on a wire rack.

RYE WITH HAVARTI CHEESE

Task	Approximate Time	Comments
Prepreparation		Ferment sourdough.
Preparation	5 min.	Calculate temperatures. Assemble ingredients. Mix.
Knead	15 min.	Take temperature of final dough.
Ferment	2 hr., 30 min.	Moderate: 74°–80°F. until doubled in volume.
Divide	5 min.	Deflate and cut into 2 equal portions.
Shape	10 min.	Deflate: Form into balls for round loaves. Place on floured board.
Proof	2 hr.	Moderate: 74°–80°F. until doubled in volume.
Bake	40 min.	With steam. 450°F.–400°F.
Cool	20 min.	On rack or in baskets.

Cumulative Total Time: 6 hr., 50 min.

LEMON DILL RYE

Allow 8 hours to make the starter.
Total preparation and baking time (not including starter):
7 hours, 35 minutes

Dill and lemon are the lively flavors that jump forth in this light, refreshing, Scandinavian-inspired bread. Enjoy it thinly sliced as an unusual sandwich bread. It's terrific with Danish fontina, tomatoes, and cucumbers!

Makes 2 10-inch round loaves

1 medium onion, chopped	¾ cup	6 ounces
Vegetable oil	2 teaspoons	
Fresh dill, chopped	¾ cup	
Grated zest of 2 lemons	4 teaspoons	
Rye sourdough starter (page 124)	2 cups	18 ounces
Spring water	3 cups	24 fluid ounces
Rye flour,* preferably coarse ground	2 cups	11 ounces
Fine sea salt	1 tablespoon	¾ ounce
20% bran wheat flour*	4–5 cups	20–25 ounces
Cornmeal, for dusting		

* See Flours (pages 42–49). These are good approximate measures. You may use more or less depending on the weight and absorbency of your flours.

PREPARE THE ONIONS, DILL, AND LEMON (40 minutes, including cooling) Preheat the oven to 400°F. Combine the onion and vegetable oil in a bowl and toss well. Spread onion on a baking sheet and bake, stirring occasionally, until golden and tinged with dark brown, 20 to 25 minutes. Transfer to a platter and place in the refrigerator to cool completely, about 20 minutes. Stir in the dill and lemon zest. Set aside.

MIX AND KNEAD THE FINAL DOUGH (20 minutes) Measure the remaining ingredients and calculate the temperatures (see page 58). Combine the starter and water in a 6-quart bowl. Break up the starter well with a wooden spoon and stir until it loosens and the mixture is slightly frothy. Add the rye flour and stir until well combined. Add the salt and just enough of the bran flour to make a thick mass that is difficult to stir. Turn onto a well-floured surface and knead 10 minutes. Gradually knead in ¾ of the onion mixture and continue kneading adding remaining flour when needed, until dough is soft and smooth, 15 to 17 minutes total. (Or make in a heavy-duty mixer; see page 67.) This dough will need extra flour during the last 5 minutes of kneading because of the added moisture of the onion mixture. Be cautious, however, about adding too much flour during kneading, as the final dough should be slightly sticky. The dough is ready when a little pulled from the mass springs back quickly (see Kneading and Kneading In, pages 66 and 76).

FERMENT THE DOUGH (3 to 4 hours) Shape the dough into a ball and let it rest on a lightly floured surface while you scrape, clean, and lightly oil the large bowl. Place the dough in the bowl and turn once to coat with oil. Take the dough's temperature: the ideal is 78°F. (see page 58). Cover with a clean damp towel or plastic wrap and place in a moderately warm (74°–80°F.) draft-free place until doubled in volume.

> Note: If the dough temperature is higher than 78°F., put it in a cooler than 78°F. place like the refrigerator, until the dough cools to 78°F. If it is lower than 78°F., put it in a warmer than 78°F. place until the dough warms to 78°F. The point is to try to keep the dough at 78°F. during its fermentation. If you do have to move the dough, be gentle and don't jostle it, or the dough may deflate.

DIVIDE THE DOUGH AND SHAPE THE LOAVES (10 minutes) Deflate the dough by pushing down in the center and pulling up on the sides. Transfer to a lightly floured work surface and knead briefly. Cut into 2 equal pieces and flatten each with the heel of your hand. Shape into tight balls for round loaves (see Taking Shape, page 68).

PROOF THE LOAVES (1½ to 2 hours) Place the loaves seam side down on a board dusted with cornmeal. Cover with a clean damp towel or plastic wrap and put in a moderately warm (74°–80°F.) draft-free place until almost doubled in volume, or until a slight indentation remains when the dough is pressed with a fingertip.

(continued)

(35 to 40 minutes) Forty-five minutes to 1 hour before baking, preheat the oven and homemade hearth or baking stone on the center rack of the oven (see Equipment, page 52) to 450°F.

The oven rack must be in the center of the oven. If it is in the lower third of the oven, the bottoms of the breads may burn, and if it is in the upper third, the top crusts may burn.

Using a very sharp, serrated knife or a single-edged razor blade, score the loaves by making quick shallow cuts ¼ to ½ inch deep along the surface. Sprinkle the tops evenly with the reserved onion, and press to help it adhere. Using a well-floured peel, slide the loaves onto the hearth. Quickly spray the inner walls and floor of the oven with cold water from a spritzer bottle. If there's an electric light bulb in the oven, avoid spraying it directly—it may burst. Spray for several seconds until steam has filled the oven. Quickly close the door to trap the steam and bake 3 minutes. Spray again in the same way, closing the door immediately so that steam doesn't escape. Reduce heat to 400°F. and bake until loaves are a rich caramel color and the crust is firm, 30 to 35 minutes.

To test the loaves for doneness, remove and hold the loaves upside down. Strike the bottoms firmly with your finger. If the sound is hollow, the breads are done. If it doesn't sound hollow, bake 5 minutes longer. Cool completely on a wire rack.

LEMON DILL RYE

Task	Approximate Time	Comments
Prepreparation		Ferment sourdough. Prepare herbs, onion, and lemon.
Preparation	5 min.	Calculate temperatures. Assemble ingredients. Mix.
Knead	15 min.	Take temperature of final dough.
Ferment	4 hr.	Moderate: 74°–80°F. until doubled in volume.
Divide	5 min.	Deflate and cut into 2 equal portions.
Shape	5 min.	Deflate: Form into balls for round loaves. Place on floured board.
Proof	2 hr., 30 min.	Moderate: 74°–80°F. until doubled in volume.
Bake	35 min.	With steam. 450°F.–400°F.
Cool	20 min.	On rack or in baskets.

Cumulative Total Time: 7 hr., 55 min.

FINNISH SOUR RYE BREAD

Allow 8 hours to make the starter.
Total preparation and baking time (not including the starter):
9 hours, 20 minutes

This is a full-flavored rye bread with a good sour taste. The Finns make it in the shape of large disks that don't rise very much. The finished loaf is richly dark and looks like a large bagel, dense and chewy with a thick crust. Slice it in 2-inch widths for stews and soups.

This dough is very sticky to work with, so keep your hands wet. It won't come together like a regular dough until at least ten or twelve minutes of kneading. Don't be alarmed and thereby add a lot of extra flour, as that will make it very tough. Give this bread a long, cool first fermentation to develop flavor more than texture.

Makes 2 thick 10-inch loaves

Rye sourdough starter (page 124)	2 cups	18 ounces
Spring water	3 cups	24 fluid ounces
Rye flour,* preferably medium ground	2½ cups	13½ ounces
Cracked rye	2¼ cups	12 ounces
Fine sea salt	1 tablespoon	¾ ounce
Whole wheat flour,* preferably medium ground	3¾ cups	19 ounces
Cornmeal, for dusting		

---

* See Flours (pages 42–49). These are good approximate measures. You may use more or less depending on the weight and absorbency of your flours.

MIX AND KNEAD THE FINAL DOUGH (20 minutes) Measure out the ingredients and calculate temperatures for a 70°F. dough (see page 58). Combine the starter and water in a 6-quart bowl. Break up the starter well with a wooden spoon and stir until it loosens and the mixture is slightly frothy. Add the rye flour and stir until well combined. Add the cracked rye, salt and just enough of the whole wheat flour to make a thick mass that is difficult to stir. Turn onto a lightly floured surface and knead, adding remaining flour when needed, until dough is soft and smooth, 15 to 17 minutes. (Or make in a heavy-duty mixer; see page 67.) This dough will be very sticky up until almost 12 minutes of kneading. Use a dough scraper to help lift and fold the dough while you are kneading. The dough is ready when it springs back when pressed with a finger. (See Kneading, page 66).

FERMENT THE DOUGH (5 to 6 hours or overnight in the refrigerator) Shape the dough into a ball and let it rest on a lightly floured surface while you scrape, clean, and lightly oil the large bowl. Place the dough in the bowl and turn once to coat with oil. Take the dough's temperature. The ideal is 70°F. (see page 58). Cover with a clean damp towel or plastic wrap and place in a moderate (68°–70°F.) draft-free place until increased in volume about one-half or place in the refrigerator overnight.

> *Note: If the dough temperature is higher than 70°F., put it in a cooler than 70°F. place like a cool basement or unheated room, until the dough cools to 70°F. If it is lower than 70°F., place it in a warmer than 70°F. place until the dough warms to 70°F. The point is to try to keep the dough at 70°F. during its fermentation. If you do have to move the dough, be gentle and don't jostle it, or the dough may deflate.*

DIVIDE THE DOUGH AND SHAPE THE LOAVES (10 minutes) Deflate the dough by pushing down in the center and pulling up on the sides. Transfer to a lightly floured work surface and knead briefly. Cut into 2 equal pieces and flatten each with the heel of your hand. Shape each piece into a tight ball (see Taking Shape, page 68). Place each ball on a board that has been well dusted with cornmeal. Using a rolling pin, roll each into a 9-inch disk about 1 inch thick. Flour the end of the rolling pin and poke and stretch a 1-inch hole in the center of each disk. Dust generously with more rye flour.

PROOF THE LOAVES (1½ to 2 hours; 3 hours if dough has been refrigerated) Cover with a clean damp towel or plastic wrap and put in a moderately warm (74°–80°F.) draft-free place. The dough will barely rise perceptively.

BAKE THE LOAVES (45 minutes) Forty-five minutes to 1 hour before baking, preheat the oven and homemade hearth or baking stone on the center rack of the oven (see Equipment, page 52) to 400°F.

(continued)

The oven rack must be in the center of the oven. If it is in the lower third of the oven, the bottoms of the breads may burn, and if it is in the upper third, the top crusts may burn.

Bake the loaves one at a time, keeping the other loaf covered until ready to bake. Gently slip one loaf onto a floured peel. Using the peel, slide the loaf onto the hearth and quickly spray the inner walls and floor of the oven with cold water from a spritzer bottle. If there's an electric light bulb in the oven, avoid spraying it directly— it may burst. Spray for several seconds until steam has filled the oven. Quickly close the door to trap the steam and bake 3 minutes. Spray again in the same way, closing the door immediately so that steam doesn't escape, and bake until the loaf is a rich caramel color and the crust is firm, 35 to 45 minutes.

To test the loaf for doneness, remove and hold upside down. Strike the bottom firmly with your finger. If the sound is hollow, allow the bread to cool on a rack. If it doesn't sound hollow, bake 5 minutes longer. Repeat baking with the second disk.

FINNISH SOUR RYE BREAD

Task	Approximate Time	Comments
Prepreparation		Ferment sourdough.
Preparation	5 min.	Calculate temperatures. Assemble ingredients. Mix.
Knead	15 min.	Take temperature of final dough.
Ferment	6 hr.	Cool: 68°–70°F. or in fridge overnight until increased 50%.
Divide	5 min.	Deflate and cut dough into 2 equal portions.
Shape	10 min.	Form into balls. Roll out into 9-inch disks on lightly floured board.
Proof	2 hr.	Moderate: 74°–80°F. Cover with a clean damp towel or plastic wrap.
Bake	45 min.	With steam. 400°F.
Cool	20 min.	On rack or in basket.

Cumulative Total Time: 9 hr., 40 min.

100 PERCENT WHOLE RYE

Allow 8 hours to make the starter.
Total preparation and baking time (not including the starter):
12 hours, 10 minutes

This traditional northern European bread is created completely with rye flour. Since the dough lacks wheat flour, it has no gluten to form free-standing loaves. It is more a batter than a dough and must be baked in pans. The resulting bread is moist and very dense. Sliced into very thin rectangles, it is perfection for a Scandinavian smörgasbord, where it can partner cheeses, pickled herring, or smoked salmon and trout.

Makes two 8 by 4-inch loaves

Rye sourdough starter (page 124)	2 cups	18 ounces
Spring water (70°F.)	3 cups	24 fluid ounces
Rye flour,* preferably medium ground	6 cups	2 pounds
Fine sea salt	1 tablespoon	¾ ounce

* See Flours (pages 42–49). This is a good approximate measure. You may use more or less depending on the weight and absorbency of your flour.

MIX THE FINAL DOUGH (20 minutes) Measure the ingredients and calculate the necessary temperatures (see page 58). Combine the starter and water in a 6-quart bowl. Break up the starter well with a wooden spoon and stir until it loosens and the mixture is slightly frothy. Gradually add 11 ounces (2 cups) of the flour and stir until well combined. Add the salt and remaining flour and stir until the batter is thick and pasty. Don't expect a heavy, typical bread dough. This is very wet dough—more like a thick batter.

FERMENT THE DOUGH (5 to 6 hours) Take the dough's temperature: the ideal is 78°F. (see page 58). Cover with a clean damp towel or plastic wrap and put in a moderately warm (74°–80°F.) draft-free place.

Note: If the dough temperature is higher than 78°F., put it in a cooler than 78°F. place like the refrigerator, until the dough cools to 78°F. If it is lower than 78°F., put it in a warmer than 78°F. place until the dough warms to 78°F.

(continued)

The point is to try to keep the dough at 78°F. during its fermentation. If you do have to move the dough, be gentle and don't jostle it, or the dough may deflate.

The dough/batter will only increase in volume about one-third and will feel wet and spongy when pressed lightly with your finger.

DIVIDE DOUGH INTO LOAF PANS (10 minutes) Generously grease two 8 × 4 × 2¾-inch bread pans with vegetable shortening and dust with rye flour. Turn the dough into the pan and level the top using a wet metal thin-blade spatula.

PROOF THE LOAVES (2 to 3 hours) Cover with a clean damp towel or plastic wrap and place in a warm moderately (74°–80°F.) draft-free place to rise again. The batter will not double in volume, but it will increase by about one-quarter and become slightly domed.

BAKE THE LOAVES (2½ to 3 hours) Preheat the oven and home-made hearth or baking stone in the center rack of the oven to 300°F. Bake until the loaves have shrunk from the sides of the pan, the tops are dark brown, and a toothpick inserted in the center comes out clean, 2½ to 3 hours. Remove the loaves from the pans and hold them upside down. Strike the bottoms firmly with your finger. If the sound is hollow, allow the breads to cool on a wire rack. If it doesn't sound hollow, bake 15 minutes longer. Cool for 10 minutes, then remove from the pans to cool completely on wire racks.

<u>Note:</u> This bread improves in flavor and texture if allowed to rest for at least 12 hours before serving.

100 PERCENT WHOLE RYE

Task	Approximate Time	Comments
Prepreparation		Ferment sourdough.
Preparation	10 min.	Calculate temperatures. Assemble ingredients. Mix.
Ferment	6 hr.	Moderate: 74°–80°F. or in fridge overnight until increased 30%.
Proof	3 hr.	Moderate: 74°–80°F. In two 8 × 4-inch pans until increased 20%.
Bake	3 hr.	300°F. Until toothpick comes out clean.
Cool	12 hr.	Unmold. Cool on rack.

Cumulative Total Time: 12 hr., 10 min.

VOLLKORNBROT

Allow 8 hours to soak the rye berries.
Allow 8 to 10 hours to make the starter.
Total preparation and baking time (not including the starter):
12 hours, 25 minutes

The name means "whole kernel bread" and it's a tradition in Germany and Scandinavia. The large amount of whole rye berries give it a toothsome, very moist texture. It is a rich, heavy loaf that must be baked in pans so you can slice it as thin as possible. Don't plan on eating this the day you bake it—it will be too moist. It must sit for at least twenty-four hours while the flavors meld and the crumb stabilizes. This isn't a sandwich bread, but rather a bread to accompany sausage, cheese, and other northern European delicacies.

Makes two 9 by 5-inch loaves

Whole rye berries	2 cups	13 ounces
Spring water heated to boiling	8 cups, approximately	64 fluid ounces, approximately
Rye sourdough starter (page 124)	2 cups	18 ounces
Rye flour,* preferably medium ground	8 cups	40 ounces
Cracked rye	2 cups	9 ounces
Fine sea salt	1 tablespoon	¾ ounce

* See Flours (pages 42–49). This is a good approximate measure. You may use a little more or less depending on the weight and absorbency of your flour.

PREPARE THE RYE BERRIES (allow 8 hours or overnight) Soak the berries in about 6 cups of the hot spring water, or at least enough to cover the berries by 1 inch. Let stand 8 hours or overnight. (If the water becomes completely absorbed before soaking time has ended, add more hot spring water to cover.) Drain and reserve the soaking liquid. Add enough fresh room-temperature spring water to the reserved soaking liquid to measure 6 cups total. Reserve.

MIX THE FINAL DOUGH (10 minutes) Measure the ingredients and calculate the temperatures (see page 58). Combine the starter, rye berries, and reserved 6 cups water in a 6-quart bowl. Break up the starter well with a wooden spoon and stir until it loosens and the mixture is slightly frothy. Add 1 cup (5½ ounces) of the rye flour and all the cracked rye; stir until well combined. Add the salt and remaining flour; stir until combined and the mixture is wet and sticky.

FERMENT THE DOUGH (4 to 6 hours) Take the dough's temperature: the ideal is 78°F. (see page 58). Cover with a clean damp towel and put in a moderately warm (74°–80°F.) draft-free place.

> *Note: If the dough temperature is higher than 78°F., put it in a cooler than 78°F. place like the refrigerator, until the dough cools to 78°F. If it is lower than 78°F., put it in a warmer than 78°F. place until the dough warms to 78°F. The point is to try to keep the dough at 78°F. during its fermentation. If you do have to move the dough, be gentle and don't jostle it, or the dough may deflate.*

The dough will become spongy but not springy, distinctly sour-smelling and increased in volume by about one-quarter.

DIVIDE THE DOUGH INTO LOAF PANS (10 minutes) Generously grease two 5 × 9 × 3-inch loaf pans with vegetable shortening and dust with rye flour. Turn the dough into the prepared pans. Smooth the tops with a wet thin flexible cake spatula.

PROOF THE LOAVES (2½ to 3 hours) Cover with a clean damp towel or plastic wrap and put in a moderately warm (74°–80°F.) draft-free place, until the dough has domed slightly and increased in volume again by one quarter.

BAKE (3 to 3½ hours) Preheat the oven and homemade hearth or baking stone on the center rack of the oven to 300°F. Bake until the loaves have shrunk from the sides of the pan and the tops are dark brown and a toothpick inserted in the center comes out clean, 2½ to 3 hours. Remove the loaves from the pans and hold the loaves upside down. Strike the bottoms firmly with your finger. If the sound is hollow, the breads are done. If it doesn't sound hollow, bake 15 minutes longer. Cool in the pans for 10 minutes, then remove and cool completely on wire racks.

(continued)

Let this bread rest at least 24 (or even 36) hours before eating. It is very moist in the center when removed from the oven, but as it cools the moisture distributes evenly throughout the bread. It will keep for weeks at room temperature wrapped tightly in plastic wrap.

VOLLKORNBROT

Task	Approximate Time	Comments
Prepreparation		Ferment sourdough. Soak rye berries.
Preparation	10 min.	Calculate temperatures. Assemble ingredients. Mix.
Mix	10 min.	Dough will be sticky until last minute. Take temperature of final dough.
Ferment	6 hr.	Moderate: 74°–80°F. or in fridge overnight until increased 25%.
Divide	5 min.	Turn into two 5 × 9 × 3-inch pans.
Proof	3 hr.	Moderate: 74°–80°F. until increased 20%.
Bake	3 hr.	300°F. until toothpick tests clean.
Cool	Completely.	Unmold. On rack.
Wait	24 hr.	Serve.

Cumulative Total Time: 12 hr., 15 min.

TWELVE

BOULANGER BASIL

A BAKER'S STORY

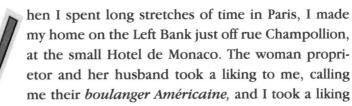

When I spent long stretches of time in Paris, I made my home on the Left Bank just off rue Champollion, at the small Hotel de Monaco. The woman proprietor and her husband took a liking to me, calling me their *boulanger Américaine,* and I took a liking to them, bringing them breads each night from the bakeries I had visited during the day. I learned then that it wasn't just bakers who loved talking about bread. One night I presented my hostess with a large five-pound loaf of a rich caramel-colored *pain au levain* and her face exploded with pleasure.

"In Normandy," she said, while she cradled the huge loaf against her chest, "we would hold the big breads up like this and slice them paper thin." She pantomimed drawing a long knife across the top of the bread, cutting off fine, invisible slices. Then she hurried off to show her husband the big loaf. I learned from her that the French people don't merely talk about bread, they behold it—with instantaneous passion and pleasure.

Coming home each evening was like stepping into the pages of literature I had relished in college. Here was the Paris I had discovered in Jean-Paul Sartre, Albert Camus, and Jean Genet—a diverse, unpredictable, challenging city of neighborhoods where ancient museums stood alongside new Arab restaurants. Fresh vegetable markets dotted every street. Around one corner, and not far from my door, was the Latin Quarter, busy and noisy with tourists. Right around another corner was a quiet residential street where people casually gazed from their balconies, and where a cat (always a cat) dozed on a windowsill or doorstep. Very close by my hotel was the place de Sorbonne, the center of the Sorbonne in Paris, and students and teachers streamed into my neighborhood to frequent the bookstores and revival movie houses.

One drizzling evening in September I returned home very tired. I had only a few days left before returning to the United States, and I had been cramming last-minute business into the final hours. I was so tired I took with great difficulty every one of the narrow creaking stairs to the third floor and finally collapsed, clothes and all, onto the bed. I don't remember falling asleep.

Late in the night I was awakened by a loud and relentless ugly buzzing noise. I bolted for the alarm clock but the awful buzzing continued. By then I was awake enough to realize that the sound was coming from the telephone on the wall above my head (I had never used this phone; no one ever called me in my room here.) I pulled the receiver from the cradle.

A man's voice speaking English quickly apologized for the late hour. He said his name was Basil Kamir, and that he was a baker here in Paris, that he had heard I was exploring *boulangeries,* and that I had a connection with a miller in the United States who had organic wheat for sale. He said that he wanted to meet me before I left Paris, that he wanted me to see his bakery, and that he was very interested in talking about organic wheat.

By then I was not only wide awake but *very* curious. Here was a French baker who spoke English with an elegant accent, who was interested in discussing organic wheat (a passion of mine), and who owned a bakery in a district of Paris that was so far off my beaten track I had never even heard of it—and had no clue how to find it.

"Just get on the Metro and follow the Yellow Line," he said, referring to one of the many color-keyed routes of Paris's underground system.

A few mornings later, after two elaborate Metro changes involving long subterranean walks—one at Odéon, then again at Montparnasse, I came up out of the ground at Pernety in the Fourteenth *Arrondissement*. I was stunned by what I saw. The neighborhood looked bombed, looted, and abandoned. Many old shops and houses stood empty; others were gutted. Then I saw bulldozers, dumpsters, and cranes suspending demolition balls, and I realized that the area was being demolished. What I found out later was that this was urban redevelopment, Paris style. The city had earmarked several blocks for development and had enticed, cajoled, and finally forced residents to leave so that it could build *moderne.* Most of the people had given in and left, a very few stubborn ones had stayed.

The street signs had been removed and the sidewalks had been torn up, so I was forced to guess which way to go as I stumbled through a muddy mix of potholes and piles of cobblestones. I was looking for rue Vercingétorix, a very long name for a French street. When I stopped a man to ask for help, my college French was so labored that I mercilessly pounded each syllable of the long street name—"*Esque-vous connais où est le rue Ver-cin-gé-tor-ix?*" The Frenchman must have thought I was asking for six different things, so he gave me a helpless shrug and went on. Then a workman, dressed in the familiar French bright blue pants and jacket, gave me three patient listenings before he understood what I was asking. He pointed me in the right direction—back where I had started.

A half-hour later I turned onto what I thought was the right street, which just happened to be a block from where I had started out. Now I was walking on wood planks that had been stretched to bridge mud puddles, sand, and debris. On either side of what used to be a cobblestone street were half-standing buildings, new ones, or nothing. I had a sinking feeling that I was lost again; there couldn't possibly be a bakery around here. I was discouraged and yearned to get back to some familiar ground. Before turning back I squinted into the distance. Something slowly came into focus: an old storefront standing between two vacant lots. As I got closer I saw that the little building was vulnerably perched between two building sites that had been excavated twenty feet below street level. By then I could read the faded painted word above the window—*Boulangerie*—a nineteenth-century Beaux Arts sign on an elegant and stately storefront. Neither had been repainted in years. My sense of relief at finding the bakery was exceeded by a sense of caution that I still can't explain. I went in slowly.

Inside was a truly classic and beautiful bakery: marble counter, rich wood cabinets and copper fixtures, tiled walls with murals depicting large women holding armfuls of wheat at harvest. Painted on the ceiling was another mural of the four seasons of the farm. There were antique bakers' tools, elaborate wrought-iron oven doors, wooden peels worn thin from use, and bakers' artifacts. The front window was trimmed in gold leaf and filled with a display of breads that looked unlike any others I had seen in Paris. These were large earthy loaves with heavy crusts, some thick with flour, some with small cracks and ridges. They were like the rustic breads that country people in France have eaten for hundreds of years.

The unmistakable aroma of *levain* was heavy in the air—also unlike any bakery in Paris—and I was beginning to feel that I was in a very different and unusual place.

In spite of the demolition going on outside, there was a steady stream of customers coming in and buying loaves. Each would linger a while to talk, tearing into a *baguette* while they made conversation. At one point three workmen from one of the construction crews came in and left with arms loaded with bread.

"Basil est toujours en retard," the young woman behind the counter said after I had waited some time. Her smile made me feel free to look around while I continued to wait. I wandered to the back where the pastry bakers were at work, then I went down a very narrow stairway to the oven below. Downstairs, the cracks between the old floor stones were packed with spilled flour. The work bench, cabinets, even the incidental pieces of equipment were so old and well worn they looked to be from another era or a museum. I moved slowly like a tourist among relics. The only thing of this century was an electric mixer. The oven itself bore an embossed iron plate with the date: 1893. I was so taken with its beauty—brick and wood fired—that I tried to get a better look at it. I fumbled with the lamp hanging at the opening, trying to look inside when a sudden nervousness came over me, a flush of anxiety that made my hands tremble. You'd think I were a little kid sneaking a touch of the Torah. I backed away, deciding to wait for a formal introduction by Basil.

When Basil arrived I was startled to see how young he was, a man not much older than my twenty-eight years. Here was a young *boulanger* whose bakery was a vestige of the past. I expected someone much older.

Basil was, in fact, an hour late that day and has been consistently late for our appointments ever since. In spite of this habit, which plagues all his friends, he and I have built a close friendship. I've had to accept the fact that Basil lives a life full of unplanned encounters, conversations, and spontaneous journeys that take him farther and teach him even more than he already knows about bread and baking. I have seen him miss airplanes because he can't end a conversation with a baker he has just met. Once Basil and I dropped in for what was supposed to be a quick trip through the Musée Français du Pain, which had just opened in Paris. The museum was a small private collection of antique bakers' tools, books about baking, paintings, and the like—an individual curator's tribute to bread making. I found it interesting enough, but was ready to leave after about forty-five minutes. Not Basil! He touched everything twice, running his fingers over every wooden handle, picking up each gadget to look at it carefully. He drew pictures of the old iron tools and fixtures, and he engaged the curator in a long and intense conversation. Wherever else we were headed that day, we would be late!

I have never known a baker young or old with Basil's keen sensitivity to the past and his insatiable appetite for knowledge of the things of quality that have preceded him. And he adheres to the old methods he learns; his breads are made from recipes garnered from seventeenth-century baking books. The wholesome loaves are works of beauty with flavors that can come only from the well-attended dough of an artisan.

Basil thinks, talks, and dreams bread. When he returns from a trip, he describes the breads of where he's been. When he remembers his childhood in the rugged Auvergne mountains of the south, he describes the stout farmers sharing bread by bending large loaves of dark *levain* over their knees until they break. When he doodles on the pad by the telephone, it's spikelets of wheat or shapes of loaves that he draws.

It's not only the idea of bread that holds Basil captive; his whole life revolves around the baking of the bread. We have been out together with friends when Basil will suddenly become quiet and withdrawn.

"What's up?" I ask. "Why are you so quiet?" Like a parent whose thoughts suddenly go to the kids who are home with the sitter, Basil is thinking about that day's *levain* that is growing at the bakery.

"I didn't like the way it looked earlier today," he says. "I think I should adjust the temperature." So after dinner we all go out of our way to his bakery so he can turn the retarder down five degrees. Wherever we were going that night, we were late!

Basil even came late to baking. He was first a scholar, then a sailor, then an African music promoter. It was only a few years before I met him that he wandered into what would one day be his bakery. The beautiful shop had been sitting empty, as had many other businesses in the area after rumors flew about demolition of the district. Shop owners vacated one after another in search of a more secure location. Basil was promoting African music, and he rented the old bakery for his store. He loved the feel of the shop and the rent was cheap.

The music business was good, but each day someone would come through the door expecting to find a bakery (Basil had never removed the sign from the front). The remaining residents needed a bakery. They told Basil they thought it sacrilegious to use a bakery for anything other than bread. Basil accepted their complaints with good grace. He had quickly come to admire the resistance of the old guard, the ones who had stayed in the neighborhood. But what could he do? He was in the music business.

He hadn't been open a year when the city began to pressure Basil to leave the block, threatening to condemn the building. Basil resisted! He had become attached to the beauty and dignity of the old bakery and to the fighting spirit of the residents. He called the minister of culture, Michelle D'Ornano, who, according to press reports, had been opposed to the development from the beginning. D'Ornano was on Basil's side.

"If we declare your bakery a landmark," he said, "the city can't condemn it." That was all Basil needed to hear. Then came the stipulations. "But if it is a *boulangerie*," said D'Ornano, "then it must be activated. If there is an oven, it must bake the bread that is sold there."

Basil was ready to do anything to save the building. He would even consider baking bread and selling African music in the same shop.

Downstairs, beneath thick blankets of cobwebs, he uncovered the original brick oven. He needed to know: Could the oven work? Was there any way to bring life back to the chimney and bricks? There was a large plate above the oven door *"Jean LeFort et Fils 1893."* This gave Basil his first lead. He opened the phone book and set out to call every LeFort until he found someone who knew of the oven builder. Finally someone said, "Jean and his sons have been dead a long time, but the nephew André is still alive and is carrying on the tradition. In fact, he is the last one left in Paris."

Basil made two more phone calls. One was to André LeFort asking him to come and look at the oven. The other was to Lionel Poilâne, the famous Parisian baker whom Basil did not know but whose passion for wood-fired brick ovens was well known. Basil hoped he would come for the sake of tradition.

In a few days, Poilâne, LeFort, and Basil stood together in front of the old oven. Poilâne was instantly taken with its beauty—the shaped inner dome, the slope of the floor, the well-lighted openings, and the almost perfect alignment of the bricks, hardly a bump or a ridge.

"You must bake bread here!" he cried. "You *must* bake bread in this oven."

LeFort was thrilled to uncover and revive the master work of his uncle. He told Basil that he thought the oven had actually been built in 1850 and rebuilt in 1893. He would fix the firebox and clean the chimney, and that was all it needed.

They all celebrated that day at a local café. Basil announced to the bartender as they entered, "We're going to save the bakery! We're going to light the oven and bake good bread—bread like from my country." He referred to the Auvergne, the remote region of south-central France where he had grown up, as his country. In the Auvergne, an area of volcanic rock and rough agricultural land, the people are like Basil—sure, tough, hard-working, and honest. They know the interdependency of people and nature, and have learned to take life seriously but not themselves. In the Auvergne, wholesome bread is as valued as friendship and good soil.

"So who will bake your bread?" asked the bartender. "Not you?"

"Don't worry," said Basil, pouring some red wine, "I will find a good baker . . . a very good baker."

"I know of a good baker," said the bartender, and he pointed to a man eating lunch at a table by himself. Jean LeFleur was the baker's name, and in a handshake he became Basil's first teacher and an instant partner in reviving the bakery. The two spent the next day collecting equipment donated to the cause, and André went to work on the oven.

In a few days they lit the first fire to begin heating the bricks, and LeFleur started to grow the first *levain*. Within a week the first breads of the new *boulangerie* were baking on the fired bricks, and the aroma of hot bread filled the neighborhood again.

Basil was elated, but his celebration was cut short by a notice from the mayor's office advising him of the date for demolition. He called D'Ornano immediately.

"If they come to demolish this building," he said, "they will have to pull me first from the oven. I am not going to leave. I am crawling into the oven with a rifle. If they try to take me, I will come out shooting."

The day after Basil's emotional threats, D'Ornano sent a committee to verify the bakery as a historic site, but the signed declaration of landmark status was slow getting to Basil and the wrecking crew came to the building. They hadn't heard of the status change. At the eleventh hour, the documentation arrived and the bulldozers retreated.

That was the day Basil became a baker, deciding to gradually let go of his music business and dedicate himself to making the traditional breads of France. He began to travel, seeking the advice of old bakers. He also scoured libraries for baking books; and in an eighteenth-century manuscript he found a recipe for *pain au levain,* which he developed into the bread he makes today at his bakery, Le Moulin de la Vierge ("The Virgin's Mill"). He has passed the recipe on to me, passionately insisting that I re-create the bread for my customers. It is, in fact, the *pain au levain* I make at Bread Alone— I've never tasted a finer one. And it is the same recipe I pass on to you in the following chapter.

LEVAIN

MAKING THE *CHEF* AND THE *LEVAIN*

evain (pronounced, *luh-vahn*) is the French word meaning "leaven," and in this sense refers to a sourdough cultured by wild yeasts. The sourdough breads of France are called *pain au levain* (bread from a sourdough or wild yeast). Unlike the United States, Germany, or Japan, where bakers have the option of buying dehydrated sourdough cultures, *levain* is not something you can buy in France. French tradition has kept the process of making *levain* a highly individual one, definitely not one of mass production. Each bakery has its own conditions. Each baker builds the *chef* (the seed the sourdough is built upon) and ripens the *levain* according to his or her own taste. Some will follow old family formulas to develop a soupy *levain* often resulting in a very sour *pain au levain*. Others may work with a firm and tough *levain*, which often creates a milder flavor in the final loaf. Then there are bakers, especially young ones, who constantly experiment.

All these different approaches have a pronounced effect on the mildness or sourness, the weight, texture and look of *pain au levain*. I like the variety! I like tasting the difference from baker to baker within the same region, even within the same neighborhood of the city. But this array tends to puff up the mystique of *pain au levain* and all sourdough breads, since most bakers keep their process secret, especially if their *levain* breads are popular.

ANOTHER CASE FOR WHOLE-GRAIN ORGANIC FLOUR

Recently I was approached by a new miller who had some organic flour for sale. His was more processed than most of the flours I regularly use—some of the germ had been removed and all of the bran. Because the flour had a slightly higher protein content, however, I decided to give it a try.

We put it to use as soon as it was delivered and everything seemed fine. The *levain* developed very well—it had good cell structure and all the right smells. But the final bread had no flavor! It was flat and bland, very surprising and disappointing.

I quickly returned to using 20 percent bran wheat flour. It's clear that the more wholesome the flour, the more well nourished and active the flavor-producing yeast cells—and the more vibrant and full flavored your final loaf of *pain au levain*.

The key to making good *pain au levain*—or any sourdough bread for that matter—is to bake often, tracking the process carefully. Keep descriptive lists of how the *levain* behaves and what it tastes like at its developmental stage. Take notes on how the temperature varies and the time it takes the *levain* to ripen. As you do, you will become familiar with the texture and feel of the process and will be creating your own "secret process" that satisfies your own taste. Bake every two days for fourteen days, and you will learn how to make really good *pain au levain*.

And what about the disappointments? A bad batch of bread is always followed by a good batch; disappointments are followed by success. Just keep baking.

MAKING THE *CHEF* ▦ AND THE *LEVAIN* ▦

Building a ripe *chef* and then the *levain* (or sourdough starter) is a fermentation process that demands some time and attention, although a minimum of actual work. This *chef* ferments and ripens slowly at a moderate temperature, and produces a full-flavored *levain* without overdoing the tang or sour bite. To speak more technically, the fermentation brings about a good balance of both lactic and acidic acids. The former gives the bread its overall sour tone, the latter its tang. This procedure is not the same as making a rye *chef*, so be alert to the differences.

THE *CHEF*

Begin by building the *chef*, the seed from which the *levain* will be created. Use 20 percent bran wheat flour, although you can use whole wheat flour for a very strongly flavored *chef* if you wish. Spring water ensures that there are no chemicals in your liquid to impede the *chef*'s growth. Also, the pinch of yeast is important to collect wild yeasts from the air. Eventually, you may wish to experiment with leaving the yeast out of the recipe. (See Stalking the Wild Yeast, page 186.)

Note: Be aware that each flour has its own behavioral characteristics. When I tested these *chef* recipes using different brands of 20 percent bran wheat flour, I found each batch had an individual personality. The main point of difference is thickness: One brand of flour will absorb water at a rate different from another. This is not a serious problem. Just observe the visual descriptions I give for the *chef* and add a little more water or flour if necessary to create the desired texture.

Observation is the key to making a healthy *chef.* Throughout the seventy-two hour fermentation period, the flour mixture will create carbon dioxide and the *chef* will evolve. It will start out as a soft dough, then transform into a thick batter, and finally become a loose batter. During fermentation, bubbles will appear where the surface was once smooth. Knowing that these dramatic changes occur will bolster your confidence as the *chef* ferments to perfection.

To help your observation, use a marker pen to show the level of the ripening *chef* each day on the side of the fermentation container. This way, you won't have to guess how much the *chef* has risen since last you looked.

DAY 1

20% bran wheat flour	¾ cup plus 2 tablespoons	4 ounces
Spring water	½ cup	4 fluid ounces
Moist yeast or dry yeast	a pinch	less than ¹⁄₁₆ teaspoon

Combine the flour, water, and yeast in a tall 2- to 3-quart clear plastic container with a lid. Stir well to make a thick, soft dough. The exact consistency of the dough will vary with the brand of flour, but don't add more flour or water at this point to adjust the texture. Scrape down the sides with a rubber spatula, cover tightly with lid, and let stand in a moderate (about 70°F.) place for 24 hours.

DAY 2

| 20% bran wheat flour | ¾ cup plus 2 tablespoons | 4 ounces |
| Spring water | ½ cup | 4 fluid ounces |

The *chef* should have almost doubled in volume. You will see tiny bubbles on the surface, and you might notice a slight musty smell. Add the flour and water to the mixture and stir vigorously to distribute the fresh ingredients and add fresh oxygen to the *chef.* The texture will still be like a soft dough. You may add a little more flour or water to make this texture, if necessary. Scrape down the sides, cover and place in a moderate (70°F.), draft-free place for 24 hours.

DAY 3

20% bran wheat flour	¾ cup plus 2 tablespoons	4 ounces
Spring water	½ cup	4 fluid ounces

The *chef* will now have the texture of a thick batter. It will have almost doubled in volume and be quite bubbly. Taste it! It will have a pronounced musty, but not bitter, flavor. The scent will be aggressively vinegary—that's fine.

Hold the container and notice the network of tiny bubbles throughout the *chef.* Add the flour and water, and stir well to make a thick batter. (You may have to add a little more water if your flour's absorbtion level is high.) Lift up the spoon slowly and notice the texture of the *chef.* It will attach itself to the spoon in sticky, gummy strands. With a marker pen, mark the level of the *chef* on the side of the container. Scrape down the sides, cover tightly, and let stand in a moderate (70°F.) draft-free place for 24 hours.

The *chef* is now ripe. It should be very loose in texture, like a pancake batter. It will have doubled in volume from the last addition of flour and water (use the marked level on the side of the container to check the expansion.) The *chef* may rise and fall, but as long as it doubles at some point during this last period, it's fine. It will be very lively with tiny bubbles of a well-developed cellular structure; you will see a honeycomb of large and small holes through the clear plastic container. Taste the *chef*—the acidic flavor may make you pucker at first, but the bitter-sour sensation will be followed by a mild woodlike taste. Don't be put off by the strong vinegarlike scent and the sometimes unpleasant character of the ripe *chef.* Better yet, get into it! If your *chef* is pungent and tangy, you're on your way to great *levain.*

You now have a fully ripe *chef* ready to transform into a *levain.* If you don't want to make the *levain* immediately, the chef can be refrigerated for up to 3 days.

THE *LEVAIN*

Once the ripe *chef* is full of bubbles and has a batterlike consistency, it is ready to turn into *levain*. Each of the *levain* bread recipes in this section calls for a certain amount of *levain* starter, usually 18 ounces. The *chef* is the seed that you will use to grow the starter. This is another process that takes time, but not effort. Also, it is only a matter of hours, not days. (The recipe for *levain* is different from the recipe for rye sourdough. In *levain* you use the whole batch of *chef*, whereas in the rye sourdough you use only a portion of the *chef*.)

Approximately 8 hours before you intend to start mixing your dough, you will have to make the *levain* sourdough starter. Follow this recipe for creating enough *levain* for baking.

LEVAIN STARTER

20% bran wheat flour	1 ¼ cups	6 ounces
Chef	full batch	

Add the flour directly into the container with the full batch of room-temperature, batterlike ripe *chef*. Stir vigorously to add fresh oxygen to the mixture. This will form a stiff consistency more like a stiff dough than a batter. This firm texture is important for ripening *levain*, because a dense rather than loose *levain* creates delicious sour bread without an overpowering tangy bite. Scrape down the sides, cover tightly, and let stand in a cool to moderate (about 70°F.) draft-free place for 8 to 10 hours.

The *levain* should have doubled in volume. The texture will be somewhat light, with many tiny bubbles throughout. Do not let the *levain* stand for longer than 10 hours, or the yeast will become exhausted and not raise the final dough. This recipe yields 18 ounces of *levain*.

You are now ready to make your final dough, which starts by weighing out the ripe *levain*, which you can do in either of these methods:

1. Place your mixing bowl on a scale, and note the bowl's weight. For example, suppose your bowl is 22 ounces. You want the total weight to equal the bowl plus the *levain*, or 40 ounces if you are using 18 ounces of *levain*. So, spoon out 18 ounces (or whatever the recipe calls for) of the *levain* directly into the bowl to make your 40 ounces.

STALKING THE WILD YEAST

In my bakery in the Catskills, the fresh mountain air is lush with invisible spores of wild yeast. All I have to do is mix up some flour and water, and the brew attracts these wild cultures, fermenting without the addition of commercial yeast.

Try as I might, I could not predictably catch wild yeasts in home kitchens however. Especially in an urban setting, where I suspect wild yeasts have a hard time surviving the pollution, my *chefs* remained stubbornly sullen and refused to ferment. Even professional bakers have this problem occasionally, and will add a pinch of yeast (just the tiniest amount) to their sourdough *chefs* and doughs to ensure success. While I prefer the taste of my wild yeast sours, the pinch of yeast might work for you, the home baker.

As you continue to bake on a regular basis, your kitchen's air will become alive with wild yeast. Once you become familiar with what a *chef* looks like at its different stages, you should experiment by making them without commercial yeast. Remember that if at any time during your wild yeast catching you feel insecure, add that pinch of commercial yeast so you won't have wasted three or four days of "stalking."

2. If you have a small scale that only measures 1 pound, you will have to measure the *levain* in batches directly into the scale's container. Rinse out the container with water (this helps avoid sticking), and spoon in the *levain*. Use a rubber spatula to scrape out the *levain* into your mixing bowl.
3. You can also measure out the *chef* into a rinsed metal measuring cup. Stir the *chef* well before measuring to expel any gas bubbles, and use a level measure of *chef*.

MAINTAINING THE *CHEF*

Having an active sour culture alive and fermenting will allow you to make a wonderful *pain au levain* every two days, once a week, once a month, or as often as you like. It's a simple process of turning the remaining *levain* back into a *chef* by feeding it and storing the *chef* in the refrigerator, which slows down the fermentation process.

20% bran wheat flour	½ cup	2½ ounces
Spring water	¾ cup plus 2 tablespoons	7 fluid ounces
Remaining *levain*		

Add the water and flour to the remaining *levain* and pour into your *chef* container. Stir well to make a loose, pancake batterlike consistency. Scrape down the sides of the container with a rubber spatula.

If you will want to make *levain* bread again within the next 36 hours, cover the mixture with its lid and let stand in a moderate (about 70°F.) draft-free place for 24 hours; it will double in volume and be very bubbly. Otherwise, refrigerate the mixture for up to 1 week.

NOURISHING THE *CHEF*

Nourishing the chef once a week makes sure the yeast cells have fresh food, oxygen, and water to feed on.

Chef	full batch	
20% bran wheat flour	¾ cup plus 2 tablespoons	4 ounces
Spring water	½ cup	4 fluid ounces

Every 7 days, use or discard 1 scant cup (8 ounces) of the *chef*. Add the flour and water, and stir well to bring oxygen into the mixture. Scrape down the sides of the container and cover tightly.

If a clear liquid forms on the surface, just stir it in. If the liquid has a pink tinge, the *chef* has spoiled. Throw it away and make a new starter. Otherwise, refrigerate the *chef* for up to 1 week.

Remember that you must feed the *chef* every week. If you are going on vacation, leave instructions with a neighbor. Healthy *chefs* can often last longer, so you can experiment with a longer period without feeding if you want. Also, *chefs* can sometimes be frozen for up to two months, but I don't recommend either timing variation as some *chefs* may not survive and you'll have to make a new one if there's a problem.

FOURTEEN

A FAMILY OF TRADITIONAL PAIN AU LEVAIN

BASIL'S *PAIN AU LEVAIN*

Allow 8 to 10 hours to ferment the *levain*.
Total preparation and baking time (not including the *levain*):
5 hours, 30 minutes

This is the bread developed by Basil Kamir in the early days of his bakery in Paris. It is a "mother" *pain au levain*! All the breads in this chapter are variations on this basic recipe. Like a good beef stock is the basis for any number of sauces and soups, this mother *levain* can be used for rolls, pizza, *focaccia*—whatever your taste desires. Once you can bake this bread, the uses and variations are limited only by what you can imagine.

Among bakers in France, the nickname for this classic loaf is *boulot*, which means "to work." It's a time-consuming chore to make large quantities of these torpedo-shaped loaves. The bakers must hand-shape them all, first into round loaves, then again into the more complicated torpedoes. The small ones are *petit boulot*, the large, *grand boulot*. Don't let this bit of trivia discourage you. You will be doing *un petit travail*—making only two loaves and the extra bit of work it takes to shape the torpedo will give you a classic bread with a time-honored look.

Take note: *Pain au Levain* doesn't ferment like other breads in this book. It gets a *very specific two-hour first rise*, a brief rest of thirty minutes, and a *two-hour third rise*.

Makes 2 long 14-inch loaves

Levain (page 185)	2 cups	18 ounces
Spring water	2¼ cups	18 fluid ounces
20% bran wheat flour*	4½–5½ cups	24–29 ounces
Fine sea salt	1 tablespoon	¾ ounce

* See Flours (pages 42–49). This is a good approximate measure. You may use more or less depending on the weight and absorbency of your flour.

MIX AND KNEAD THE FINAL DOUGH (20 minutes) Measure the ingredients and calculate the temperatures (see page 58). Combine the *levain* and water in a 6-quart bowl. Break up the *levain* well with a wooden spoon, or squeeze it through your fingers until broken up. Continue stirring until the *levain* is partly dissolved and the mixture is slightly frothy. Add 1 cup (5 ounces) of the flour and stir until well combined. Add the salt and just enough of the remaining flour to make a thick mass that is difficult to stir. Turn out onto a

(continued)

lightly floured surface and knead, adding remaining flour when needed, until dough is firm and smooth, 15 to 17 minutes total. (Or make in a heavy-duty mixer; see page 67.) The dough is ready when a little dough pulled from the mass springs back quickly (see Kneading, page 66).

FERMENT THE DOUGH (2 hours) Shape the dough into a ball and let it rest on a lightly floured surface while you scrape, clean, and lightly oil the large bowl. Place the dough in the bowl and turn once to coat with oil. Take the dough's temperature: the ideal is 78°F. (see page 66). Cover with a clean damp towel or plastic wrap and place in a moderately warm (74°–80°F.) draft-free place until increased in volume about one-quarter.

> *Note: If the dough temperature is higher than 78°F., put it in a cooler than 78°F. place like the refrigerator, until the dough cools to 78°F. If it is lower than 78°F., put it in a warmer than 78°F. place until the dough warms to 78°F. The point is to try to keep the dough at 78°F. during its fermentation. If you do have to move the dough, be gentle and don't jostle it, or the dough may deflate.*

This dough will not behave like an ordinary yeasted bread dough. It won't rise to a puffy state.

DIVIDE THE DOUGH AND REST (35 minutes) Deflate the dough by pushing down in the center and pulling up on the sides. Transfer the dough to a lightly floured work surface and knead briefly. Cut into 2 equal pieces. Shape each into a tight round ball and place on a lightly floured board. Cover with a clean damp towel or plastic wrap and place in a moderately warm (74°–80°F.) draft-free spot for 30 minutes.

SHAPE THE LOAVES (5 minutes) Flatten each ball with the heel of your hand on a lightly floured surface into a disk 8 inches in diameter. Shape into torpedoes (see Taking Shape, page 68).

PROOF THE LOAVES (2 hours) Place the loaves seam side up in a well-floured *couche* (see Equipment, page 52). Cover with a clean damp towel or plastic wrap and place in a moderately warm (74°–80°F.) draft-free spot until almost doubled in volume, or until a slight indentation remains when the dough is pressed with a fingertip.

BAKE THE LOAVES (about 30 minutes) Forty-five minutes to 1 hour before baking, preheat the oven and homemade hearth or baking stone on the center rack of the oven (see Equipment, page 52) to 450°F.

The oven rack must be in the center of the oven. If it is in the lower third of the oven, the bottoms of the breads may burn, and if it is in the upper third, the top crusts may burn.

Using the *couche* as an aid, gently roll one loaf from the *couche* onto a lightly floured peel so that it sits seam side down. Using a very sharp, serrated knife or a single-edged razor blade, score the loaf by making quick shallow cuts ¼ to ½ inch deep along the surface. Using the peel, slide the loaf onto the hearth. Repeat the process with the second loaf. Quickly spray the inner walls and floor of the oven with cold water from a spritzer bottle. If there's an electric light bulb in the oven, avoid spraying it directly—it may burst. Spray for several seconds until steam has filled the oven. Quickly close the door to trap the steam and bake 3 minutes. Spray again in the same way, closing the door immediately so that steam doesn't escape. Bake until loaves are a rich caramel color and the crust is firm, 25 to 30 minutes.

To test the loaves for doneness, remove and hold the loaves upside down. Strike the bottoms firmly with your finger. If the sound is hollow, the breads are done. If it doesn't sound hollow, bake 5 minutes longer. Cool completely on a wire rack.

PAIN AU LEVAIN AND VARIATIONS

Task	Approximate Time	Comments
Prepreparation	8–10 hr.	Build the *levain*. For variations, prepare the fresh ingredients.
Preparation	5 min.	Calculate temperatures. Assemble ingredients, mix.
Knead	15 min.	Take temperature of dough.
Ferment	2 hr.	Moderate: 74°–80°F. until increased 25% in volume.
Divide	5 min.	Deflate. Cut into 2 equal portions. Form round balls. Place on floured board.
Rest	30 min.	Moderate: 74°–80°F.
Shape	5 min.	Flatten with heel of hand. Shape into torpedoes.
Proof	2 hr.	Moderate: 74°–80°F. in *couche*.
Bake	30 min.	With steam. 450°F.
Cool	20 min.	On rack or in basket.

Cumulative Total Time: 5 hr., 50 min.

PAIN AU LEVAIN WITH OLIVES AND ROSEMARY

Allow 8 to 10 hours to ferment the *levain*.
Total preparation and baking time (not including the *levain*)
5 hours, 50 minutes

This loaf is inspired by the foods of Provence, where combining rosemary and olives is a culinary way of life. The olives make the bread moist and chewy, and their slightly bitter flavor heightens the flavor of the *levain*. I use firm-fleshed Provençal oil-cured black olives, often called *nyons*. The tiny brine-cured Niçoise olives are tasty snacks, but too moist to add to bread dough. I can usually easily find fresh rosemary for sale in small plastic bags at the supermarket. When you eat a slice of this with a glass of red wine and a salad, close your eyes and you will be in the South of France!

Makes 2 long 14-inch loaves

Levain (page 185)	2 cups	18 ounces
Spring water	2¼ cups	18 fluid ounces
20% bran wheat flour*	4½–5½ cups	24–29 ounces
Fine sea salt	1 tablespoon	¾ ounces
Mediterranean black olives, pitted	1 cup	4½ ounces
Chopped fresh rosemary	¼ cup	¼ ounce

* See Flours (pages 42–49). This is a good approximate measure. You may use more or less depending on the weight and absorbency of your flour.

MIX AND KNEAD THE FINAL DOUGH   (20 minutes) Measure the ingredients and calculate the temperatures (see page 78). Combine the *levain* and water in a 6-quart bowl. Break up the *levain* well with a wooden spoon or squeeze it through your fingers until broken up. Continue stirring until the *levain* is partly dissolved and the mixture is slightly frothy. Add 1 cup (5 ounces) of the flour and stir until well combined. Add the salt and just enough of the remaining flour to make a thick mass that is difficult to stir. Turn onto a well-floured surface and knead, adding remaining flour when needed, until dough is fairly soft, about 10 minutes. Gradually knead in the olives and rosemary, again adding more flour as needed. Continue kneading until the dough is firm and smooth, 15 to 17 minutes total. (Or make in a heavy-duty mixer; see page 67.) The dough is ready when a little dough pulled from the mass springs back quickly (see Kneading and Kneading In, pages 66 and 76).

FERMENT THE DOUGH (2 hours) Shape the dough into a ball and let it rest on a lightly floured surface while you scrape, clean, and lightly oil the large bowl. Place the dough in the bowl and turn once to coat with oil. Take the dough's temperature: the ideal is 78°F. (see page 58). Cover with a clean damp towel or plastic wrap and place in a moderately warm (74°–80°F.) draft-free spot until increased in volume about one-quarter.

> *Note: If the dough temperature is higher than 78°F., put it in a cooler than 78°F. place like the refrigerator, until the dough cools to 78°F. If it is lower than 78°F., put it in a warmer than 78°F. place until the dough warms to 78°F. The point is to try to keep the dough at 78°F. during its fermentation. If you do have to move the dough, be gentle and don't jostle it, or the dough may deflate.*

This dough will not behave like an ordinary yeasted bread dough. It won't rise to a puffy state.

DIVIDE THE DOUGH AND REST (35 minutes) Deflate the dough by pushing down in the center and pulling up on the sides. Transfer to a lightly floured work surface and knead briefly. Cut into 2 equal pieces. Shape each into a tight round ball and place on a lightly floured board. Cover with a clean damp towel or plastic wrap and place in a moderately warm (74°–80°F.) draft-free spot for 30 minutes.

SHAPE THE LOAVES (5 minutes) Flatten each ball with the heel of your hand into a disk 8 inches in diameter. Shape into torpedoes (see Taking Shape, page 68).

PROOF THE LOAVES (2 hours) Place the loaves seam side up in a well-floured *couche* (see Equipment, page 52). Cover with a clean damp towel or plastic wrap and put in a moderately warm (74°–80°F.) draft-free place until almost doubled in volume, or until a slight indentation remains when the dough is pressed with a fingertip.

BAKE THE LOAVES (about 30 minutes) Forty-five minutes to 1 hour before baking, preheat the oven and homemade hearth or baking stone on the center rack of the oven (see Equipment, page 52) to 450°F.

The oven rack must be in the center of the oven. If it is in the lower third of the oven, the bottoms of the breads may burn, and if it is in the upper third, the top crusts may burn.

Using the *couche* as an aid, gently roll one loaf from the *couche* onto a lightly floured peel so that it sits seam side down. Using a very sharp, serrated knife or a single-edged razor blade, score the loaf by making quick shallow cuts ¼ to ½ inch deep along the surface. Using the peel, slide the loaf onto the hearth. Quickly repeat the process with the second loaf. Spray the inner walls and floor of the oven with cold water from a spritzer bottle. If there's an electric light bulb in the oven, avoid spraying it directly—it may burst. Spray for several seconds until steam has filled the oven. Quickly close the door to trap the steam and bake 3 minutes. Spray again in the same way, closing the door immediately so that steam doesn't escape. Bake until loaves are a rich caramel color and the crust is firm, 25 to 30 minutes.

To test the loaves for doneness, remove and hold the loaves upside down. Strike the bottoms firmly with your finger. If the sound is hollow, the breads are done. If it doesn't sound hollow, bake 5 minutes longer. Cool completely on a rack.

PAIN AU LEVAIN WITH FRESH HERBS AND SUN-DRIED TOMATOES

Allow 8 to 10 hours to ferment the *levain*.
Total preparation and baking time (not including the *levain*):
5 hours, 50 minutes

Sun-dried tomatoes packed in olive oil are available in Italian delicatessens and specialty food stores. They bring a tangy sensation to the fresh herb flavor that permeates the crumb and crust of this bread. Because it ferments so long, the flavors develop together.

Makes 2 long 14-inch loaves

Levain (page 185)	2 cups	18 ounces
Spring water	2¼ cups	18 fluid ounces
20% bran wheat flour*	4½–5½ cups	24–29 ounces
Fine sea salt	1 tablespoon	¾ ounce
Chopped fresh sage	½ cup	½ ounce
Chopped fresh basil	½ cup	½ ounce
Sun-dried tomatoes packed in oil, drained, patted dry, and chopped	½ cup	1½ ounces

---

* See Flours (pages 42–49). This is a good approximate measure. You may use more or less depending on the weight and absorbency of your flour.

MIX AND KNEAD THE FINAL DOUGH (20 minutes) Measure the ingredients and calculate the temperatures (see page 58). Combine the *levain* and water in a 6-quart bowl. Break up the *levain* well with a wooden spoon or squeeze through your fingers until it is broken up. Continue stirring until the *levain* is partly dissolved and the mixture is slightly frothy. Add 1 cup (5 ounces) of the flour and stir until well combined. Add the salt and just enough of the remaining flour to make a thick mass that is difficult to stir. Turn out onto a lightly floured surface and knead, adding remaining flour when needed, until dough is fairly soft, about 10 minutes. Gradually knead in the sage, basil, and tomatoes, adding more flour as needed. Continue kneading until dough is firm and smooth, 15 to 17 minutes total. (Or make in a heavy-duty mixer; see page 67.) The dough is ready when a little dough pulled from the mass springs back quickly (see Kneading and Kneading In, pages 66 and 76).

FERMENT THE DOUGH (2 hours) Shape the dough into a ball and let it rest on a lightly floured surface while you scrape, clean, and lightly oil the large bowl. Place the dough in the bowl and turn once to coat with oil. Take the dough's temperature: the ideal is 78°F. (see page 58). Cover with a clean damp towel or plastic wrap and put in a moderately warm (74°–80°F.) draft-free place until increased in volume about one-quarter.

> *Note: If the dough temperature is higher than 78°F., put it in a cooler than 78°F. place like the refrigerator, until the dough cools to 78°F. If it is lower than 78°F., put it in a warmer than 78°F. place until the dough warms to 78°F. The point is to try to keep the dough at 78°F. during its fermentation. If you do have to move the dough, be gentle and don't jostle it, or the dough may deflate.*

This dough will not behave like an ordinary yeasted bread dough. It won't rise to a puffy state.

DIVIDE THE DOUGH AND REST (35 minutes) Deflate the dough by pushing down in the center and pulling up on the sides. Transfer to a lightly floured work surface and knead briefly. Cut into 2 equal pieces. Shape each into a tight round ball and place on a lightly floured board. Cover with a clean damp towel or plastic wrap and put in a moderately warm (74°–80°F.) draft-free place for 30 minutes.

SHAPE THE LOAVES (5 minutes) Flatten each ball with the heel of your hand into a disk 8 inches in diameter. Shape into torpedoes (see Taking Shape, page 68).

PROOF THE LOAVES (2 hours) Place the loaves seam side up in a well-floured *couche* (see Equipment, page 52). Cover with a clean damp towel or plastic wrap and put in a moderately warm (74°–80°) draft-free place until almost doubled in volume, or until a slight indentation remains when the dough is pressed with a fingertip.

BAKE THE LOAVES (about 30 minutes) Forty-five minutes to 1 hour before baking, preheat the oven and homemade hearth or baking stone on the center rack of the oven (see Equipment, page 52) to 450°F.

(continued)

The oven rack must be in the center of the oven. If it is in the lower third of the oven, the bottoms of the breads may burn, and if it is in the upper third, the top crusts may burn.

Using the *couche* as an aid, gently roll one loaf from the *couche* onto a lightly floured peel so that it sits seam side down. Using a very sharp, serrated knife or a single-edged razor blade, score the loaf by making quick shallow cuts ¼ to ½ inch deep along the surface. Using the peel, slide the loaf onto the hearth. Repeat the process with the second loaf. Quickly spray the inner walls and floor of the oven with cold water from a spritzer bottle. If there's an electric light bulb in the oven, avoid spraying it directly—it may burst. Spray for several seconds until steam has filled the oven. Quickly close the door to trap the steam and bake 3 minutes. Spray again in the same way, closing the door immediately so that steam doesn't escape. Bake until loaves are a rich caramel color and the crusts are firm, 25 to 30 minutes.

To test the loaves for doneness, remove and hold the loaves upside down. Strike the bottoms firmly with your finger. If the sound is hollow, the breads are done. If it doesn't sound hollow, bake 5 minutes longer. Cool completely on wire racks.

PAIN AU LEVAIN WITH PECANS AND DRIED CHERRIES

> Allow 1 hour to prepare the pecans and cherries.
> Allow 8 to 10 hours to ferment the *levain*.
> Total preparation and baking time (not including the *levain*):
> 5 hours, 50 minutes

This is not a traditional country bread, but I find the combination of pecans and cherries so irresistible that I believe this bread will become a modern classic. Eat it for breakfast, toasted. For lunch, it makes a wonderful sandwich with a tangy cheese. You can get the cherries by mail order; see page 322.

Makes 2 long 14-inch loaves

Pecan halves and bits	2 cups	6 ounces
Dried cherries	2 cups	10 ounces
Spring water, heated to boiling	2½ cups, approximately	20 fluid ounces
Levain (page 185)	2 cups	18 ounces
20% bran wheat flour*	4½–5½ cups	24–29 ounces
Fine sea salt	1 tablespoon	¾ ounce

* See Flours (pages 42–49). This is a good approximate measure. You may use more or less depending on the weight and absorbency of your flour.

PREPARE THE PECANS AND CHERRIES (1 hour) Preheat the oven to 350°F. Arrange the pecans in a single layer on a baking sheet and bake, stirring occasionally, until the nuts are fragrant and lightly toasted, about 10 minutes. Transfer to a plate and cool completely. Chop coarsely and set aside.

Place the cherries and spring water in a medium bowl. Let stand until just softened, 10 to 30 minutes, depending on the dryness of the cherries. Drain well; reserve soaking liquid. Add more water, if needed, to make 2¼ cups. Pat dry with paper towels. Chop coarsely and set aside.

MIX AND KNEAD THE FINAL DOUGH (20 minutes) Measure the remaining ingredients and calculate the temperatures (see page 58). Combine the *levain* and the reserved soaking liquid in a 6-quart bowl. Break up the *levain* well with a wooden spoon or squeeze through your fingers until it is broken up. Continue stirring until the

(continued)

levain is partly dissolved and the mixture is slightly frothy. Add 1 cup (5 ounces) of the flour and stir until well combined. Add the salt and just enough of the remaining flour to make a thick mass that is difficult to stir. Turn out onto a lightly floured surface and knead, adding remaining flour when needed, until dough is fairly soft, 10 minutes. Gradually knead in the pecans and cherries, adding more flour as necessary. Continue kneading until the dough is firm and smooth, 15 to 17 minutes total. (Or make in a heavy-duty mixer; see page 67.) The dough is ready when a little dough pulled from the mass springs back quickly (see Kneading and Kneading In, pages 66 and 76).

FERMENT THE DOUGH (2 hours) Shape the dough into a ball and let it rest on a lightly floured surface while you scrape, clean, and lightly oil the large bowl. Place the dough in the bowl and turn once to coat with oil. Take the dough's temperature: the ideal is 78°F. (see page 58). Cover with a clean damp towel or plastic wrap and put in a moderately warm (74°–80°F.) draft-free place until increased in volume about one-quarter.

> *Note: If the dough temperature is higher than 78°F., put it in a cooler than 78°F. place like the refrigerator, until the dough cools to 78°F. If it is lower than 78°F., put it in a warmer than 78° F. place until the dough warms to 78°F. The point is to try to keep the dough at 78°F. during its fermentation. If you do have to move the dough, be gentle and don't jostle it, or the dough may deflate.*

This dough will not behave like an ordinary yeasted bread dough. It won't rise to a puffy state.

DIVIDE THE DOUGH AND REST (35 minutes) Deflate the dough by pushing down in the center and pulling up on the sides. Transfer to a lightly floured work surface and knead briefly. Cut into 2 equal pieces. Shape each into a tight round ball and place on a lightly floured board. Cover with a clean damp towel or plastic wrap and place in a moderately warm (74°–80°F.) draft-free place for 30 minutes.

SHAPE THE LOAVES (5 minutes) Flatten each ball with the heel of your hand on a lightly floured surface into a disk 8 inches in diameter. Shape into torpedoes (see Taking Shape, page 68).

PROOF THE LOAVES (2 hours) Place the loaves seam side up in a well-floured *couche* (see Equipment, page 52). Cover with a clean damp towel or plastic wrap and put in a moderately warm (74°–80°F.) draft-free place until almost doubled in volume, or until a slight indentation remains when the dough is pressed with a fingertip.

BAKE THE LOAVES (about 30 minutes) Forty-five minutes to 1 hour before baking, preheat the oven and homemade hearth or baking stone on the center rack of the oven (see Equipment, page 52) to 450°F.

The oven rack must be in the center of the oven. If it is in the lower third of the oven, the bottoms of the breads may burn, and if it is in the upper third, the top crusts may burn.

Using the *couche* as an aid, gently roll one loaf from the *couche* onto a lightly floured peel so that it sits seam side down. Using a very sharp, serrated knife or a single-edged razor blade, score the loaf by making quick shallow cuts ¼ to ½ inch deep along the surface. Using the peel, slide the loaf onto the hearth. Quickly repeat the process with the second loaf. Spray the inner walls and floor of the oven with cold water from a spritzer bottle. If there's an electric light bulb in the oven, avoid spraying it directly—it may burst. Spray for several seconds until steam has filled the oven. Quickly close the door to trap the steam and bake 3 minutes. Spray again in the same way, closing the door immediately so that steam doesn't escape. Bake until loaves are a rich caramel color and the crusts are firm, 25 to 30 minutes.

To test the loaves for doneness, remove and hold the loaves upside down. Strike the bottoms firmly with your finger. If the sound is hollow, the breads are done. If it doesn't sound hollow, bake 5 minutes longer. Cool completely on a wire rack.

PAIN AU LEVAIN WITH WALNUTS

> Allow 1 hour to prepare the walnuts.
> Allow 8 to 10 hours to ferment the *levain*.
> Total preparation and baking time (not including the *levain*):
> 5 hours, 50 minutes

As a traditional favorite in France, thin slices of this bread are served with the cheese course in many restaurants. I like it toasted with thick preserves spread on top. It also makes any sandwich a better-tasting whole meal. The bread may have an unusual purple cast from the walnut skins, but what flavor!

Makes 2 long 14-inch loaves

Walnut pieces	2 cups	7 ounces
Levain (page 185)	2 cups	18 ounces
Spring water	2¼ cups	18 fluid ounces
20% bran wheat flour*	5½–6½ cups	27–32 ounces
Fine sea salt	1 tablespoon	¾ ounce

* See Flours (pages 42–49). This is a good approximate measure. You may use more or less depending on the weight and absorbency of your flour.

PREPARE THE WALNUTS (1 hour) Preheat the oven to 350°F. Arrange the walnuts in a single layer on a baking sheet and bake, stirring occasionally, until fragrant and lightly toasted. Transfer to a plate and place in the refrigerator to cool completely.

Remove ¾ cup (3 ounces) of the cooled walnuts and place in the container of a food processor. Sprinkle with 2 tablespoons of the flour and process by pulsing until very finely ground. (The flour helps absorb the walnut oil and reduce the chances of the mixture turning greasy.) Set aside.

Coarsely crush the remaining walnuts. Set aside.

MIX AND KNEAD THE FINAL DOUGH (20 munites) Measure the remaining ingredients and calculate the temperatures (see page 58). Combine the *levain* and water in a 6-quart bowl. Break up the *levain* well with a wooden spoon or squeeze through your fingers until it is broken up. Continue stirring until the *levain* is partly dissolved and the mixture is slightly frothy. Add 1 cup (5 ounces) of the remaining flour and stir until well combined. Add the salt, ground walnuts, and just enough of the remaining flour to make a thick mass that is difficult to stir. Turn out onto a lightly floured surface and knead, adding remaining flour when needed, until dough is fairly soft, 10 minutes. Gradually knead in the crushed walnuts. Continue kneading until the dough is firm and smooth, 15 to 17 minutes total. (Or make in a heavy-duty mixer; see page 67.) The dough is ready when a little dough pulled from the mass springs back quickly (see Kneading and Kneading In, pages 66 and 76).

FERMENT THE DOUGH (2 hours) Shape the dough into a ball and let it rest on a lightly floured surface while you scrape, clean, and lightly oil the large bowl. Place the dough in the bowl and turn once to coat with oil. Take the dough's temperature: the ideal is 78°F. (see page 58). Cover with a clean damp towel or plastic wrap and put in a moderately warm (74°–80°F.) draft-free place until increased in volume about one-quarter.

> *Note: If the dough temperature is higher than 78°F., put it in a cooler than 78°F. place like the refrigerator, until the dough cools to 78°F. If it is lower than 78°F., put it in a warmer than 78°F. place until the dough warms to 78°F. The point is to try to keep the dough at 78°F. during its fermentation. If you do have to move the dough, be gentle and don't jostle it, or the dough may deflate.*

This dough will not behave like an ordinary yeasted bread dough. It won't rise to a puffy state.

DIVIDE THE DOUGH AND REST (35 minutes) Deflate the dough by pushing down in the center and pulling up on the sides. Transfer to a lightly floured work surface and and knead briefly. Cut into 2 equal pieces. Shape each into a tight round ball and place on a lightly floured board. Cover with a clean damp towel or plastic wrap and put in a moderately warm (74°–80°F.) draft-free place for 30 minutes.

SHAPE THE LOAVES (5 minutes) Flatten each ball with the heel of your hand on a lightly floured surface into a disk 8 inches in diameter. Shape into torpedoes (see Taking Shape, page 68).

(continued)

PROOF THE LOAVES (2 hours) Place the loaves seam side up in a well-floured *couche* (see Equipment, page 52). Cover with a clean damp towel or plastic wrap and put in a moderately warm (74°–80°F.) draft-free place until almost doubled in volume, or until a slight indentation remains when the dough is pressed with a fingertip.

BAKE THE LOAVES (about 30 minutes) Forty-five minutes to 1 hour before baking, preheat the oven and homemade hearth or baking stone on the center rack of the oven (see Equipment, page 52) to 450°F.

The oven rack must be in the center of the oven. If it is in the lower third of the oven, the bottoms of the breads may burn, and if it is in the upper third, the top crusts may burn.

Using the *couche* as an aid, gently roll one loaf from the *couche* onto a lightly floured peel so that it sits seam side down. Using a very sharp, serrated knife or a single-edged razor blade, score the loaf by making shallow cuts ¼ to ½ inch deep along the surface. Using the peel, slide the loaf onto the hearth. Quickly repeat the process with the second loaf. Spray the inner walls and floor of the oven with cold water from a spritzer bottle. If there's an electric light bulb in the oven, avoid spraying it directly—it may burst. Spray for several seconds until steam has filled the oven. Quickly close the door to trap the steam and bake 3 minutes. Spray again in the same way, closing the door immediately so that steam doesn't escape. Bake until loaves are a rich caramel color and the crusts are firm, 25 to 30 minutes.

To test the loaves for doneness, remove and hold the loaves upside down. Strike the bottoms firmly with your finger. If the sound is hollow, the breads are done. If it doesn't sound hollow, bake 5 minutes longer. Cool completely on a wire rack.

MY PERSONAL FAVORITE *PAIN AU LEVAIN*

Allow 8 to 10 hours to ferment the *levain*.
Total preparation and baking time (not including the *levain*):
7 hours, 45 minutes

This is a showpiece! A huge almost four-pound *pain au levain* in the tradition of the big country breads of Europe. When village baking was done only once a week, the breads were made large enough to last for days. This is a beautiful deep golden loaf you'll want to make for parties.

Makes 1 large 14-inch loaf, about 3½ pounds

Levain (page 185)	2 cups	18 ounces
Spring water	2¼ cups	18 fluid ounces
20% bran wheat flour*	4–4¾ cups	20–24 ounces
Fine sea salt	1 tablespoon	¾ ounces

* See Flours (pages 42–49). This is a good approximate measure. You may use more or less depending on the weight and absorbency of your flour.

MIX AND KNEAD THE FINAL DOUGH (20 minutes) Measure the ingredients and calculate the temperatures (see page 58). Combine the *levain* and water in a 6-quart bowl. Break up the *levain* well with a wooden spoon or squeeze through your fingers until it is broken up. Continue stirring until the *levain* is partially dissolved and the mixture is slightly frothy. Add 1 cup (5 ounces) of the flour and stir until well combined. Add the salt and just enough of the remaining flour to make a thick mass that is difficult to stir. Turn out onto a lightly floured surface and knead, adding remaining flour when needed, until dough is firm and smooth, 15 to 17 minutes total. (Or make in a heavy-duty mixer; see page 67.) The dough is ready when a little dough pulled from the mass springs back quickly (see Kneading, page 66).

FERMENT THE DOUGH (2 hours) Shape the dough into a ball and let it rest on a lightly floured surface while you scrape, clean, and lightly oil the large bowl. Place the dough in the bowl and turn once to coat with oil. Take the dough's temperature: the ideal is 78°F. (see page 58). Cover with a clean damp towel or plastic wrap and put in a moderately warm (74°–80°F.) draft-free place until increased in volume about one-quarter to one-half.

(continued)

Note: If the dough temperature is higher than 78°F., put it in a cooler than 78°F. place like the refrigerator, until the dough cools to 78°F. If it is lower than 78°F., put it in a warmer than 78°F. place until the dough warms to 78°F. The point is to try to keep the dough at 78°F. during its fermentation. If you do have to move the dough, be gentle and don't jostle it, or the dough may deflate.

This dough will not behave like an ordinary yeasted bread dough. It won't rise to a puffy state.

DIVIDE THE DOUGH AND REST (35 minutes) Deflate the dough by pushing down in the center and pulling up on the sides. Transfer to a lightly floured work surface and knead briefly. Shape into a tight ball and place on a lightly floured board. Cover with a clean damp towel or plastic wrap and put in a moderately warm (74°–80°F.) draft-free place for 30 minutes.

SHAPE THE LOAF (5 minutes) Flatten the ball with the heel of your hand on a lightly floured work surface into a disk. Shape into an oblong loaf about 14 inches long (see Taking Shape, page 68).

PROOF THE LOAF (3 to 4 hours) Place the loaf seam side up in a well-floured *couche* (see Equipment, page 52). Cover with a clean damp towel or plastic wrap and put in a moderately warm (74°–80°F.) draft-free place until almost doubled in volume, or until a slight indentation remains when the dough is pressed with a fingertip. This dough gets softer, lighter, and very delicate as it proofs—more so than any other dough in this book. After 4 hours there will be a pronounced difference between the dough you set in the *couche* and the final light dough.

BAKE THE LOAF (about 30 minutes) Forty-five minutes to 1 hour before baking, preheat the oven and homemade hearth or baking stone on the center rack of the oven (see Equipment, page 52) to 450°F. If you are using tiles or brick for a hearth, make sure that they cover at least a 14- × 12-inch area of the oven rack. This is a big loaf and will need a lot of oven space.

The oven rack must be in the center of the oven. If it is in the lower third of the oven, the bottoms of the breads may burn, and if it is in the upper third, the top crusts may burn.

Using the *couche* as an aid, gently roll the loaf from the *couche* onto a lightly floured peel so that it sits seam side down. Using a very sharp, serrated knife or a single-edged razor blade, score the loaf by making quick shallow cuts ¼ to ½ inch deep along the surface. Using the peel, slide the loaf onto the hearth. Quickly spray the inner walls and floor of the oven with cold water from a spritzer bottle. If there's an electric light bulb in the oven, avoid spraying it directly—it may burst. Spray for several seconds until steam has filled the oven. Quickly close the door to trap the steam and bake 3 minutes. Spray again in the same way, closing the door immediately so that steam doesn't escape. Bake until the loaf begins to color, about 20 minutes. Reduce heat to 400°F. and continue baking until deep golden in color and the crust is firm, 20 to 25 minutes.

To test the loaf for doneness, remove and hold the loaf upside down. Strike the bottom firmly with your finger. If the sound is hollow, the bread is done. If it doesn't sound hollow, bake 5 minutes longer. Cool completely on a wire rack.

MY PERSONAL FAVORITE *PAIN AU LEVAIN*

Task	Approximate Time	Comments
Prepreparation	8–10 hr.	Build *levain*.
Preparation	5 min.	Calculate temperatures. Assemble ingredients, combine, mix.
Knead	15 min.	Take temperature of dough.
Ferment	2 hr.	Cool: 70°F. until increased 25–40%.
Divide	5 min.	Shape into ball on lightly floured board.
Rest	30 min.	Cool: 70°F.
Shape	5 min.	Flatten with heel of hand and shape into oblong loaf. Place in *couche* or basket.
Proof	4 hr.	Cool: 70°F. until doubled in volume.
Bake	45 min.	With steam. 450°F.–400°F.
Cool	25 min.	On rack or in basket.

Cumulative Total Time: 8 hr., 10 min.

FOUGASSE WITH OLIVES

Allow 8 to 10 hours to ferment the *levain*.
Total preparation and baking time (not including *levain*):
4 hours, 50 minutes

This is a flat country bread traditionally made in a variety of shapes or fantasies, often a ladder or a tree. It's a great bread for family dinners of spaghetti or stew, because you simply break off or tear off what you want. The legend or unofficial truth is that *fougasse* was made and used originally to even out the scales when bakers sold bread. In France bread is sold by weight. If a customer's purchase didn't come to an even weight, the baker tore off portions of *fougasse* and added it to the scale to ensure full weight. A *fougasse* can be made with a straight dough, but I like using a *levain* because of the added flavor and interesting texture.

Makes one 9 by 12-inch loaf

Levain (page 185)	1 cup	9 ounces
Spring water	1 cup plus 2 tablespoons	9 fluid ounces
20% bran wheat flour*	2¼–3 cups	12–15 ounces
Sea salt	2 teaspoons	½ ounce
Mediterranean black olives, pitted (not chopped)	½ cup	2½ ounces

* See Flours (pages 42–49). This is a good approximate measure. You may use more or less depending on the weight and absorbency of your flour.

MIX AND KNEAD THE FINAL DOUGH (20 minutes) Measure out the ingredients and calculate the temperatures (see page 58). Combine the *levain* and water in a 6-quart bowl. Break up the *levain* well with a wooden spoon or squeeze through your fingers until it is broken up. Continue stirring until the *levain* is partially dissolved and the mixture is slightly frothy. Add 1 cup (5 ounces) of the flour and stir until well combined. Add the salt and just enough of the remaining flour to make a thick mass that is difficult to stir. Turn out onto a lightly floured surface and knead, adding remaining flour when needed, about 14 minutes. Gradually knead in the olives.

Don't add the olives too early or they will release their juices into the dough, turning it purple. Continue kneading until the dough is firm and smooth, 15 to 17 minutes total. The dough is ready when a little dough pulled from the mass springs back quickly (see Kneading and Kneading In, pages 66 and 76).

FERMENT THE DOUGH (1 hour) Shape the dough into a ball and let it rest on a lightly floured surface while you scrape, clean, and lightly oil the large bowl. Place the dough in the bowl and turn once to coat with oil. Take the dough's temperature: the ideal is 78°F. (see page 58). Cover with a clean damp towel or plastic wrap and put in a moderately warm (74°–80°F.) draft-free place until increased in volume about one-quarter.

> *Note: If the dough temperature is higher than 78°F., put it in a cooler than 78°F. place like the refrigerator, until the dough cools to 78°F. If it is lower than 78°F., place it in a warmer than 78°F. place until the dough warms to 78°F. The point is to try to keep the dough at 78°F. during its fermentation. If you do have to move the dough, be gentle and don't jostle it, or the dough may deflate.*

This dough will not behave like an ordinary yeasted bread dough. It won't rise to a puffy state.

DIVIDE THE DOUGH AND REST (35 minutes) Deflate the dough by pushing down in the center and pulling up on the sides. Transfer to a lightly floured work surface and knead briefly. Shape into a tight ball and place on a lightly floured board. Cover with a clean damp towel or plastic wrap and in a moderately warm (74°–80°F.) draft-free place for 30 minutes.

FERMENT THE DOUGH A SECOND TIME (1½ hours) Flatten the dough into a disk with the heel of your hand. Shape into a tight ball and place on a lightly floured board. Cover with a clean damp cloth or plastic wrap and put in a moderately warm (74°–80°F) draft-free place until increased in volume by three-quarters.

SHAPE THE LOAF (5 minutes) Using a rolling pin, roll out the dough onto a large piece of parchment paper peel into an oblong 12 inches long, 9 inches wide, and 1 inch thick.

(continued)

PROOF THE LOAF (45 minutes) Cover with a clean damp towel or plastic wrap and place in a moderately warm (74°–80°F.) draft-free place until almost doubled in volume, or until a slight indentation remains when the dough is pressed with a fingertip.

BAKE THE LOAF (about 30 minutes) Forty-five minutes to 1 hour before baking, preheat the oven and homemade hearth or baking stone on the center rack of the oven (see Equipment, page 52) to 450°F.

The oven rack must be in the center of the oven. If it is in the lower third of the oven, the bottoms of the breads may burn, and if it is in the upper third, the top crusts may burn.

Using a very sharp, serrated knife or a single-edged razor blade, cut 5 or 6 random slits 3 inches long in the dough. Open the slits slightly with your fingers. Using the peel, slide the loaf on the parchment paper onto the hearth. Quickly spray the inner walls and floor of the oven with cold water from a spritzer bottle. If there's an electric light bulb in the oven, avoid spraying it directly—it may burst. Spray for several seconds until steam has filled the oven. Quickly close the door to trap the steam and bake 3 minutes. Spray again in the same way, closing the door immediately so that steam doesn't escape. Bake until golden in color and crust is very firm, 25 to 30 minutes.

To test for doneness, remove and hold the loaf upside down. Strike the bottom firmly with your finger. If the sound is hollow, discard the parchment paper and allow the bread to cool on a rack. If it doesn't sound hollow, bake 5 minutes longer.

FOUGASSE WITH OLIVES

Task	Approximate Time	Comments
Prepreparation		Build *levain* if necessary. Prepare fresh ingredients.
Preparation	5 min.	Calculate temperatures. Assemble ingredients. Mix.
Knead	15 min.	Take temperature of dough.
Ferment	1 hr.	Moderate: 74°–80°F. until 25–40% of volume.
Shape	5 min.	Round ball on floured board.
Rest	30 min.	Cool: 70°F. Cover with a clean damp towel or plastic wrap.
Shape	5 min.	Flatten with heel of hand. Round again on lightly floured board.
Ferment	1 hr., 30 min.	Cool: 70°F. Cover with a clean damp towel or plastic wrap.
Shape	5 min.	Flatten with heel of hand. Roll out into oblong 12 × 9 inches and 1 inch thick.
Proof	45 min.	Moderate: 74°–80°F. Cover with a clean damp towel or plastic wrap. Cut slits randomly and open with fingers.
Bake	30 min.	With steam. 450°F.
Cool	20 min.	On rack.

Cumulative Total Time: 5 hr., 10 min.

SAN FRANCISCO SOURDOUGH

Allow 8 to 10 hours to ferment the *levain*.
Allow 24 hours to ferment the *poolish*.
Total preparation and baking time (not including *levain* and *poolish*):
5 hours, 35 minutes

This famous light and airy California bread gets its tang from the traditional French technique of using some ripe *levain* mixed with a little flour and water to develop a *poolish* before mixing the final dough. A very long fermentation of the *poolish* develops the highly acidic acids that give the popular bread its pronounced flavor. But remember, the older your *chef*, the stronger sour punch your bread will have.

Makes 2 long 14-inch loaves or 2 round 9-inch loaves

POOLISH

Levain (page 185)	⅔ cup	8 ounces
Spring water	1 cup	8 fluid ounces
Organic white flour with germ*	1½ cups	8 ounces

FINAL DOUGH

Spring water	2 cups	16 fluid ounces
Organic white flour with germ*	5½–6½ cups	27–32 ounces
Fine sea salt	1 tablespoon	¾ ounce

---

* See Flours (pages 42–49). These are good approximate measures. You may use more or less depending on the weight and absorbency of your flour.

MAKE THE *POOLISH* (allow 24 hours) Combine the *levain* and water in a 2-quart clear plastic container with a lid. Break up the *levain* well with a wooden spoon or squeeze through your fingers until it is broken up. Stir until the *levain* is partly dissolved and the mixture is slightly frothy. Add the flour and stir with a wooden spoon until very thick and sticky. Scrape down the sides with a rubber spatula. Cover with plastic wrap and put in a moderately warm (74°–80°F.) place.

MIX AND KNEAD THE FINAL DOUGH (20 minutes) Measure the ingredients and calculate the temperatures (see page 58). Combine the *poolish* and water in a 6-quart bowl. Break up the *poolish* well with a wooden spoon and stir until the *poolish* becomes loose and the mixture slightly frothy. Add 2 cups (10 ounces) of the flour and the salt; stir until well combined. Add just enough of the remaining flour to make a thick mass that is difficult to stir. Turn out onto a lightly floured surface and knead, adding remaining flour when needed, until dough is firm and smooth, 15 to 17 minutes total. (Or make in a heavy-duty mixer; see page 67.) The dough is ready when a little dough pulled from the mass springs back quickly (see Kneading, page 66).

FERMENT THE DOUGH (2½ hours) Shape the dough into a ball and let it rest on a lightly floured surface while you scrape, clean, and lightly oil the large bowl. Place the dough in the bowl and turn once to coat with oil. Take the dough's temperature: the ideal is 78°F. (see page 58). Cover with a clean damp towel or plastic wrap and put in a moderately warm (74°–80°F.) draft-free place until doubled in volume.

> *Note: If the dough temperature is higher than 78°F., put it in a cooler than 78°F. place like the refrigerator, until the dough cools to 78°F. If it is lower than 78°F., put it in a warmer than 78°F. place until the dough warms to 78°F. The point is to try to keep the dough at 78°F. during its fermentation. If you do have to move the dough, be gentle and don't jostle it, or the dough may deflate.*

FIRST REST (30 minutes) Deflate the dough by pushing down in the center and pulling up on the sides. Cover with a clean damp towel or plastic wrap and put in a moderately warm (74°–80°F.) draft-free place for 30 minutes.

SECOND REST (30 minutes) Transfer the dough to a lightly floured board and knead briefly. Shape into a tight ball. Cover with a clean damp towel or plastic wrap, and put in a moderately warm (74°–80°F.) draft-free place for 30 minutes.

DIVIDE THE DOUGH AND SHAPE INTO LOAVES (5 minutes) Divide the dough into 2 equal portions. Flatten each with the heel of your hand on a lightly floured board. The dough may be very soft

(continued)

and loose at this point. Shape into 12-inch-long torpedoes (see Taking Shape, page 68). The torpedo is the classic San Francisco sourdough shape. You may also choose to shape the dough into rounds.

PROOF THE LOAVES (1 hour) Place the torpedoes, seam side up in a well-floured *couche* (see Equipment, page 52). Cover with a clean damp towel or plastic wrap. Put in a moderately warm (74°–80°F.) draft-free place until increased in volume about 1½ times, or until a slight indentation remains when the dough is pressed with a fingertip. (Place rounds on a cornmeal-dusted surface to rise.)

BAKE THE LOAVES (about 35 minutes) Forty-five minutes to 1 hour before baking, preheat the oven and homemade hearth or baking stone on the center rack of the oven (see Equipment, page 52) to 450°F.

The oven rack must be in the center of the oven. If it is in the lower third of the oven, the bottoms of the breads may burn, and if it is in the upper third, the top crusts may burn.

Gently roll one loaf from the *couche* onto a lightly floured peel so that it sits seam side down. Using a very sharp, serrated knife or a single-edged razor blade, score the loaf by making quick shallow cuts ¼ to ½ inch deep along the surface. Using the peel, slide the loaf onto the hearth. Quickly repeat the process with the second loaf. Quickly spray the inner walls and floor of the oven with cold water from a spritzer bottle. If there's an electric light bulb in the oven, avoid spraying it directly—it may burst. Spray for several seconds until steam has filled the oven. Quickly close the door to trap the steam and bake 3 minutes. Spray again in the same way, closing the door immediately so that steam doesn't escape. Bake until loaves begin to color, about 15 minutes. Reduce heat to 425°F. and bake until loaves are a rich caramel color and the crust is firm, 15 to 20 minutes.

To test for doneness, remove and hold the loaves upside down. Strike the bottoms firmly with your finger. If the sound is hollow, the breads are done. If it doesn't sound hollow, bake 5 minutes longer. Cool completely on a wire rack.

SAN FRANCISCO SOURDOUGH

Task	Approximate Time	Comments
Prepreparation	8–10 hr.	Build *levain*.
	24 hr.	Ferment *poolish*.
Preparation	5 min.	Calculate temperatures. Assemble ingredients, combine, mix.
Knead	15 min.	Take temperature of dough.
Ferment	2 hr., 30 min.	Moderate: 74°–80°F. until doubled.
Rest	30 min.	Deflate and rest.
Rest	30 min.	Moderate: 74°–80°F.
Divide	5 min.	2 equal pieces.
Shape	5 min.	Flatten with heel of hand. Cover with a clean damp towel or plastic wrap.
Proof	1 hr.	Moderate: 74°–80°F. until 1½ × in volume.
Bake	35 min.	With steam. 450°F.–425°F.
Cool	25 min.	On rack or in basket.

Cumulative Total Time: 6 hr.

FOCACCIA MADE WITH *LEVAIN*

> Allow 8 to 10 hours to ferment the *levain*.
> Total preparation and baking time (not including *levain*):
> 5 hours

This is my favorite dough for focaccia and pizza. It has a chewy, light crumb plus the complex taste of *levain* that's so delicious you won't want to smother it with elaborate toppings. With this dough, less is more. Try the classic topping of simple oil and salt (see page 280).

Makes 2 round 16-inch focaccia or 4 round 12-inch focaccia

Levain (page 185)	2 cups	18 ounces
Spring water	2¼ cups	18 fluid ounces
20% bran wheat flour*	4–5 cups	20–25 ounces
Fine sea salt	1 tablespoon	¾ ounce
Focaccia topping (page 280)		

---

* See Flours (pages 42–49). This is a good approximate measure. You may use more or less depending on the weight and absorbency of your flour.

MIX AND KNEAD THE FINAL DOUGH   (20 minutes) Measure the ingredients and calculate the temperatures (see page 58). Combine the *levain* and water in a 6-quart bowl. Break up the *levain* well with a wooden spoon or squeeze through your fingers until it is broken up. Continue stirring until the *levain* is partially dissolved and the mixture is slightly frothy. Add 1 cup (5 ounces) of the flour and stir until well combined. Add the salt and just enough of the remaining flour to make a thick mass that is difficult to stir. Turn out onto a lightly floured surface and knead, adding remaining flour when needed, until dough is firm and smooth, 15 to 17 minutes total. (Or make in a heavy-duty mixer, see page 67.) The dough is ready when a little dough pulled from the mass springs back quickly (see Kneading, page 66).

FERMENT THE DOUGH (1 hour) Shape the dough into a ball and let it rest on a lightly floured surface while you scrape, clean, and lightly oil the large bowl. Place the dough in the bowl and turn once to coat with oil. Take the dough's temperature: the ideal is 78°F. (see page 58). Cover with a clean damp towel or plastic wrap and put in a moderately warm (74°–80°F.) draft-free place until increased in volume about one-quarter.

Note: If the dough temperature is higher than 78°F., put it in a cooler than 78°F. place like the refrigerator, until the dough cools to 78°F. If it is lower than 78°F., put it in a warmer than 78°F. place until the dough warms to 78°F. The point is to try to keep the dough at 78°F. during its fermentation. If you do have to move the dough, be gentle and don't jostle it, or the dough may deflate.

This dough will not behave like an ordinary yeasted bread dough. It won't rise to a puffy state.

DIVIDE THE DOUGH AND REST (35 minutes) Deflate the dough by pushing down in the center and pulling up on the sides. Transfer to a lightly floured work surface and knead briefly. Cut into 2 equal pieces. Shape each into a tight round ball and place on a lightly floured board. Cover with a clean damp towel or plastic wrap and put in a moderately warm (74°–80°F.) draft-free place for 30 minutes.

SHAPE THE LOAVES (5 minutes) Flatten each ball with the heel of your hand into a disk 8 inches in diameter. The dough is too delicate to roll out on a work surface and then transfer after proofing. Using a rolling pin, roll out the dough directly onto a lightly floured peel or rimless baking sheet into circles 16 inches in diameter and ½ inch thick.

PROOF THE LOAVES (1½ hours) Cover with a clean damp towel or plastic wrap and put in a moderately warm (74°–80°F.) draft-free place until almost doubled in thickness, or until a slight indentation remains when the dough is pressed with a fingertip.

PREPARE THE TOPPING (20 minutes) Prepare a topping.

BAKE THE LOAVES (about 15 minutes) Forty-five minutes to 1 hour before baking, preheat the oven and homemade hearth or baking stone on the center rack of the oven (see Equipment, page 52) to 425°F.

The oven rack must be in the center of the oven. If it is in the lower third of the oven, the bottoms of the breads may burn, and if it is in the upper third, the top crusts may burn.

(*continued*)

Work with one dough at a time, keeping the other dough covered. Finger-poke one of the doughs in a random pattern of dimples. Add the topping and then using the peel, slide the bread onto the hearth. Bake until bread is golden brown, 12 to 15 minutes. Cool on a rack for 5 to 10 minutes. Repeat the process with the second loaf.

FOCACCIA MADE WITH LEVAIN

Task	Approximate Time	Comments
Prepreparation	8–10 hr.	Build *levain*.
Preparation	5 min.	Calculate temperatures. Assemble ingredients, combine, mix.
Knead	15 min.	Take temperature of dough.
Ferment	1 hr.	Cool: 68°–70°F. until increased 25–40%.
Divide	5 min.	Deflate. Cut into 2 equal portions. Shape into balls on lightly floured board.
Rest	30 min.	Cool: 68°–70°F.
Shape	10 min.	Flatten with heel of hand and shape again into balls on floured board.
Ferment	1 hr.	Cool: 68°–70°F.
Shape	5 min.	Roll out into 16-inch disks, ½ inch thick.
Proof	1 hr., 30 min.	Cool: 68°–70°F. until almost doubled in volume.
Prepare Toppings		Recipes: pages 280–281.
Bake	15 min.	One at a time with choice of toppings. 425°F.
Cool	10 min.	On rack.

Cumulative Total Time: 5 hr., 10 min.

BOULANGER DELFOSSE

ANOTHER BAKER'S STORY

Paul Delfosse is an elderly baker in Paris who lives alone now and runs his bakery all by himself. Early in the morning he mixes the dough, and by 9:00 A.M. he has a few varieties of large warm loaves and dozens of *baguettes* that he sells himself. He closes at 1:00 P.M., mixes more dough, takes a nap in his apartment above the bakery, then comes back to bake in the late afternoon. He sells bread until 7:00 or 8:00 at night.

Delfosse is unlike any other baker I've met. Far from being open or gregarious, he's very insulated and doesn't enjoy conversation. Instead of the broad and round bakers I have known, he is short, withered, and thin. His back is bowed from years of mixing hundreds of pounds of dough by hand; at least half his life was spent without a mixing machine.

"It wasn't so bad then," he says. "The flour was much better than today." His hair is slicked back under an old canvas hat he has fashioned from a flour sack, and silver wire-rim glasses make him appear intensely intellectual.

It was on a spring afternoon that Basil and I accompanied the mason André LeFort, who had been called in to make repairs on Delfosse's oven, that I first met the old baker. I had heard that he was a rude and cranky man. Basil had tried to befriend him, as he does any baker with a brick oven, but he had been rebuked—literally thrown out several times. André was the only one with any relationship with Delfosse, simply because he was needed for oven repairs.

Delfosse and I stood alone together in an awkward silence while André made repairs and Basil watched. Then for some reason, when I asked him how long he'd been a baker, Delfosse began to open up.

"All my life," he answered. "This is the only bakery I've worked in and this is the only oven I've used. Except for the war."

"What happened during the war?" I asked.

Delfosse told me that his father and mother had owned the bakery and that he'd been baking since he was ten years old. Soon after he was drafted, he was captured by the Germans and sent to a POW farm in Belgium, where he worked as a potato farmer.

"I was no good. What did I know about farming?" he said. "I mimicked everyone else. They did this with the hoe, I did this. They did that with the hoe, I did that. But it wasn't so bad; we had plenty of potatoes to eat." Delfosse fell silent then, as if the story was ended or as if he'd already told me too much.

"Then what happened?" I asked.

He continued slowly. "One day a German officer came to the farm and called me in. He said he had met my mother in Paris and that he wanted to help me. I didn't believe him for one minute. I was cold and stubborn and I told him to leave me alone. So, he left."

Delfosse suddenly became enthusiastic about the story.

"But the odd thing was that he had in fact been in my parents' bakery in Paris and had bought an armload of *baguettes*. While there, he accidently left his wallet with a great amount of money stuffed in it on the counter. This counter!" he said, slapping the gray marble. "But the next day he came back retracing his steps, and was astonished to find that my mother had put his wallet in a safe place and hadn't taken any of the money. He was very grateful and asked if there was anything he could do for her.

"She, of course, told him that her son was a prisoner of war. She also told him that I was her only son and only child. Then she asked if he could see to it that I be kept safe until the war was over. And the German promised to do what he could to look out for me.

"So you see," Delfosse said smiling at me, "he had come in truth to help me but I sent him away. I thought it was a trick of the enemy."

Delfosse fell silent again. He saw that André and Basil were both listening to his story. But I picked up my cue quickly.

"What happened?"

"On another trip to Paris the German went to the bakery. 'Your son would have nothing to do with me,' he complained to my mother. 'There's no way I can help him unless he trusts me.'

"My mother said to him, 'When you see him again you tell him that I say he should listen to you and do as you say.' That's what my mother would say, too. Listen to me and do as I say."

"So eventually the officer returned to the potato farm and called me in again. The words from my mother softened me and I cooperated. The next day I was on my way to what I thought was a new camp. But it was not. It was a village that looked as if it were somewhere in Austria. The whole village had been taken over by the highest German military, and it was staffed by prisoners of war: the butcher, the tailor, the dairymen, the vegetable farmer—all were prisoners. They tried to create the ideal of a prosperous town in the midst of the carnage of war, a fantasy place for rest and respite for the officers. So I became a baker in the village bakery. The officer had told them to have me reproduce my father's crispy *baguettes*. I did, of course, gladly. One day I was digging potatoes for the German troops, the next day I was pulling hot loaves from the oven for their commanders. I was baking again. And I was safe.

"On his next trip to Paris he stopped in to assure my mother that I was out of harm's way and would survive the war and come home safely. When the war was over, I hitchhiked back to Paris and I've been baking right here ever since."

I looked around. The tiled floors and muraled walls, the marble and wood, and the large frame of a store window all were evidence of a once warm and classic bakery. But now the window was fogged with dust and grease, and the worn wooden shelves displayed only a few varieties of breads. The tall baskets for the *baguettes* were empty. A hand-scrawled piece of cardboard hung on the murky glass door—"Bread at 9:00 A.M., Bread at 7:00 P.M." Delfosse had no time or energy to make more of the grand old bakery.

The neighborhood is built up around the nearby Ecole des Beaux-Arts. Stretching to either side of Delfosse's *boulangerie* are fancy galleries, bookstores, and art supply shops. It's no wonder he has become insulated and rude; he told us that most people who show interest in the bakery want to gut it and turn it into a gallery or café.

André had finished his repairs and Delfosse returned to work. He began to cut dough and shape it into long *baguettes* that he then put in individual canvas *couches* for proofing. Next, he fired the oven for baking. Within minutes the roar of the oven pulled Delfosse away. Back to the world he has never really left.

THE BAGUETTE

French history is filled with events in which bread (having it or not having it) was a hot issue. Ever since the Revolution, which as legend says started with Marie Antoinette's incendiary comment "Let them eat cake," the price and size of bread have been passionately controlled. In France today politicians endear themselves when they make speeches and pass laws that keep the price of bread down and thereby available to the masses. Since World War II the popular long and slender *baguette*, traditionally bought over the counter and eaten hot from the oven, has been the political loaf.

The government regulated the size and price of the *baguette*, and the people of France were overjoyed, at least at first. With a guaranteed weight of 250 grams and at a cost of 2 francs 80, one could always afford to buy the popular loaf. However, a couple of unfortunate things happened. While the price couldn't go up, the cost of baking the *baguettes* did. In order to make a profit, bakers had to make and sell more and more *baguettes*. As a consequence, the long, slim loaves became mass produced in huge quantities from vats of ill-attended dough. Over thirty years the quality went way down. What was once a crackling fresh, chewy and crusty national treasure with rich robust flavor was fast becoming a feeble crusted, overly aerated, and bland and empty tribute to the past.

Some bakers skirted the profit-and-loss issue by selling their *baguettes* not as baguettes at all. They molded the same dough into a variety of new shapes, creating "*pain de fantaisie*" that they then could sell at a fair market price.

Then came creative bakers who appealed to consumers who were disappointed by all the bad *baguettes* in the bakeries. These bakers returned to or had never abandoned the classic *baguette*. However, in order to make enough money to stay afloat, they began making husky country breads familiar in the provinces but not necessarily known to Parisians. Their shop shelves were full of the "new breads"—loaves baked with olives and onions, hazelnuts, dried figs, and fresh herbs in an array of shapes. It worked! Food writers and critics began to feature these bakers and business boomed.

Fortunately, it is possible to find a great *baguette* not only in Paris but in this book—a *baguette* that has weight, density, good color, and the classic slender form; one that is a pleasure to hold in your hands. When you tear into a good *baguette* warm from the hearth, the crust resists with a seductive crackle. As you chew on the golden thick crumb, you'll know why the French wanted a law making the *baguette* affordable forever!

When you shop in a good French bakery, you will notice that the loaves in the *baguette* section come in different thicknesses and lengths. There are five members of the *baguette* family, each with a specific weight and character, but all made from the same dough and shaped and scored in the same manner.

1. The classic *baguette* is an 8-ounce (250 grams) loaf 30 inches long. It has a thick and crackly crust and a good amount of crumb. It's good for snacking or for small sandwiches.
2. The *ficelle* is a 4-ounce (125 grams) loaf 30 inches long. At half the weight but the same length as the *baguette,* this loaf is very thin and crusty—great for dipping into sauces.
3. The *bâtard* is an 8-ounce (250 grams) loaf. It's the same weight as the classic *baguette* but is shaped to 24 inches long. It's a plumper loaf with more crumb and less crust, good for larger sandwiches.
4. The *parisienne* is a big 1-pound (500 grams) loaf 30 inches long. The same length as the classic but twice the volume.
5. The *marchand du vin* is a loaf you will probably not see for sale in the United States. The name means the "Merchant of

Wine," and the loaf is seen mostly on bars in bistros. It is 1 pound (500 grams) and very long and thin—42 inches. The bistros cut them in half and make mini-sandwiches to set out on the bar. People drink wine, eat sandwiches, and buy more wine so as to eat more sandwiches.

s with most French breads, you make the *baguette* by making a *poolish* first. The small batch of fermented dough brings flavor and moisture to the final dough. If you baked *baguettes* every day, you would use some of the dough of the previous day's batch for the new day's bread, but here we simply make a *poolish*.

These loaves will not be as long and slender as you have seen them in bakeries, unless your oven is unusually deep and wide. You'll have to mold your *baguettes* into fourteen-inch lengths to fit your oven.

CLASSIC *BAGUETTE*

Allow 24 hours to ferment the *poolish*.
Total preparation and baking time (not including the *poolish*):
6 hours

This is the long and slender classic French loaf with a light and airy crumb, and a golden crunchy crust. It's best warm from the oven and is delicious by itself with butter for a snack, or as a complement to soups, stews, or other meal. A good *baguette* will stale quickly since the proportion of crust to crumb is 50-50. So bake it and eat it, or freeze it, but don't plan on it for the next day.

Makes 4 baguettes *12 to 14 inches long, 1 inch wide*

POOLISH

Spring water (75°F.)	1 cup	8 fluid ounces
Moist yeast	½ teaspoon	⅛ ounce
or dry yeast	¼ teaspoon	1⁄16 ounce
Organic all-purpose white flour*	1½ cups	8 ounces

FINAL DOUGH

Spring water	1 cup	8 fluid ounces
Moist yeast	½ teaspoon	⅛ ounce
or dry yeast	¼ teaspoon	1⁄16 ounce
Organic all-purpose white flour*	4¼–5¼ cups	21–26 ounces
Fine sea salt	1 tablespoon	¾ ounce

---

* See Flours (pages 42–49). These are good approximate measures. You may use more or less depending on the weight and absorbency of your flours.

MAKE AND FERMENT THE *POOLISH* (allow 24 hours) Combine the water and yeast in a medium bowl. Let stand 1 minute, then stir with a wooden spoon until yeast is dissolved. Add the flour, and stir until the consistency of a thick batter. Continue stirring for about 100 strokes or until the strands of gluten come off the spoon when you press the back of the spoon against the bowl. Scrape down the sides of the bowl with a rubber spatula. Cover with a clean damp towel or plastic wrap, and put in a moderately warm (74°F-80°F.) draft-free place until it doubles in volume.

MIX AND KNEAD THE FINAL DOUGH (20 minutes) Measure the ingredients and calculate the necessary temperatures (see page 58). Measure and transfer 1 cup (9 ounces) of the *poolish* to a 6-quart bowl. (Discard remaining *poolish*.) Add the water and yeast. Break up the *poolish* well with a spoon and stir until it loosens and the mixture foams slightly. Add 1 cup (5 ounces) of the flour and stir until well combined. Add the salt and only enough of the remaining flour to make a thick mass that is difficult to stir. Turn out onto a well-floured surface. Knead, adding more of the remaining flour when needed, until dough is soft and smooth, 15 to 17 minutes. (Or make in a heavy-duty mixer; see page 67.) The dough is ready when a small amount pulled from the mass springs back quickly (see Kneading, page 66).

FERMENT THE DOUGH (2 to 3 hours) Shape the dough into a ball and let it rest on a lightly floured surface while you scrape, clean, and lightly oil the large bowl. Place the dough in the bowl and turn the dough to coat the top with oil. Take the dough's temperature: the ideal is 78°F. (see page 58). Cover with a clean damp towel or plastic wrap and put in a moderately warm (74°–80°F.) draft-free place until doubled in volume, and a slight indentation remains after pressing a finger into the dough.

> *Note: If the dough temperature is higher than 78°F., put it in a cooler than 78°F. place like the refrigerator, until the dough cools to 78°F. If it is lower than 78°F., put it in a warmer than 78°F. place until the dough warms to 78°F. The point is to try to keep the dough at 78°F. during its fermentation. If you do have to move the dough, be gentle and don't jostle it, or the dough may deflate.*

DIVIDE THE DOUGH AND REST (35 minutes) Deflate the dough by pushing down in the center and pulling up on the sides. Transfer the dough to a lightly floured board. Knead briefly. Divide into 4 equal portions. Flatten with the heel of your hand and shape each into a tight ball. Cover with a clean damp towel or plastic wrap and put in a moderately warm (74°–80°F.) draft-free place for 30 minutes.

SHAPE THE DOUGH INTO LOAVES (10 minutes) Flatten each ball with the heel of your hand on an unfloured board. Shape each into a 14-inch loaf (see Taking Shape, page 68).

PROOF THE LOAVES (1½ hours) Place the loaves seam side up in a well-floured *couche* (see Equipment, page 52). Cover with a clean damp towel or plastic wrap and put in a moderately warm (74°–80°F.) draft-free place until increased in volume about 1½ times, or until a slight indentation remains when the dough is pressed with a fingertip.

BAKE THE LOAVES (20 to 25 minutes) Forty-five minutes to 1 hour before baking, preheat the oven and homemade hearth or baking stone on the center rack of the oven (see Equipment, page 52) to 450°F.

The oven rack must be in the center of the oven. If it is in the lower third of the oven, the bottoms of the breads may burn, and if it is in the upper third, the top crusts may burn.

Using the *couche* as an aid, gently roll one loaf from the *couche* onto a lightly floured peel so that it sits seam side down. Repeat with a second loaf. Using a very sharp, serrated knife or a single-edged razor blade, score the 2 loaves by making quick shallow cuts ¼ to ½ inch deep along the surface. Using the peel, slide the loaves onto the hearth. Quickly repeat the process with the next 2 loaves. Spray the inner walls and floor of the oven with cold water from a spritzer bottle. If there's an electric light bulb in the oven, avoid spraying it directly—it may burst. Spray for several seconds until steam has filled the oven. Quickly close the door to trap the steam and bake 3 minutes. Spray again in the same way, closing the door immediately so that steam doesn't escape, and bake until loaves are a rich caramel color and the crusts are firm, 15 to 20 minutes.

To test the loaves for doneness, remove and hold the loaves upside down. Strike the bottoms firmly with your finger. If the sound is hollow, the breads are done. If it doesn't sound hollow, bake 5 minutes longer. Cool 5 minutes.

Note: It is not necessary to cool *baguettes* completely. In fact, they are best eaten warm.

See chart on page 232.

BAGUETTE VARIATION

Allow 24 hours to ferment the *poolish*.
Total preparation and baking time (not including *poolish*):
5 hours, 25 minutes

This *baguette* has the same wonderful flavor and chewy crisp crust as the Classic (page 226). But by combining a very light organic white flour and coarse whole wheat flour, you produce a loaf with an even lighter texture.

Makes 6 baguettes, 12–14 inches long, 1 inch wide

POOLISH

Spring water (75°F.)	1 cup	8 fluid ounces
Moist yeast	½ teaspoon	⅛ ounce
or dry yeast	¼ teaspoon	⅟₁₆ ounce
Organic all-purpose white flour*	1¼ cups	6 ounces
Whole wheat flour,* preferably coarse ground	⅔ cup	2 ounces

FINAL DOUGH

Spring water	1 cup	8 fluid ounces
Moist yeast	½ teaspoon	⅛ ounce
or dry yeast	¼ teaspoon	⅟₁₆ ounce
Whole wheat flour,* preferably coarse ground	¼ cup	1¼ ounces
Fine sea salt	1 tablespoon	¾ ounce
Organic all-purpose white flour*	2½–3 cups	12–15 ounces

---

* See Flours (pages 42–49). These are good approximate measures. You may use more or less depending on the weight and absorbency of your flours.

MAKE AND FERMENT THE *POOLISH* (allow 24 hours) Combine the water and yeast in a medium bowl. Let stand 1 minute, then stir with a wooden spoon until yeast is dissolved. Add the all-purpose flour and whole wheat flour. Stir until the consistency of a thick batter. Continue stirring for about 100 strokes or until the strands of gluten come off the spoon when you press the back of the spoon against the bowl. Scrape down the sides of the bowl with a rubber

(continued)

spatula. Cover with a clean damp towel or plastic wrap, and place in a cool to moderate (70°F.) draft-free place.

MIX AND KNEAD THE FINAL DOUGH (20 minutes) Measure the ingredients and calculate the necessary temperatures (see page 58). Measure and transfer 1 cup (9 ounces) of the *poolish* to a 6-quart bowl. (Discard remaining *poolish*.) Add the water and yeast. Break up the *poolish* well with a wooden spoon and stir until it loosens and the mixture foams slightly. Add ¼ cup (1¼ ounces) whole wheat flour and stir until well combined. Add the salt and only enough of the all-purpose flour to make a thick mass that is difficult to stir. Turn out onto a well-floured surface. Knead, adding more of the remaining all-purpose flour when needed, until dough is soft and smooth, 15 to 17 minutes. (Or make in a heavy-duty mixer; see page 67.) The dough is ready when a small amount pulled from the mass springs back quickly (see Kneading, page 66).

FERMENT THE DOUGH (2½ hours) Shape the dough into a ball and let it rest on a lightly floured surface while you scrape, clean, and lightly oil the large bowl. Place the dough in the bowl and turn the dough to coat the top with oil. Take the dough's temperature: the ideal is 78°F. (see page 58). Cover with a clean damp towel or plastic wrap and put in a moderately warm (74°–80°F.) draft-free place until doubled in volume, and a slight indentation remains after pressing a finger into the dough.

> *Note: If the dough temperature is higher than 78°F., place it in a cooler than 78°F. place like the refrigerator, until the dough cools to 78°F. If it is lower than 78°F., place it in a warmer than 78°F. place until the dough warms to 78°F. The point is to try to keep the dough at 78°F. during its fermentation. If you do have to move the dough, be gentle and don't jostle it, or the dough may deflate.*

DIVIDE THE DOUGH AND REST (35 minutes) Deflate the dough by pushing down in the center and pulling up on the sides. Transfer the dough to a lightly floured board. Divide into 4 equal portions. Knead briefly, flatten with the heel of your hand, and shape into tight balls. Cover with a clean damp towel or plastic wrap and put in a moderately warm (74°–80°F.) draft-free place for 30 minutes.

SHAPE THE DOUGH INTO LOAVES (10 minutes) Flatten each ball with the heel of your hand on an unfloured board. Shape each into a 14-inch loaf (see Taking Shape, page 68).

PROOF THE LOAVES (1½ hours) Place the loaves seam side up in a well-floured *couche* (see Equipment, page 52). Cover with a clean damp towel or plastic wrap and place in a moderately warm (74°–80°F.) draft-free place until increased in volume about 1½ times, or until a slight indentation remains when the dough is pressed with a fingertip.

BAKE THE LOAVES (20 to 25 minutes) Forty-five minutes to 1 hour before baking, preheat the oven and homemade hearth or baking stone on the center rack of the oven (see Equipment, page 52) to 450°F.

The oven rack must be in the center of the oven. If it is in the lower third of the oven, the bottoms of the breads may burn, and if it is in the upper third, the top crusts may burn.

Using the *couche* as an aid, gently roll one loaf from the *couche* onto a lightly floured peel so that it sits seam side down. Repeat with a second loaf. Using a very sharp, serrated knife or a single-edged razor blade, score the 2 loaves by making quick shallow cuts ¼ to ½ inch deep along the surface. Using the peel, slide the loaves onto the hearth. Quickly repeat the process with the next 2 loaves. Quickly spray the inner walls and floor of the oven with cold water from a spritzer bottle. If there's an electric light bulb in the oven, avoid spraying it directly—it may burst. Spray for several seconds until steam has filled the oven. Quickly close the door to trap the steam and bake 3 minutes. Spray again in the same way, closing the door immediately so that steam doesn't escape, and bake until loaves are a rich caramel color and the crust is firm, 15 to 20 minutes.

To test the loaves for doneness, remove and hold the loaves upside down. Strike the bottoms firmly with your finger. If the sound is hollow, the breads are done. If it doesn't sound hollow, bake 5 minutes longer. Cool 5 minutes.

> *Note:* It is not necessary to cool *baguettes* completely. In fact, they are best eaten warm.

CLASSIC *BAGUETTE* AND VARIATION

Task	Approximate Time	Comments
Prepreparation		Ferment *poolish*.
Preparation	5 min.	Calculate temperatures. Assemble ingredients. Mix.
Knead	15 min.	Take temperature of final dough.
Ferment	2 hr., 30 min.	Moderate: 74°–80°F. until double.
Divide	5 min.	Deflate and cut 4 equal portions. Form 4 balls.
Rest	30 min.	Moderate: 74°–80°F. on floured board.
Shape	10 min.	Classic *baguette*. Place in well-floured *couche*.
Proof	1 hr., 30 min.	Moderate: 74°–80°F. until doubled.
Bake	20 min.	With steam. 450°F.
Cool	5 min.	On rack or in basket.

Cumulative Total Time: 5 hr., 25 min.

BASIL'S *BAGUETTE*

Allow 5 hours to ferment the *poolish*.
Allow 12 hours or overnight to ferment and warm the dough.
Total preparation and baking time (not including *poolish* or the long fermentation of the dough):
1 hour

The specialty of Le Moulin de la Vierge, Basil Kamir's bakery in Paris, this *baguette* has a more complex texture than others—not as light or airy. The crust is chewier and thicker than most and the crumb has the full-bodied flavor of the grain. Basil mixes the *poolish* and lets it ferment five hours. Then he mixes the dough and lets it sit another ten hours. I suggest you mix the *poolish* about 5:00 P.M. and the final dough about 10:00 P.M. the night before you bake.

Makes 6 baguettes 14 inches long and 2 inches wide

POOLISH

Spring water (75°F.)	2¼ cups	18 fluid ounces
Moist yeast	¾ teaspoon	⅝ ounce
or dry yeast	generous ¼ teaspoon	¼ ounce
Organic all-purpose white flour*	2 cups plus 2 tablespoons	11 ounces

FINAL DOUGH

Spring water	1 cup	8 fluid ounces
Moist yeast	¾ teaspoon	⅝ ounce
or dry yeast	generous ¼ teaspoon	¼ ounce
Organic all-purpose white flour*	3¾–4¾ cups	19–24 ounces
Fine sea salt	1 tablespoon plus 1½ teaspoons	1 ounce

* See Flours (pages 42–49). These are good approximate measures. You may use more or less depending on the weight and absorbency of your flour.

MAKE AND FERMENT THE *POOLISH* (allow 24 hours) Combine the water and yeast in a 6-quart bowl. Let stand 1 minute, then stir with a wooden spoon until yeast is dissolved. Add the flour, and stir until the consistency of a thick batter. Continue stirring for about 100 strokes. Cover with a clean damp towel or plastic wrap, and put in a moderately warm (74°–80°F.) draft-free place.

(continued)

MIX AND KNEAD THE FINAL DOUGH (20 minutes) Measure the remaining ingredients and calculate the necessary temperatures (see page 58). Bring the bowl with the *poolish* to your work space. Add the water and yeast. Break up the *poolish* well with a wooden spoon and stir until it loosens and the mixture foams slightly. Add 1 cup (5 ounces) of the flour and stir until well combined. Add the salt and only enough of the remaining flour to make a thick mass that is difficult to stir. Turn out onto a well-floured surface. Knead, adding more of the remaining flour when needed, until dough is soft and smooth, 15 to 17 minutes. (Or make in a heavy-duty mixer; see page 67.) The dough is ready when a small amount pulled from the mass springs back quickly (see Kneading, page 66).

FERMENT THE DOUGH (allow 10 hours in the refrigerator and 2 hours to bring the dough to room temperature) Shape the dough into a ball and let it rest on a lightly floured surface while you scrape, clean, and lightly oil the large bowl. Place the dough in the bowl and turn the dough to coat the top with oil. Take the dough's temperature: the ideal is 78°F. (see page 58). Cover with a clean damp towel or plastic wrap and put in a very cool (50°F.) draft-free place or in the refrigerator for 10 hours or overnight.

Move dough to a warm (80°–85°F.) place until it comes to room temperature, about 2 hours.

DIVIDE THE DOUGH AND SHAPE THE LOAVES (10 minutes) Deflate the dough by pushing down in the center and pulling up on the sides. Transfer the dough to an unfloured board. Divide into 6 equal portions. Knead briefly, flatten with the heel of your hand, and shape each into a 14-inch loaf (see Taking Shape, page 68).

PROOF THE LOAVES (25 minutes) Place the loaves seam side up in a well-floured *couche* (see Equipment, page 52). Cover with a clean damp towel or plastic wrap and put in a moderately warm (74°–80°F.) draft-free place and allow to rest 20 minutes.

BAKE THE LOAVES (20 to 25 minutes) Forty-five minutes to 1 hour before baking, preheat the oven and homemade hearth or baking stone on the center rack of the oven (see Equipment, page 52) to 450°F.

The oven rack must be in the center of the oven. If it is in the lower third of the oven, the bottoms of the breads may burn, and if it is in the upper third, the top crusts may burn.

Using the *couche* as an aid, gently roll one loaf from the *couche* onto a lightly floured peel so that it sits seam side down. Repeat with a second and third loaf. Using a very sharp, serrated knife or a single-edged razor blade, score the 2 loaves by making quick shallow cuts ¼ to ½ inch deep along the surface. Using the peel, slide the loaves onto the hearth. Quickly repeat the process with the next 3 loaves. Quickly spray the inner walls and floor of the oven with cold water from a spritzer bottle. If there's an electric light bulb in the oven, avoid spraying it directly—it may burst. Spray for several seconds until steam has filled the oven. Quickly close the door to trap the steam and bake 3 minutes. Spray again in the same way, closing the door immediately so that steam doesn't escape, and bake until loaves are a rich caramel color and the crust is firm, 20 to 25 minutes.

To test the loaves for doneness, remove and hold the loaves upside down. Strike the bottoms firmly with your finger. If the sound is hollow, the breads are done. If it doesn't sound hollow, bake 5 minutes longer. Cool 5 minutes.

<u>Note:</u> It is not necessary to cool *baguettes* completely. In fact, they are best eaten warm.

BASIL'S BAGUETTE

Task	Approximate Time	Comments
Prepreparation		Ferment *poolish*.
Preparation	5 min.	Calculate temperatures. Assemble ingredients, mix.
Knead	15 min.	Take temperature of final dough. Place in large bowl.
Ferment	10 hr.	Very cool! 50°F. or in refrigerator.
Come to room temperature	2 hr.	Warm: 80°–85°F.
Divide	5 min.	Deflate. Cut into 6 equal portions.
Shape	10 min.	Classic *baguette*. Place in well-floured *couche*.
Proof	20 min.	Moderate: 74°–80°F.
Bake	25 min.	With steam. 450°F.
Cool	5 min.	On rack or in baskets.

Cumulative Total Time: 13 hr., 20 min.

BAGUETTE AU LEVAIN

Allow 8 hours to ferment the *levain*.
Total preparation and baking time (not including the *levain*):
5 hours, 25 minutes

Shaped into a *baguette*, the *levain* dough produces a sweet and wildly crunchy crust. For those who love the crisp crust of a *baguette* and the earthy flavor of *levain*, this golden loaf is a dream come true. If you want fewer *baguettes*, simply halve this recipe, but I prefer to freeze any excess loaves.

Makes 6 baguettes 14 inches long

Levain (page 185)	2 cups	18 ounces
Spring water	2¼ cups	18 fluid ounces
Organic all-purpose white flour*	4¾–5¾ cups	24–29 ounces
Fine sea salt	1 tablespoon	¾ ounce

* See Flours (pages 42–49). This is a good approximate measure. You may use more or less depending on the weight and absorbency of your flour.

MIX AND KNEAD THE FINAL DOUGH (20 minutes) Measure the ingredients and calculate the temperatures (see page 58). Combine the *levain* and water in a 4-quart bowl. Break up the *levain* well with a wooden spoon or squeeze it through your fingers until broken up. Continue stirring until the *levain* is partially dissolved and the mixture is slightly frothy. Add 1 cup (5 ounces) of the flour and stir until well combined. Add the salt and just enough of the remaining flour to make a thick mass that is difficult to stir. Turn onto a well-floured surface and knead, adding remaining flour when needed, until dough is firm and smooth, 15 to 17 minutes total. (Or make in a heavy-duty mixer; see page 67). The dough is ready when a little dough pulled from the mass springs back quickly (see Kneading, page 66).

FERMENT THE DOUGH (2 hours) Shape the dough into a ball and let it rest on a lightly floured surface while you scrape, clean, and lightly oil the large bowl. Place the dough in the bowl and turn once to coat with oil. Take the dough's temperature: the ideal is 78°F. (see page 58). Cover with a clean damp towel or plastic wrap and put in a moderately warm (74°–80°F.) draft-free place until increased in volume about one-quarter.

Note: If the dough temperature is higher than 78°F., put it in a cooler than 78°F. place like the refrigerator, until the dough cools to 78°F. If it is lower than 78°F., put it in a warmer than 78°F. place until the dough warms to 78°F. The point is to try to keep the dough at 78°F. during its fermentation. If you do have to move the dough, be gentle and don't jostle it, or the dough may deflate.

This dough will not behave like an ordinary yeasted bread dough. It won't rise to a puffy state.

DIVIDE THE DOUGH AND REST (35 minutes) Deflate the dough by pushing down in the center and pulling up on the sides. Transfer the dough to a lightly floured work surface. Knead briefly and cut into 6 equal pieces. Shape each into a tight round ball and place on an unfloured board. Cover with a clean damp towel or plastic wrap and put in a moderately warm (74°–80°F.) draft-free place for 30 minutes.

SHAPE THE LOAVES (10 minutes) Flatten each ball with the heel of your hand into a disk 8 inches in diameter. Shape into *baguettes* (see Taking Shape, page 68).

PROOF THE LOAVES (2 hours) Place the loaves seam side up in a well-floured *couche* (see Equipment, page 52). Cover with a clean damp towel or plastic wrap and put in a moderately warm (74°–80°F.) draft-free place until almost doubled in volume, or until a slight indentation remains when the dough is pressed with a fingertip. This dough becomes softer, lighter, and very delicate as it proofs—more so than any other dough in the book. After 2 hours, there will be a pronounced difference between the firm dough you placed in the *couche* and the final very light proofed dough.

BAKE THE LOAVES (about 20 minutes) Forty-five minutes to 1 hour before baking, preheat the oven and homemade hearth or baking stone on the center rack of the oven (see Equipment, page 52) to 450°F.

The oven rack must be in the center of the oven. If it is in the

(continued)

lower third of the oven, the bottoms of the breads may burn, and if it is in the upper third, the top crusts may burn.

Using the *couche* as an aid, gently roll 2 loaves from the *couche* onto a lightly floured peel so that they sit seam side down. Using a very sharp, serrated knife or a single-edged razor blade, score the loaves by making quick shallow cuts ¼ to ½ inch deep along the surface. Using the peel, slide the loaves onto the hearth. Quickly repeat the process with the remaining loaves. Spray the inner walls and floor of the oven with cold water from a spritzer bottle. If there's an electric light bulb in the oven, avoid spraying it directly—it may burst. Spray for several seconds until steam has filled the oven. Quickly close the door to trap the steam and bake 3 minutes. Spray again in the same way, closing the door immediately so that steam doesn't escape. Bake until loaves are a rich caramel color and the crusts are firm, 20 to 25 minutes.

To test the loaves for doneness, remove and hold the loaves upside down. Strike the bottoms firmly with your finger. If the sound is hollow, the breads are done. If it doesn't sound hollow, bake 5 minutes longer. Cool the baguettes slightly on a wire rack.

BAGUETTE AU LEVAIN

Task	Approximate Time	Comments
Prepreparation	8 hr.	Ferment *levain*.
Preparation	5 min.	Calculate temperatures. Assemble ingredients, combine, mix.
Knead	15 min.	Take temperature of dough.
Ferment	2 hr.	Moderate: 74°–80°F. until increased by 25%.
Divide	5 min.	Deflate and cut into 6 equal pieces. Shape into balls on lightly floured board.
Rest	30 min.	Moderate: 74°–80°F.
Shape	10 min.	Flatten with heel of hand and shape into *baguettes*.
Proof	2 hr.	Moderate: 74°–80°F. until doubled in volume.
Bake	20 min.	With steam. 450°F.
Cool	10 min.	On rack or in basket.

Cumulative Total Time: 5 hr., 35 min.

EIGHTEEN

A FAMILY OF BREADS INSPIRED BY TRADITIONAL FRENCH AND ITALIAN BREADS

HONEY BRIOCHE LOAVES

> Allow 1 hour to make the *poolish*.
> Total preparation and baking time (not including the *poolish*):
> 6 hours, 30 minutes

A loaf variation on the classic brioche, this golden bread has a light honey taste. Baked in ordinary loaf pans instead of the traditional fluted molds, it's delicious when sliced, toasted, and slathered with butter. This sticky dough needs to be prepared in a heavy-duty mixer.

Makes two 8 by 4-inch loaves

POOLISH

Moist yeast	1 tablespoon	¾ ounces
or dry yeast	1½ teaspoons	½ ounce
Milk, at room temperature	1 cup	8 fluid ounces
Organic all-purpose white flour*	1½ cups	7½ ounces

FINAL DOUGH

Honey, preferably wildflower	¼ cup	1 ounce
2 large eggs, at room temperature		
3 large egg yolks at room temperature		
Organic all-purpose white flour*	2½ cups	12½ ounces
Fine sea salt	1¼ teaspoons	
Unsalted butter, softened, cut into 8 pieces	8 tablespoons	4 ounces

---

* See Flours (pages 42–49). These are good approximate measures. You may use more or less depending on the weight and absorbency of your flour.

MAKE AND FERMENT THE *POOLISH* (allow 1 hour) Combine the yeast, milk, and flour in the bowl of a heavy-duty mixer. Beat on medium speed with the paddle blade until the yeast is dissolved and the mixture is the consistency of a batter, about 2 minutes. Remove the blade, scrape down the sides of the bowl, and cover with a clean damp towel or plastic wrap. Put in a moderate (74°–80°F.) draft-free place until the dough is puffy and domed.

MIX AND KNEAD THE FINAL DOUGH (20 minutes) Measure the ingredients and calculate the necessary temperatures (see page 58). Reattach the bowl to the mixer fitted with a paddle blade. Add the honey, whole eggs, and yolks; beat on medium-high speed 5 minutes. Reduce speed to medium and gradually add the flour and salt. Fit the mixer with the dough hook and continue beating at medium speed for 10 minutes. The dough will be sticky and batterlike. It will not clean the sides of the bowl. Add the butter and beat, scraping the bowl once, until it is completely incorporated, about 5 minutes longer.

FERMENT THE DOUGH (3 hours) Shape the dough into a ball and place smooth side down in a well-buttered 4-quart bowl. Turn the dough to coat the top with butter. Take the dough's temperature: the ideal is 78°F. (see page 58). Cover with a clean damp towel or plastic wrap and put in a moderately warm (74°–80°F.) draft-free place until doubled in volume, about 2 hours.

> _Note:_ *If the dough temperature is higher than 78°F., put it in a cooler than 78°F. place like the refrigerator, until the dough cools to 78°F. If it is lower than 78°F., put it in a warmer than 78°F. place until the dough warms to 78°F. The point is to try to keep the dough at 78°F. during its fermentation. If you do have to move the dough, be gentle and don't jostle it, or the dough may deflate.*

Place the dough in the refrigerator for 1 hour and chill slightly to make it easier to handle. (This dough can also ferment in the refrigerator for 8 hours or overnight. Be sure to allow about 2 hours for it to come to cool room temperature before shaping and proofing the loaves.)

DIVIDE THE DOUGH AND SHAPE INTO LOAVES (10 minutes) Deflate the dough by pushing down in the center and pulling up on the sides. Transfer the dough to a well-floured work surface and knead briefly, adding more flour if needed to make a very soft, slightly sticky dough. Cut into 2 equal portions. Shape into two 8-inch-long logs (see Taking Shape, page 68).

PROOF THE LOAVES (1½ to 2 hours) Butter two 8 × 4 × 2½-inch loaf pans. Place the loaves smooth side up in the pans. Cover with a clean damp towel or plastic wrap and put in a moderately warm (74°–80°F.) draft-free place until the dough rises in a dome above the rim of the pans.

BAKE THE LOAVES (30 minutes) Forty-five minutes to 1 hour before baking, preheat the oven and homemade hearth or baking stone on the center rack of the oven (see Equipment, page 52) to 400°F.

The oven rack must be in the center of the oven. If it is in the lower third of the oven, the bottoms of the breads may burn, and if it is in the upper third, the top crusts may burn.

Place the loaves in the oven and bake until the tops are golden, 25 to 30 minutes. To test the loaves for doneness, remove from the pans and hold the loaves upside down. Strike the bottoms firmly with your finger. If the sound is hollow, the breads are done. If it doesn't sound hollow, return the loaves to the pans and bake 5 minutes longer. Cool in the pans for 10 minutes, then remove and cool completely on a wire rack.

HONEY BRIOCHE LOAVES

Task	Approximate Time	Comments
Prepreparation	1 hr.	Ferment *poolish*.
Preparation	5 min.	Assemble ingredients. Mix.
Knead	15 min.	In mixer.
Ferment	2 hr.	Moderate: 74°–80°F. until doubled. In refrigerator.
Divide	5 min.	Knead 3 minutes, then cut into 2 equal pieces.
Shape	5 min.	Into logs. Place in prepared loaf pans.
Proof	1 hr., 30 min.	Moderate: 74°–80°F.
Bake	30 min.	400°F.
Cool	Completely	Unmolded on rack.

Cumulative Total Time: 6 hr., 30 min.

ORANGE VANILLA BRIOCHE

Allow 12 hours for the candied peels to dry.
Allow 1 hour to ferment the *poolish*.
Total preparation and baking time (not including the candied peels or the *poolish*):
6 hours, 20 minutes

This is a nontraditional brioche with a delicious sweet and fruity flavor, and an airy texture. Use a heavy-duty mixer to work this rich egg-and-butter dough and bake in a large brioche mold for dramatic effect.

Makes 1 large 8-inch loaf

CANDIED ORANGE PEELS

1 medium orange		
Sugar	½ cup	3½ ounces
Spring water	¼ cup	2 fluid ounces

POOLISH

Moist yeast	1 tablespoon	¾ ounce
or dry yeast	1½ teaspoons	½ ounce
Milk, at room temperature	¼ cup	2 fluid ounces
Spring water	½ cup	4 fluid ounces
Organic all-purpose white flour*	¾ cup	4 ounces

FINAL DOUGH

1 vanilla bean, halved horizontally, or vanilla extract	1 teaspoon	
1 large egg, lightly beaten		
Sugar	1½ tablespoons	
Unsalted butter, softened	3 tablespoons	1½ ounces
Organic all-purpose white flour*	1⅔ cups	9 ounces
Fine sea salt	1¼ teaspoons	
1 large egg yolk, beaten with 1 tablespoon water, for glaze		

---

* See Flours (pages 42–49). These are good approximate measures. You may use more or less depending on the weight and absorbency of your flour.

(continued)

PREPARE THE CANDIED ORANGE PEELS (40 minutes plus 12 hours to dry) Using a serrated knife, cut the peel (zest) and white pith off the orange in wide slices. (Don't worry if there's a little of the fruit remaining on the pith.) Cut the peel into ¼-inch-wide slivers.

Place the peel in a medium saucepan and add enough tap water to cover by 1 inch. Bring to a boil over high heat, then cook for exactly 4 minutes. Drain well, then repeat the procedure with fresh water. Drain again, and do again for the third time. (This removes any bitterness from the peel.)

In the same saucepan, combine the sugar, water, and blanched peel. Bring to a simmer over medium heat, stirring to help dissolve the sugar. When the syrup comes to a boil, stop stirring. Do not actually stir with a spoon from this point on, or the syrup may crystallize. Reduce the heat to medium-low and cook, swirling the pan by the handle occasionally to avoid scorching, until the peel has absorbed the syrup and is tender and translucent, about 20 minutes.

Using 2 forks, transfer the peel to a lightly oiled wire cake rack set over waxed paper. Use the forks to separate the peel pieces. Allow the peel to dry at room temperature at least 12 hours.

Using a sharp knife rinsed in hot water, chop the peel into ¼-inch pieces. Use the candied peel within 24 hours of making.

MAKE AND FERMENT THE *POOLISH* (allow 1 hour) Combine the yeast, milk, water, and flour in the bowl of a heavy-duty mixer. Beat on medium speed with the paddle blade until the yeast is dissolved and the mixture is the consistency of a batter, about 2 minutes. Remove the blade, scrape down the sides of the bowl, and cover with a clean damp towel or plastic wrap. Put in a moderately warm (74°–80°F.) draft-free place until the *poolish* is puffy and domed.

MIX AND KNEAD THE FINAL DOUGH (25 minutes) Measure the ingredients and calculate the necessary temperatures (see page 58). Reattach the bowl with the *poolish* to the mixer fitted with a paddle blade. Using the tip of a small sharp knife, scrape the seeds out of the vanilla bean pod. Discard the pod or use in Vanilla Bean Butter Loaf (see page 310). Add the egg, sugar, vanilla seeds or extract, flour, and salt. Beat on medium speed until a batter forms. Fit the mixer with the dough hook and continue beating on medium speed for 10 minutes. The dough will take a while to form on the hook. It will be sticky and will leave a film on the sides of the bowl.

Add the butter and beat, scraping the bowl once, until it is completely incorporated, about 3 minutes longer. Add the candied orange peels and beat 1 minute. Turn out onto a lightly floured surface and knead briefly to distribute oranges evenly. The dough will be very soft.

FERMENT THE DOUGH (3 hours) Shape the dough into a ball and place smooth side down in a large well-buttered 4-quart bowl. Turn the dough to coat the top with butter. Take the dough's temperature: the ideal is 78°F. (see page 58). Cover with a clean damp towel or plastic wrap and put in a moderately warm (74°–80°F.) draft-free place until doubled in volume, about 2 hours.

> *Note: If the dough temperature is higher than 78°F., put it in a cooler than 78°F. place like the refrigerator, until the dough cools to 78°F. If it is lower than 78°F., put it in a warmer than 78°F. place until the dough warms to 78°F. The point is to try to keep the dough at 78°F. during its fermentation. If you do have to move the dough, be gentle and don't jostle it, or the dough may deflate.*

Place the dough in the refrigerator for 1 hour to slightly chill it and make it easier to handle. (This dough can also ferment in the refrigerator for 8 hours or overnight. Be sure to allow about 2 hours for it to come to cool room temperature before shaping and proofing the brioche.)

DIVIDE THE DOUGH AND SHAPE (10 minutes) Deflate the dough by pushing down in the center and pulling up on the sides. Transfer to a well-floured work surface and knead briefly, adding more flour if needed to make a very soft, slightly sticky dough. Remove a small portion of the dough, about the size of a golf ball and shape it into a ball. Shape the remaining dough into a tight ball.

PROOF THE LOAF (about 2 hours) Generously butter an 8-inch brioche mold. Place the large ball of dough smooth side up in the mold. Poke a hole in the center of the dough with a well-floured finger.

(continued)

Place the small ball in the hole to make a topknot. Cover loosely with a clean damp towel or plastic wrap and put in a moderately warm (74°–80°F.) draft-free place until doubled in volume.

BAKE THE LOAF (35 to 45 minutes) Forty-five minutes to 1 hour before baking, preheat the oven and homemade hearth or baking stone on the center rack of the oven (see Equipment, page 52) to 375°F.

The oven rack must be in the center of the oven. If it is in the lower third of the oven, the bottoms of the breads may burn, and if it is in the upper third, the top crusts may burn.

Lightly brush the top of the brioche with the egg yolk mixture. Place the brioche in the oven and bake until the top is golden, 35 to 45 minutes. To test for doneness, remove from the mold and hold the brioche upside down. Strike the bottom firmly with your finger. If the sound is hollow, the brioche is done. If it doesn't sound hollow, return the brioche to the mold and bake 5 minutes longer. Cool completely on a wire rack.

ORANGE VANILLA BRIOCHE

Task	Approximate Time	Comments
Prepreparation	12 hr. 1 hr.	Dry orange peels. Ferment *poolish*.
Preparation	10 min.	Assemble ingredients. Mix.
Knead	14 min.	In mixer.
Knead	1 min.	On floured board.
Ferment	1 hr. 2 hr.	Moderate: 74°–80°F. until doubled. In refrigerator.
Shape	5 min.	Into balls. Place in prepared mold.
Proof	2 hr.	Moderate: 74°–80°F. until doubled.
Bake	45 min.	375°F.
Cool	completely	Unmolded on rack.

Cumulative Total Time: 6 hr., 20 min.

PAIN DE CAMPAGNE

> Allow 24 hours to ferment the *poolish*.
> Total preparation and baking time (not including *poolish*):
> 5 hours, 40 minutes

In France, any bread made from *baguette* dough but not shaped into a *baguette* is called *pain de campagne.* This one is a high, round country loaf with a light taste, airy crumb, and chewy thick crust. The bread will store cut side down for three days.

Makes 2 round 6-inch loaves

POOLISH

Spring water (75°F.)	1 cup	8 fluid ounces
Moist yeast	½ teaspoon	⅛ ounces
or dry yeast	¼ teaspoon	¹⁄₁₆ ounce
Organic all-purpose white flour*	1½ cups	8 ounces

FINAL DOUGH

Spring water	1 cup	8 fluid ounces
Moist yeast	½ teaspoon	⅛ ounce
or dry yeast	¼ teaspoon	¹⁄₁₆ ounce
Organic all-purpose white flour*	2½–3 cups	12–15 ounces
Fine sea salt	1 tablespoon	¾ ounce

---

* See Flours (pages 42–49). These are good approximate measures. You may use more or less depending on the weight and absorbency of your flour.

MAKE AND FERMENT THE *POOLISH* (allow 24 hours) Combine the water and yeast in a medium bowl. Let stand 1 minute, then stir with a wooden spoon until yeast is dissolved. Add the flour and stir until the consistency of a thick batter. Continue stirring for about 100 strokes or until the strands of gluten come off the spoon when you press the back of the spoon against the bowl. Scrape down the sides of the bowl with a rubber spatula. Cover with a clean damp towel or plastic wrap, and put in a moderately warm (74°–80°F.) draft-free place until it doubles in volume.

MIX AND KNEAD THE FINAL DOUGH (20 minutes) Measure the ingredients and calculate the necessary temperatures (see page 58). Transfer 1 cup (9 ounces) of the *poolish* to a 6-quart bowl. (Discard remaining *poolish*.)

(continued)

Add the remaining water and the yeast. Break up the *poolish* well with a wooden spoon and stir until the *poolish* is partly dissolved and the mixture foams slightly. Add 1 cup (5 ounces) of the flour and stir until well combined. Add the salt and only enough of the remaining flour to make a thick mass that is difficult to stir. Turn out onto a well-floured surface. Knead, adding more of the remaining flour when needed, until dough is soft and smooth, 15 to 17 minutes. (Or make in a heavy-duty mixer; see page 67.) The dough is ready when a small amount pulled from the mass springs back quickly (see Kneading, page 66).

FERMENT THE DOUGH (about 2 hours) Shape the dough into a ball and let it rest on a lightly floured surface while you scrape, clean, and lightly oil the large bowl. Place the dough in the bowl and turn the dough to coat the top with oil. Take the dough's temperature: the ideal is 78°F. (see page 58). Cover with a clean damp towel or plastic wrap and put in a moderately warm (74°–80°F.) draft-free place until doubled in volume, and a slight indentation remains after pressing a finger into the dough.

> *Note: If the dough temperature is higher than 78°F., put it in a cooler than 78°F. place like the refrigerator, until the dough cools to 78°F. If it is lower than 78°F., put it in a warmer than 78°F. place until the dough warms to 78°F. The point is to try to keep the dough at 78°F. during its fermentation. If you do have to move the dough, be gentle and don't jostle it, or the dough may deflate.*

DIVIDE THE DOUGH AND REST (35 minutes) Deflate the dough by pushing down in the center and pulling up on the sides. Transfer the dough to a lightly floured board. Divide into 2 equal portions. Knead briefly, flatten with the heel of your hand, and shape into tight balls. Cover with a clean damp towel or plastic wrap and put in a moderately warm (74°–80°F.) draft-free place for 30 minutes.

SHAPE THE DOUGH INTO LOAVES (5 minutes) Flatten each ball with the heel of your hand on a lightly floured board. Shape again into tight balls for round loaves (see Taking Shape, page 68).

PROOF THE LOAVES (1½ hours) Line 2 bowls or baskets about 6 inches in diameter and 3 inches deep with well-floured towels, and place the loaves smooth side down in each bowl. Dust the tops of the dough with flour. Cover with a clean damp towel or plastic wrap. Place in a moderately warm (74°–80°F.) draft-free place until almost doubled in volume, and a slight indentation remains when the dough is pressed with a fingertip.

BAKE THE LOAVES (30 minutes) Forty-five minutes to 1 hour before baking, preheat the oven and homemade hearth or baking stone on the center rack of the oven (see Equipment, page 52) to 450°F.

The oven rack must be in the center of the oven. If it is in the lower third of the oven, the bottoms of the breads may burn, and if it is in the upper third, the top crusts may burn.

Gently invert one loaf from the bowl onto a lightly floured peel so that it sits seam side down. Using a very sharp, serrated knife or a single-edged razor blade, score the loaf by making quick shallow cuts ¼ to ½ inch deep along the surface. Using the peel, slide the loaf onto the hearth. Quickly repeat the process with the remaining loaf. Quickly spray the inner walls and floor of the oven with cold water from a spritzer bottle. If there's an electric light bulb in the oven, avoid spraying it directly—it may burst. Spray for several seconds until steam has filled the oven. Quickly close the door to trap the steam and bake 3 minutes. Spray again in the same way, closing the door immediately so that steam doesn't escape. Bake until loaves are a rich caramel color and the crust is firm, 25 to 30 minutes.

To test the loaves for doneness, remove and hold the loaves upside down. Strike the bottoms firmly with your finger. If the sound is hollow, the breads are done. If it doesn't sound hollow, bake 5 minutes longer. Cool completely on a wire rack.

PAIN DE CAMPAGNE

Task	Approximate Time	Comments
Prepreparation		Ferment *poolish*.
Preparation	5 min.	Calculate temperatures. Assemble ingredients. Mix.
Knead	15 min.	Take temperature of dough.
Ferment	2 hr.	Moderate: 74°–80°F. until doubled.
Divide	5 min.	Deflate and cut 2 equal portions. Shape into balls.
Rest	30 min.	Moderate: 74°–80°F. on floured board until doubled.
Shape	5 min.	Deflate. Shape into round loaves. Place in well-floured linen-lined bowl or basket.
Proof	1 hr., 30 min.	Moderate: 74°–80°F. until doubled.
Bake	30 min.	With steam. 450°F.
Cool	20 min.	On rack or in basket.

Cumulative Total Time: 6 hr.

PAIN NORMANDE

Allow 8 hours or overnight to ferment the final dough.
Total preparation and baking time (not including fermenting the dough):
8 hours, 35 minutes

In Normandy, baking and cooking with apples is a way of life; this dark moist bread with sweet apple chunks is a standard among Normandy bakers. The apples are kneaded into the dough at the end of the first fermentation, after the chilled dough has come to room temperature.

Makes 1 round 10-inch loaf

Sparkling cider, at room temperature (the nonalcoholic variety, such as Martinelli's)	1½ cups	12 fluid ounces
Moist yeast or dry yeast	4 teaspoons 2 teaspoons	¾ ounce
Whole wheat flour,* preferably coarse	½ cup	2¾ ounces
Fine sea salt	1 tablespoon	¾ ounce
Organic white flour with germ*	2¼–2¾ cups	12–14 ounces
2 tart green apples, such as Pippins, Greenings, or Granny Smiths, cored, peeled, finely chopped	1 cup	4 ounces
Cornmeal, for dusting		

* See Flours (pages 42–49). These are good approximate measures. You may use more or less depending on the weight and absorbency of your flours.

MIX AND KNEAD THE FINAL DOUGH (20 minutes) Combine the cider and yeast in a 6-quart bowl. Let stand 1 minute, then stir with a wooden spoon until the yeast is dissolved. Add the whole wheat flour; stir until well combined. Add the salt and only enough of the white flour to make a thick mass that is difficult to stir. Turn out onto a well-floured surface. Knead, adding more of the remaining flour when needed, until dough is soft and smooth, 15 to 17 minutes. (Or make in a heavy-duty mixer; see page 67.) The dough is ready when a small amount pulled from the mass springs back quickly (see Kneading, page 66).

(continued)

FERMENT THE DOUGH (8 hours or overnight) Shape the dough into a ball and let it rest on a lightly floured surface while you scrape, clean, and lightly oil the large bowl. Place the dough in the bowl and turn the dough to coat the top with oil. Cover with plastic wrap and place in the refrigerator.

FERMENT THE DOUGH A SECOND TIME (4 to 5 hours) Place the bowl with the dough in a moderately warm (74°–80°F.) draft-free place and allow to come to room temperature, about 2 hours.

Deflate by pulling up on the sides and pushing down in the center. Transfer the dough to a lightly floured surface. Flatten with the heel of your hand and knead in the chopped apples. Add more flour when needed as the apples will give off moisture into the dough. Shape the dough into a ball and place back in the bowl. Take the dough's temperature: the ideal is 78°F. (see page 58). Cover with a clean damp towel or plastic wrap and put in a moderately warm (74°–80°F.) draft-free place until doubled in volume, and a slight indentation remains after pressing a fingertip into the dough, 2 to 3 hours.

> *Note: If the dough temperature is higher than 78°F., put it in a cooler than 78°F. place like the refrigerator, until the dough cools to 78°F. If it is lower than 78°F., put it in a warmer than 78°F. place until the dough warms to 78°F. The point is to try to keep the dough at 78°F. during its fermentation. If you do have to move the dough, be gentle and don't jostle it, or the dough may deflate.*

SHAPE THE DOUGH INTO A LOAF (5 minutes) Deflate the dough and knead briefly on a lightly floured board. Shape into a tight ball for a round loaf (see Taking Shape, page 68).

PROOF THE LOAF (1½ hours) Place the loaf on a board that has been dusted with cornmeal. Cover with a clean damp towel or plastic wrap and put in a moderately warm (74°–80°F.) draft-free place until almost doubled in volume, and a slight indentation remains when the dough is pressed with a fingertip.

BAKE THE LOAF (40 minutes) Forty-five minutes to 1 hour before baking, preheat the oven and homemade hearth or baking stone on the center rack of the oven (see Equipment, page 52) to 450°F.

The oven rack must be in the center of the oven. If it is in the lower third of the oven, the bottoms of the breads may burn, and if it is in the upper third, the top crusts may burn.

Gently slip the loaf onto a lightly floured peel. Using a very sharp, serrated knife or a single-edged razor blade, score the loaf by making quick shallow cuts ¼ to ½ inch deep along the surface. Using the peel, slide the loaf onto the hearth. Quickly spray the inner walls and floor of the oven with cold water from a spritzer bottle. If there's an electric light bulb in the oven, avoid spraying it directly—it may burst. Spray for several seconds until steam has filled the oven. Quickly close the door to trap the steam and bake 3 minutes. Spray again in the same way, closing the door immediately so that steam doesn't escape. Bake until the loaf begins to color, 15 minutes. Reduce the heat to 400°F. and continue baking until the loaf is a rich caramel color and the crust is firm, 20 to 25 minutes.

To test for doneness, remove and hold the loaf upside down. Strike the bottom firmly with your finger. If the sound is hollow, the bread is done. If it doesn't sound hollow, bake 5 minutes longer. Cool completely on a wire rack.

PAIN NORMANDE

Task	Approximate Time	Comments
Preparation	5 min.	Assemble ingredients. Mix.
Knead	15 min.	
Ferment	8 hr.	Cold: In refrigerator.
Come to room temperature	2 hr.	Moderate: 74°–80°F.
Ferment	3 hr.	Moderate: until doubled.
Shape	5 min.	Into balls for round loaves.
Proof	1½ hr.	Moderate: 74°–80°F. until almost doubled.
Bake	40 min.	450°F.–400°F. With steam.
Cool	20 min.	On rack.

Cumulative Total Time: 16 hr., 55 min.

PAIN AUX NOIX (WITH HAZELNUTS)

Allow 4 to 8 hours to ferment the *poolish*.
Total preparation and baking time (not including the *poolish*):
6 hours, 35 minutes

This small, compact loaf is rich, fragrant, and studded with lots of toasted hazelnuts. It is a superlative breakfast loaf, toasted and spread with butter and preserves, or served with a soft cheese like Neufchâtel.

Makes two 8 by 4-inch loaves

POOLISH

Spring water	½ cup	4 fluid ounces
Moist yeast	1½ teaspoons	⅜ ounce
or dry yeast	¾ teaspoon	¼ ounce
Organic white flour	¾ cup	4 ounces
with germ*		
Hazelnuts	1¾ cups	7 ounces

FINAL DOUGH

Spring water	½ cup	4 fluid ounces
Moist yeast	1½ teaspoons	⅜ ounce
or dry yeast	¾ teaspoon	¼ ounce
Milk	½ cup	4 fluid ounces
Honey, preferably	¼ cup	1 ounce
wildflower		
Whole wheat flour,*	1 cup	5½ ounces
preferably coarse		
ground		
Unsalted butter,	2 tablespoons	2 ounces
softened		
Fine sea salt	2 teaspoons	½ ounce
Organic white flour	2½ cups	13 ounces
with germ*		
Milk, for brushing tops	1 tablespoon	

* See Flours (pages 42–49). These are good approximate measures. You may use more or less depending on the weight and absorbency of your flours.

MAKE AND FERMENT THE *POOLISH* (allow 4 to 8 hours) Combine the water and yeast in a medium bowl. Let stand 1 minute, then stir with a wooden spoon until yeast dissolves. Add the flour and stir until the consistency of a thick batter. Continue stirring for about 100 strokes or until the strands of gluten come off the spoon when you press the back of the spoon against the bowl. Scrape down the sides of the bowl with a rubber spatula. Cover with a clean damp towel or plastic wrap, and put in a moderately warm (74°–80°F.) draft-free place until it is bubbly and increased in volume.

PREPARE THE HAZELNUTS (1 hour) Preheat the oven to 350°F. Arrange the nuts on a baking sheet and bake, stirring once or twice, until the skins are cracked, 10 to 12 minutes. Wrap the nuts in a kitchen towel and let stand 20 minutes. Use the towel to rub as much of the skins off the nuts as possible. Place the skinned nuts in the freezer to cool completely.

Place ½ cup of the hazelnuts in the container of a food processor.

Process by pulsing until fine. Set aside.

Coarsely chop remaining hazelnuts. Set aside.

MIX AND KNEAD THE FINAL DOUGH (25 minutes) Measure the ingredients and calculate the necessary temperatures (see page 58). Transfer to a 6-quart bowl. Add the water and yeast. Break up the *poolish* well with a wooden spoon and stir until it loosens and the mixture foams slightly. Add the ground hazelnuts, chopped hazelnuts, milk, honey, whole wheat flour, and butter; stir until well combined. Add the salt and enough of the white flour to make a thick mass that is difficult to stir. Turn out onto a well-floured surface. Knead, adding more of the remaining flour when needed, until dough is soft and smooth, 15 to 17 minutes. (Or make in a heavy-duty mixer; see page 67.) The dough is ready when a small amount pulled from the mass springs back quickly (see Kneading, page 66).

FERMENT THE DOUGH (2 to 2½ hours) Shape the dough into a ball and let it rest on a lightly floured surface while you scrape, clean, and lightly oil the large bowl. Place the dough in the bowl and turn the dough to coat the top with oil. Take the dough's temperature: the ideal is 78°F. (see page 58). Cover with a clean damp towel or plastic wrap and put in a moderately warm (74°–80°F.) draft-free place until doubled in volume.

(continued)

Note: If the dough temperature is higher than 78°F., put it in a cooler than 78°F. place like the refrigerator, until the dough cools to 78°F. If it is lower than 78°F., put it in a warmer than 78°F. place until the dough warms to 78°F. The point is to try to keep the dough at 78°F. during its fermentation. If you do have to move the dough, be gentle and don't jostle it, or the dough may deflate.

The dough has risen enough when a finger poked ½ inch into the dough leaves indentation.

FERMENT A SECOND TIME (1½ to 2 hours) Deflate by pushing down in the center and pulling up on the sides. Cover again with a clean, damp towel or plastic wrap and put in a moderately warm (74°–80°F.) draft-free place until doubled in volume.

DIVIDE THE DOUGH AND SHAPE INTO LOAVES (5 minutes) Deflate the dough by pushing down in the center and pulling up on the sides. Transfer the dough to a lightly floured work surface and knead briefly. Cut into 2 equal pieces. Flatten each with the heel of your hand using firm direct strokes. Shape into 8-inch-long logs, sealing firmly and pinching closed (see Taking Shape, page 68).

PROOF THE LOAVES (about 1 hour) Lightly butter two 8 × 4 × 2½-inch loaf pans. Place the loaves in the pans seam side down. Cover with a clean damp towel or plastic wrap and put in a moderately warm (74°–80°F.) draft-free place until increased in volume about 1½ times.

BAKE THE LOAVES (30 minutes) Forty-five minutes to 1 hour before baking, preheat the oven and homemade hearth or baking stone on the center rack of the oven (see Equipment, page 52) to 400°F.

The oven rack must be in the center of the oven. If it is in the lower third of the oven, the bottoms of the breads may burn, and if it is in the upper third, the top crusts may burn.

Using a very sharp, serrated knife or a single-edged razor blade, score the loaves by making quick shallow cuts ¼ to ½ inch deep along the surface.

Place the loaves one at a time onto the hearth and quickly spray the inner walls and floor of the oven with cold water from a spritzer bottle. If there's an electric light bulb in the oven, avoid spraying it directly—it may burst. Spray for several seconds until steam has filled the oven. Quickly close the door to trap the steam and bake 3 minutes. Spray again in the same way, closing the door immediately so that steam doesn't escape. Bake until loaves are golden, 25 to 30 minutes.

To test the loaves for doneness, remove from their pans and hold the loaves upside down. Strike the bottoms firmly with your finger. If the sound is hollow, the breads are done. If it doesn't sound hollow, bake 5 minutes longer. Cool in the pans for 10 minutes, then remove and cool completely on a wire rack.

PAIN AUX NOIX (WITH HAZELNUTS)

Task	Approximate Time	Comments
Preparation	4 hr.	Ferment *poolish*.
Preparation	10 min.	Assemble ingredients. Mix.
Knead	15 min.	Check temperature of final dough.
Ferment	2 hr., 30 min.	Moderate: 74°–80°F. until doubled.
Ferment	2 hr.	Moderate: 74°–80°F.
Divide	5 min.	Cut into 2 equal pieces.
Shape	5 min.	Into logs and press into prepared pans.
Proof	1 hr.	Moderate: 74°–80°F. until increased 1½ times.
Bake	30 min.	With steam. 400°F.
Cool	20 min.	Unmold on rack.

Cumulative Total Time: 6 hr., 55 min.

CHOCOLATE-APRICOT KUGELHOPF

Allow 1 hour to ferment the *poolish*.
Total preparation and baking time (including the *poolish*):
5 hours, 20 minutes

Kugelhopf, an Alsatian yeast-risen coffee cake, baked in a fluted tube mold, comes in a mouthwatering array of variations. Here's my version embellished with bittersweet chocolate, coffee, and dried apricots. This dough requires a heavy-duty electric mixer.

Makes 1 large 9-inch coffee cake, 8 to 12 servings

POOLISH

Milk, at room temperature	1 cup	8 fluid ounces
Moist yeast	2 teaspoons	½ ounce
or dry yeast	1 teaspoon	¼ ounce
Organic white flour with germ*	1 cup	5 ounces

FINAL DOUGH

Sugar	½ cup	3½ ounces
2 large eggs, at room temperature		
Organic white flour with germ*	3¾ cups	20 ounces
Unsalted butter, softened, cut into 8 pieces	8 tablespoons	4 ounces
Fine sea salt	2 teaspoons	½ ounce

FILLING

Light brown sugar	½ cup	3 ounces
Bittersweet chocolate, finely chopped	1 cup	5 ounces
Dried apricots, finely chopped	1 cup	6 ounces
Instant coffee powder	2 teaspoons	
Unsalted butter, melted	2 tablespoons	1 ounce

* See Flours (pages 42–49). This is a good approximate measure. You may use more or less depending on the weight and absorbency of your flour.

MAKE AND FERMENT THE *POOLISH* (allow 1 hour) Combine the milk, yeast, and flour in a medium bowl. Let stand 1 minute, then stir with a wooden spoon about 100 strokes or until mixture is the consistency of a smooth batter. Scrape down the sides of the bowl with a rubber spatula. Cover with a clean damp towel or plastic wrap, and put in a moderately warm (74°–80°F.) draft-free place until it is puffy and domed.

MIX AND KNEAD THE FINAL DOUGH (15 minutes) Measure out the ingredients and calculate the necessary temperatures (see page 58). Transfer the *poolish* to the bowl of a heavy-duty mixer fitted with a paddle blade. Add the sugar, eggs, and flour. Beat on medium-low speed 5 minutes. Gradually beat in the butter pieces and continue beating 8 minutes. The dough will be slightly sticky, soft, and silky. If the dough seems too moist, gradually beat in more flour. It will spring back when pressed with a finger.

FERMENT THE DOUGH (1½ to 2 hours) Shape the dough into a ball and place smooth side down in a well buttered 6-quart bowl. Turn the dough to coat the top with butter. Take the dough's temperature: the ideal is 78°F. (see page 58). Cover with a clean damp towel or plastic wrap and put in a moderately warm (74°–80°F.) draft-free place until doubled in volume.

> *Note: If the dough temperature is higher than 78°F., put it in a cooler than 78°F. place like the refrigerator, until the dough cools to 78°F. If it is lower than 78°F., put it in a warmer than 78°F. place until the dough warms to 78°F. The point is to try to keep the dough at 78°F. during its fermentation. If you do have to move the dough, be gentle and don't jostle it, or the dough may deflate.*

MAKE THE FILLING (5 minutes) Combine the brown sugar, chocolate, apricots, and coffee in a small bowl. Set aside.

DIVIDE THE DOUGH AND SHAPE (10 minutes) Generously butter the inside of a 9-inch Kugelhopf mold or fluted 10-inch tube pan. Deflate the dough by pushing down in the center and pulling

(continued)

up on the sides. Transfer the dough to a well-floured work surface and knead briefly. Using a rolling pin, roll out the dough to a 12 × 24-inch rectangle. (If dough is too elastic to roll out, cover and let rest for 5 minutes before proceeding.) Brush the dough with the melted butter. Sprinkle with the chocolate filling mixture, leaving a 1-inch border on all sides. Starting at the long end, roll up tightly lengthwise, gently stretching the dough to 26 inches. Using a sharp knife, cut the roll into fifteen 1½-inch-wide slices.

Stand 7 of the slices upright in the prepared pan. The cut sides should face the sides of the pan. They need not fit tightly. Arrange the remaining 8 slices upright on top of the first layer.

PROOF THE LOAF (1½ to 2 hours) Cover dough with a clean damp towel or plastic wrap and put in a moderately warm (74°–80°F.) draft-free place until almost doubled in volume.

BAKE THE LOAF (35 to 45 minutes) Forty-five minutes to 1 hour before baking, preheat the oven and homemade hearth or baking stone on the center rack of the oven (see Equipment, page 52) to 350°F.

Bake until the top is dark golden brown, 35 to 45 minutes. (Cover the top of the bread loosely with foil if the bread is browning too quickly.) To test for doneness tap the top crust with a fingertip. If it doesn't sound hollow, bake 5 minutes longer. If it sounds hollow the bread is done. Unmold the bread onto a wire cake and cool completely.

CHOCOLATE-APRICOT KUGELHOPF

Task	Approximate Time	Comments
Prepreparation	1 hr.	Ferment *poolish*.
Preparation	5 min.	Assemble ingredients. Mix.
Knead	15 min.	In mixer.
Ferment	2 hr.	Moderate: 74°–80°F. until doubled.
Shape	10 min.	Roll out, cut, and arrange pieces in mold.
Proof	2 hr.	Moderate: 74°–80°F. until doubled.
Bake	45 min.	350°F.
Glaze	5 min.	On cake rack.
Cool	Completely	

Cumulative Total Time: 5 hr., 20 min.

FRUITED BARLEY MALT BREAD

Allow 8 hours to ferment the *poolish*.
Total preparation and baking times, (not including *poolish*):
6 hours, 5 minutes

Peggy Cullen, a well-known Manhattan baker, suggested using barley malt as a sweetener and flavor base for a new bread. What a terrific idea it turned out to be! She and I developed a country loaf with malt's earthy sweet flavor and the fruity accent of apples and raisins. I include it in this section as an easier-to-make version of *Pain Normande* (page 251).

Makes 2 round 7-inch loaves

POOLISH

Spring water (75°F.)	1 cup	8 fluid ounces
Moist yeast	1 teaspoon	¼ ounce
or dry yeast	½ teaspoon	⅛ ounce
Whole wheat flour,* preferably coarse ground	½ cup	2¾ ounces
Organic white flour with germ*	½ cup	2½ ounces

FINAL DOUGH

Spring water	1½ cups	12 ounces
Barley malt syrup (see Note)	⅓ cup	2¾ ounces
Moist yeast	1 teaspoon	¼ ounce
or dry yeast	½ teaspoon	⅛ ounce
Rolled oats	1½ cups	5 ounces
Ground cinnamon	½ teaspoon	
Fine sea salt	1 tablespoon	¾ ounce
20% bran wheat flour*	5–6 cups	25–30 ounces
Dried apples, coarsely chopped	1 cup	2 ounces
Seedless dark raisins	1 cup	5 ounces
Cornmeal, for dusting		

* See Flours (pages 42–49). These are good approximate measures. You may use more or less depending on the weight and absorbency of your flours.

Note: *Barley malt syrup is available in natural foods stores. Do not use diastalic malt syrup, which is too strong.*

MAKE AND FERMENT THE *POOLISH* (allow 2 to 8 hours) Combine the water and yeast in a medium bowl. Let stand 1 minute, then stir with a wooden spoon until yeast is dissolved. Add the whole wheat and white flours. Stir until the consistency of a thick batter. Continue stirring for about 100 strokes or until the strands of gluten come off the spoon when you press the back of the spoon against the bowl. Scrape down the sides of the bowl with a rubber spatula. Cover with a clean damp towel or plastic wrap, and put in a moderately warm (74°–80°F.) draft-free place until it is bubbly and increased in volume.

MIX AND KNEAD THE FINAL DOUGH (25 minutes) Measure the ingredients and calculate the necessary temperatures (see page 58). Transfer the *poolish* to a 6-quart bowl. Add the water, barley malt syrup, and yeast. Break up the *poolish* well with a wooden spoon and stir until it loosens and the mixture foams slightly. Add the oats, cinnamon, salt, and enough of the bran flour to make a thick mass that is difficult to stir. Turn out onto a well-floured surface. Knead, adding more of the remaining flour when needed, until dough is fairly soft, 12 minutes. Gradually knead in the apples and raisins, and continue kneading until dough is soft and smooth, 15 to 17 minutes total. (Or make in a heavy-duty mixer; see page 67.) The dough is ready when a small amount pulled from the mass springs back quickly (see Kneading and Kneading In, pages 66 and 76).

FERMENT THE DOUGH (2 to 3 hours) Shape the dough into a ball and let it rest on a lightly floured surface while you scrape, clean, and lightly oil the large bowl. Place the dough in the bowl and turn the dough to coat the top with oil. Take the dough's temperature: the ideal is 78°F. (see page 58). Cover with a clean damp towel or plastic wrap and place in a moderately warm (74°–80°F.) draft-free place until almost doubled in volume.

(continued)

Note: If the dough temperature is higher than 78°F., put it in a cooler than 78°F. place like the refrigerator, until the dough cools to 78°F. If it is lower than 78°F., put it in a warmer than 78°F. place until the dough warms to 78°F. The point is to try to keep the dough at 78°F. during its fermentation. If you do have to move the dough, be gentle and don't jostle it, or the dough may deflate.

DIVIDE AND SHAPE THE DOUGH INTO LOAVES (10 minutes) Deflate the dough by pushing down in the center and pulling up on the sides. Transfer the dough to a lightly floured work surface and cut into 2 equal pieces. Knead briefly and flatten each with the heel of your hand using firm direct strokes. Shape each piece into a tight ball for round loaves (see Taking Shape, page 68).

PROOF THE LOAVES (1½ to 2 hours) Place on a board lightly dusted with cornmeal. Cover with a clean damp towel or plastic wrap and place in a moderately warm (74°–80°F) draft-free place until increased in volume about 1½ times.

BAKE THE LOAVES (about 35 minutes) Forty-five minutes to 1 hour before baking, preheat the oven and homemade hearth or baking stone on the center rack of the oven (see Equipment, page 52) to 425°F.

The oven rack must be in the center of the oven. If it is in the lower third of the oven, the bottoms of the breads may burn, and if it is in the upper third, the top crusts may burn.

Using a very sharp, serrated knife or a single-edged razor blade, score the loaves by making quick shallow cuts ¼ to ½ inch deep along the surface. Using a floured peel, slide the loaves one at a time onto the hearth and quickly spray the inner walls and floor of the oven with cold water from a spritzer bottle. If there's an electric light bulb in the oven, avoid spraying it directly—it may burst. Spray for several seconds until steam has filled the oven. Quickly close the door to trap the steam and bake 3 minutes. Spray again in the same way, closing the door immediately so that steam doesn't escape. Bake until loaves are a rich caramel color and the crusts are firm, 30 to 35 minutes.

To test the loaves for doneness, remove and hold the loaves upside down. Strike the bottoms firmly with your finger. If the sound is hollow, breads are done. If it doesn't sound hollow, bake 5 minutes longer. Cool completely on a wire rack.

FRUITED BARLEY MALT BREAD

Task	Approximate Time	Comments
Prepreparation	8 hr.	Ferment *poolish*.
Preparation	10 min.	Assemble ingredients. Mix.
Knead	15 min.	Take temperature of final dough.
Ferment	3 hr.	Moderate: 74°–80°F. until doubled.
Divide	5 min.	In 2 equal pieces.
Shape		In balls for round loaves.
Proof	2 hr.	Moderate: 74°–80°F. until increased 1½ times.
Bake	35 min.	With steam. 425°F.
Cool	20 min.	On rack or in basket.

Cumulative Total Time: 6 hr., 25 min.

PANETTONE

Allow 8 hours to soak the fruits.
Allow 1 hour to ferment the *poolish*.
Total preparation and baking time (not including fermenting the *poolish* or soaking the fruits):
7 hours, 15 minutes

A classic in Italy and France at holiday time, this bread is so light and well packed with fruit that it's almost a confection. It's good anytime you want something sweet with tea or coffee. I make it in a springform pan, as authentic panettone pans are difficult to locate. If you have one, use my recipe in a well-buttered mold, but experiment with the baking time—it may take longer.

Makes 1 round 10-inch loaf

FRUIT

Seedless golden raisins	½ cup	3 ounces
Seedless dark raisins	½ cup	3 ounces
Black Mission figs, cut in ½-inch pieces	½ cup	3 ounces
Calimyrna figs, cut in ½-inch pieces	½ cup	3 ounces
Cognac	¾ cup	6 fluid ounces

POOLISH

Milk, at room temperature	½ cup	4 fluid ounces
Moist yeast	4 teaspoons	1 ounce
or dry yeast	2 teaspoons	½ ounce
Organic all-purpose white flour*	¾ cup	4 ounces

FINAL DOUGH

Unsalted butter, softened	9 tablespoons	4½ ounces
Sugar	⅓ cup	2¼ ounces
½ vanilla bean, halved horizontally, or vanilla extract	1 teaspoon	
2 large eggs, at room temperature		
4 egg yolks, at room temperature		

Fine sea salt	½ teaspoon	
Organic all-purpose white flour*	3–4 cups	15–20 ounces
Unsalted butter, melted	2 tablespoons	1 ounce

* See Flours (pages 42–49). These are good approximate measures. You may use more or less depending on the weight and absorbency of your flour.

PREPARE THE DRIED FRUIT (allow 8 hours or overnight) Combine the raisins and figs in a bowl. Heat the cognac in a small saucepan until just warm, then pour over raisin mixture. Set aside at least 8 hours or overnight. Stir occasionally if possible.

MAKE AND FERMENT THE *POOLISH* (allow 1 hour) Combine the milk and yeast in a medium bowl. Stir with a wooden spoon until yeast dissolves. Add the flour and stir until the mixture is the consistency of a batter, about 100 strokes. Scrape down the sides of the bowl with a rubber spatula. Cover with a clean damp towel or plastic wrap, and put in a moderately warm (74°–80°F.) draft-free place until it is puffy and domed.

MIX AND KNEAD THE FINAL DOUGH (20 minutes) Measure the ingredients and calculate the necessary temperatures (see page 58). Combine the butter and sugar in the bowl of a heavy-duty mixer fitted with a paddle blade. Beat on medium speed until smooth, about 1½ minutes. Using the tip of a small sharp knife, scrape the seeds out of the vanilla bean. Discard the pod, or use in Vanilla Bean Butter Loaf (page 310). Add the *poolish,* eggs and egg yolks, salt, and vanilla seeds; beat on medium speed 5 minutes, then gradually add 1 cup (5 ounces) of the flour. Fit the mixer with the dough hook. Add 2½ cups (12½ ounces) of the remaining flour and continue beating at medium speed for 10 minutes. Drain the fruit well, if necessary, and add, beating 2 minutes more. Turn out onto a lightly floured surface and knead, until smooth and slightly sticky, adding more flour if necessary, about 3 minutes.

FERMENT THE DOUGH (about 2½ hours) Shape the dough into a ball and place smooth side down in a well-buttered 6-quart bowl.

(continued)

Turn the dough to coat the top with butter. Take the dough's temperature: the ideal is 78°F. (see page 58). Cover with a clean damp towel or plastic wrap and place in a moderately warm (74°–80°F.) draft-free place until doubled in volume.

> *Note: If the dough temperature is higher than 78°F., put it in a cooler than 78°F. place like the refrigerator, until the dough cools to 78°F. If it is lower than 78°F., put it in a warmer than 78°F. place until the dough warms to 78°F. The point is to try to keep the dough at 78°F. during its fermentation. If you do have to move the dough, be gentle and don't jostle it, or the dough may deflate.*

DIVIDE THE DOUGH AND SHAPE INTO A LOAF (10 minutes) Deflate the dough by pushing down in the center and pulling up on the sides. Transfer the dough to a lightly floured work surface and knead briefly. Shape into a log (see Taking Shape, page 68).

PROOF THE LOAF (2 to 3 hours) Butter a 10-inch springform pan or panettone pan. Press the loaf into the prepared pan. Cover with a clean damp towel or plastic wrap and put in a moderately warm (74°–80°F.) draft-free place until the dough rises nearly to the rim of the pan.

BAKE THE LOAF (45 minutes) Forty-five minutes to 1 hour before baking, preheat the oven and homemade hearth or baking stone on the center rack of the oven (see Equipment, page 52) to 400°F.

Bake 20 minutes. Cover the top loosely with foil and continue baking until the loaf is golden brown and a toothpick inserted in the center comes out clean, about 25 minutes. Remove from oven and brush the top with the melted butter. Cool on a wire rack 20 minutes. Unmold and cool completely before serving.

PANETTONE

Task	Approximate Time	Comments
Prepreparation	8–10 hr. 1 hr.	Soak the fruit. Ferment *poolish*.
Preparation	10 min.	Assemble ingredients. Calculate temperatures. Mix.
Knead	17 min. 3 min.	In mixer fitted with paddle. On floured board.
Ferment	2 hr., 30 min.	Moderate: 74°–80°F. until doubled.
Shape	5 min.	Into log and press into prepared pan.
Proof	2 hr., 30 min.	Moderate: 74°–80°F.
Bake	45 min.	400°F.
Cool	Completely	Unmolded on rack.

Cumulative Total Time: 7 hr., 15 min.

SEMOLINA SESAME ROLLS

> Allow 1½ hours to ferment the *poolish*.
> Total preparation and baking time (not including the *poolish*):
> 4 hours, 35 minutes

Golden semolina flour gives these rolls a rich color and sumptuous sweet taste. Use more sesame seeds if you like for even more crunch in the crust. If you're wondering, this recipe *will* make a large round loaf, baked for about 30 minutes at 425°F. Also, if you want more rolls, this recipe is easily doubled.

Makes 8 rolls

POOLISH

Spring water (75°F.)	½ cup	4 fluid ounces
Moist yeast	1½ teaspoons	⅜ ounce
or dry yeast	¾ teaspoon	³⁄₁₆ ounce
Organic white flour with germ*	½ cup	2½ ounces

FINAL DOUGH

Spring water	½ cup	4 fluid ounces
Moist yeast	2 teaspoons	½ ounce
or dry yeast	1 teaspoon	¼ ounce
Sugar	1 teaspoon	
Semolina flour* (not Semolina meal)	1 cup	6½ ounces
Fine sea salt	2 teaspoons	
Organic white flour with germ*	1½–2 cups	7½–10 ounces
1 egg white, lightly beaten		
Sesame seeds	4 teaspoons	
Semolina meal or cornmeal, for dusting		

---

* See Flours (pages 42–49). These are good approximate measures. You may use more or less depending on the weight and absorbency of your flours.

MAKE AND FERMENT THE *POOLISH* (allow 1½ hours) Combine the water and yeast in a medium bowl. Let stand 1 minute, then stir with a wooden spoon until yeast is dissolved. Add the flour and stir until the consistency of a thick batter. Continue stirring for about

100 strokes or until the strands of gluten come off the spoon when you press the back of the spoon against the bowl. Scrape down the sides of the bowl with a rubber spatula. Cover with a clean damp towel or plastic wrap, and put in a moderately warm (74°–80°F.) draft-free place until it is puffy, bubbly, and domed.

MIX AND KNEAD THE FINAL DOUGH (20 minutes) Measure the ingredients and calculate the necessary temperatures (see page 58). Transfer the *poolish* to a 6-quart bowl. Add the water and yeast. Break up the *poolish* well with a wooden spoon and stir until it loosens and the mixture foams slightly. Add the sugar, semolina flour, salt, and 1 cup (5 ounces) white flour; stir to make a thick mass that is soft but sturdy. Turn out onto a lightly floured surface. Knead, adding more of the remaining flour when needed, until dough is soft and smooth, 15 to 17 minutes. The dough is ready when a small amount pulled from the mass springs back quickly (see Kneading, page 68).

FERMENT THE DOUGH (1½ to 2 hours) Shape the dough into a ball and let it rest on a lightly floured surface while you scrape, clean, and lightly oil the large bowl. Place the dough in the bowl and turn the dough to coat the top with oil. Take the dough's temperature: the ideal is 78°F. (see page 58). Cover with a clean damp towel or plastic wrap and place in a moderately warm (74°–80°F.) draft-free place until doubled in volume, and a slight indentation remains after pressing a finger into the dough.

> *Note: If the dough temperature is higher than 78°F., put it in a cooler than 78°F. place like the refrigerator, until the dough cools to 78°F. If it is lower than 78°F., place it in a warmer than 78°F. place until the dough warms to 78°F. The point is to try to keep the dough at 78°F. during its fermentation. If you do have to move the dough, be gentle and don't jostle it, or the dough may deflate.*

FERMENT THE DOUGH A SECOND TIME (1 hour) Deflate the dough by pushing down in the center and pulling up on the sides. Cover with a clean damp towel or plastic wrap and place in a moderately warm (74°–80°F.) draft-free place.

(continued)

DIVIDE THE DOUGH AND SHAPE INTO ROLLS (10 minutes) Deflate the dough and turn onto a lightly floured board. Knead briefly. Divide the dough into eight (2½- to 3-ounce) pieces. Flatten each with the heel of your hand and shape into tight golf–ball-sized balls (see Taking Shape, page 68). Place on a board dusted with semolina meal or cornmeal.

PROOF THE ROLLS (45 minutes) Cover with a clean, damp towel or plastic wrap and place in a moderately warm (74°–80°F) draft-free place until almost doubled in volume, and a slight indentation remains when the dough is pressed with a fingertip.

BAKE THE ROLLS (about 20 minutes) Forty-five minutes to 1 hour before baking, preheat the oven and homemade hearth or baking stone on the center rack of the oven (see Equipment, page 52) to 425°F.

The oven rack must be in the center of the oven. If it is in the lower third of the oven, the bottoms of the breads may burn, and if it is in the upper third, the top crusts may burn.

Brush the rolls lightly with the egg white and sprinkle with sesame seeds. Using a floured peel, slide the rolls a few at a time onto the hearth. Quickly spray the inner walls and floor of the oven with cold water from a spritzer bottle. If there's an electric light bulb in the oven, avoid spraying it directly—it may burst. Spray for several seconds until steam has filled the oven. Quickly close the door to trap the steam and bake 3 minutes. Spray again in the same way, closing the door immediately so that steam doesn't escape. Bake until rolls are a rich golden color, 15 to 20 minutes.

To test for doneness, remove and hold one roll upside down. Strike the bottom firmly with your finger. If the sound is hollow, allow the rolls to cool on a wire rack. If it doesn't sound hollow, bake 5 minutes longer. Cool on a rack.

SEMOLINA SESAME ROLLS

Task	Approximate Time	Comments
Preparation	1 hr., 30 min.	Ferment *poolish*.
Preparation	5 min.	Assemble ingredients. Calculate temperatures. Mix.
Knead	15 min.	Take temperature of final dough.
Ferment	2 hr.	Moderate: 74°–80°F. until doubled.
Ferment	1 hr.	Moderate: 74°–80°F.
Divide	5 min.	Cut into 8 pieces 2½ ounces each.
Shape	5 min.	Into tight balls for rolls.
Proof	45 min.	Moderate: 74°–80°F.
Bake	20 min.	With steam. 425°F.
Cool	10 min.	On rack.

Cumulative Total Time: 4 hr. 45 min.

CLASSIC *FOCACCIA*

Allow the dough to ferment 8 hours.
Total preparation and baking time (not including the fermentation of the dough):
3 hours, 45 minutes

This is the large, flat round bread—crusty, thick, and chewy moist—that most of us associate with pizza. But in Italy it's often just brushed with olive oil, sprinkled with coarse salt, and enjoyed as a snack or with soups and salads. My version is a soft dough that works best when made in a heavy-duty mixer.

Makes 2 flat 10-inch round loaves

Spring water	1¾ cups	14 fluid ounces
Fresh yeast	2 teaspoons	½ ounce
or dry yeast	1 teaspoon	¼ ounce
Organic white flour with germ*	3½–4½ cups	18–22 ounces
Whole wheat flour,* preferably coarse ground	¼ cup	1⅜ ounces
Olive oil	¼ cup	
Fine sea salt	2 teaspoons	
Cornmeal for dusting		
Topping of choice (page 280)		

---

* See Flours (pages 42–49). These are good approximate measures. You may use more or less depending on the weight and absorbency of your flours.

MIX AND KNEAD THE FINAL DOUGH (20 minutes) Measure the ingredients and calculate the necessary temperatures (see page 58). Combine the water and yeast in the bowl of a heavy-duty mixer fitted with a paddle. Let stand for 1 minute, then beat at low speed until the yeast dissolves. Add the white flour, whole wheat flour, oil, and salt; beat until just combined. Replace the paddle with a dough hook. Continue mixing at medium-low speed, adding remaining flour if needed until dough is well developed, about 15 minutes. This will be a very soft and sticky dough and it will probably not clean the sides of the bowl until the full 15 minutes of mixing. (See Kneading in the Mixer, page 68.)

FERMENT THE DOUGH (8 hours or overnight) Shape the dough into a ball and place in a lightly oiled 6-quart bowl, turning the dough once to coat the top with oil. Cover with plastic wrap and place in the refrigerator.

WARM THE DOUGH (2 hours) Place the bowl with the dough in a moderately warm (74°–80°F.) draft-free place and allow to come to room temperature.

SHAPE THE LOAVES (5 minutes) Deflate the dough by pushing down in the center and pulling up on the sides. Turn onto a lightly floured surface and knead briefly. Cut into 2 equal portions and shape into tight balls. Place on a 12-inch square of parchment paper that has been lightly dusted.

Flatten each ball with the heel of your hand into a disk and dust the top of the dough with flour. Using a rolling pin, roll out the dough directly onto the parchment paper into 10-inch circles about ½ inch thick.

PROOF THE LOAVES (1 hour) Cover with a clean damp towel or plastic wrap and place in a moderately warm (74°–80°F.) draft-free place until doubled in thickness, or until a slight indentation remains when the dough is pressed with a fingertip.

PREPARE THE TOPPING (20 minutes) Prepare the topping according to recipe instructions.

BAKE THE LOAVES (about 20 minutes) Forty-five minutes to 1 hour before baking, preheat the oven and homemade hearth or baking stone on the center rack of the oven (see Equipment, page 52) to 400°F.

The oven rack must be in the center of the oven. If it is in the lower third of the oven, the bottoms of the breads may burn, and if it is in the upper third, the top crusts may burn.

Work with one dough at a time, keeping the other dough covered. Deflate the dough by rolling out directly on the parchment paper to ½ inch thickness. Finger-poke one of the doughs in a ran-

(continued)

dom pattern of dimples. Add the topping, and using the peel and/or board or rimless baking sheet, slide the breads, still on the parchment paper, one at a time onto the hearth. Quickly spray the inner walls and floor of the oven with cold water from a spritzer bottle. If there's an electric light bulb in the oven, avoid spraying it directly—it may burst. Spray for several seconds until steam has filled the oven. Quickly close the door to trap the steam and bake 3 minutes. Spray again in the same way, closing the door immediately so that steam doesn't escape. Bake until rich golden in color, 15 to 20 minutes. Cool briefly on a rack. Repeat with the second *focaccia*. Serve warm.

CLASSIC *FOCACCIA*

Task	Approximate Time	Comments
Preparation	5 min.	Assemble ingredients. Calculate temperatures. Mix.
Knead	15 min.	In mixer.
Ferment	8 hr.	Cold: In refrigerator.
Warm to room temperature	2 hr	Cut into 2 equal pieces.
Shape	5 min.	Roll out into disks.
Proof	1 hr.	Moderate: 74°–80°F. until doubled.
Bake	20 min.	With steam. 400°F.
Cool	5 min.	Serve warm.

Cumulative Total Time: 11 hr., 45 min.

MIXED-GRAIN *FOCACCIA*

Allow the dough to ferment 8 hours.
Total preparation and baking time (not including the fermentation of the dough):
4 hours, 10 minutes

This is a darker and chewier *focaccia* with the nutlike flavor of whole wheat and the added depth of rye. The final dough is very soft and slightly wet, so I recommend kneading in the mixer. This is delicious by itself warm from the hearth.

Makes 2 round 10-inch focaccia

Spring water	1¾ cups	14 fluid ounces
Fresh yeast	2 teaspoons	½ ounce
or dry yeast	1 teaspoon	¼ ounce
Whole wheat flour,* preferably coarse ground	⅓ cup	1⅔ ounces
Rye flour,* preferably coarse ground	⅔ cup	3⅔ ounces
Organic white flour with germ*	3–4 cups	15–21 ounces
Olive oil	¼ cup	
Fine sea salt	2 teaspoons	
Topping of choice (page 280)		

* See Flours (pages 42–49). These are good approximate measures. You may use more or less depending on the weight and absorbency of your flours.

MIX AND KNEAD THE FINAL DOUGH (20 minutes) Measure the ingredients and calculate the necessary temperatures (see page 58). Combine the water and yeast in the bowl of a heavy-duty mixer fitted with a paddle. Let stand for 1 minute, then beat at low speed until the yeast is dissolved. Add the whole wheat and rye flours, 3 cups (15 ounces) of the white flour, oil, and salt; beat until just combined. Replace the paddle with a dough hook. Continue mixing at medium-low speed, adding remaining flour as needed until dough is well developed, about 15 minutes. This will be a very soft and sticky dough and it will probably not clean the sides of the bowl until the full 15 minutes of mixing (see Kneading in the Mixer, page 67).

(continued)

FERMENT THE DOUGH (8 hours or overnight) Shape the dough into a ball and place in a lightly oiled 6-quart bowl, turning the dough once to coat the top with oil. Cover with a clean damp towel or plastic wrap and place in the refrigerator.

WARM THE DOUGH (2 hours) Put the bowl with the dough in a moderately warm (74°–80°F.) draft-free place and allow to come to room temperature.

SHAPE THE LOAVES (5 minutes) Deflate the dough by pushing down in the center and pulling up on the sides. Turn onto a lightly floured surface and knead briefly. Cut into 2 equal portions and shape into tight balls. Place on a 12-inch square of parchment paper that has been lightly dusted.

Flatten each ball with the heel of your hand into a disk and dust the top of the dough with flour. Using a rolling pin, roll out the dough directly onto the parchment paper into 10-inch circles about ½ inch thick.

PROOF THE LOAVES (1½ to 2 hours) Cover with a clean damp towel or plastic wrap and place in a moderately warm (74°–80°F.) draft-free place until doubled in thickness, or until a slight indentation remains when the dough is pressed with a fingertip.

PREPARE THE TOPPING (20 minutes) Prepare a topping according to the recipe.

BAKE THE LOAVES (about 15 minutes) Forty-five minutes to 1 hour before baking, preheat the oven and homemade hearth or baking stone on the center rack of the oven (see Equipment, page 52) to 400°F.

The oven rack must be in the center of the oven. If it is in the lower third of the oven, the bottoms of the breads may burn, and if it is in the upper third, the top crusts may burn.

Work with one dough at a time, keeping the other dough covered. Deflate the dough by rolling out directly on the parchment paper to ½ inch thickness. Finger-poke the dough in a random pattern of dimples. Add the topping, and using the peel and/or board or rimless baking sheet, slide the *focaccia,* still on the parchment paper, one at a time onto the hearth. Quickly spray the inner walls and floor of the oven with cold water from a spritzer bottle. If there's an electric light bulb in the oven, avoid spraying it directly—it may burst. Spray for several seconds until steam has filled the oven. Quickly close the door to trap the steam and bake 3 minutes. Spray again in the same way, closing the door immediately so that steam doesn't escape. Bake until rich golden in color, 12 to 15 minutes. Cool briefly on a rack. Repeat with the second *focaccia.* Serve warm.

MIXED-GRAIN *FOCACCIA*

Task	Approximate Time	Comments
Preparation	5 min.	Assemble ingredients. Calculate temperatures. Mix.
Knead	15 min.	In mixer.
Ferment	8 hr.	Cold: In refrigerator.
Warm to room temperature	2 hr.	Cut into 2 equal pieces.
Shape	5 min.	Roll out into disks.
Proof	1 hr., 30 min.	Moderate: 74°–80°F. until doubled.
Bake	15 min.	With steam. 400°F.
Cool	5 min.	Serve warm.

Cumulative Total Time: 12 hr., 25 min.

FOCACCIA TOPPINGS

Fresh ingredients are the key to making a good *focaccia* topping, and the summer garden is perfect for collecting the makings. The next important ingredient is your imagination. Combine any ingredients you like and enjoy. These toppings are some of my favorites.

CLASSIC OLIVE OIL AND SALT TOPPING

2 tablespoons olive oil
1 tablespoon coarse salt

Brush dough with oil. Sprinkle with salt.

Makes enough for 2 focaccia

SLICED ONION AND GARLIC TOPPING

1 large onion, sliced very thin,
6 large cloves garlic, sliced very thin
3 tablespoons olive oil
2 teaspoons coarse salt

Combine the onion and garlic in a medium bowl. Toss with half the olive oil. Brush dough with remaining oil. Sprinkle onion-garlic mixture evenly over, then sprinkle with salt.

Makes enough for 2 focaccia

CHEESY NEW POTATO, FRESH BASIL, AND SUN-DRIED TOMATO TOPPING

3 tablespoons olive oil
1 large onion, thinly sliced
6 cloves garlic, finely chopped
6 small new potatoes, cooked and thinly sliced
3 tablespoons sun-dried tomatoes in olive oil, drained, and finely chopped
1 tablespoon chopped fresh basil
1 tablespoon chopped fresh parsley
¼ teaspoon freshly ground black pepper
3 tablespoons freshly grated Parmesan cheese

Heat 1 tablespoon of the oil in a medium skillet over medium heat. Add the onion and cook 2 minutes. Add the garlic; cook just until onion is transparent, about 2 minutes. Transfer to a bowl and toss with potatoes, tomatoes, basil, parsley, and pepper.

Brush dough with remaining 2 tablespoons olive oil. Spread potato mixture evenly over, then sprinkle with Parmesan cheese.

Makes enough for 1 focaccia

TOMATO, OLIVE, RICOTTA, AND FRESH HERB TOPPING

3 tablespoons olive oil

6 shallots, thinly sliced

6 cloves garlic, finely chopped

1 tablespoon sun-dried tomato paste, or sun-dried tomatoes in oil, drained and minced

1 cup ricotta cheese

12 Mediterranean pitted black olives, chopped

1 tablespoon chopped fresh parsley

1 teaspoon chopped fresh thyme

¼ teaspoon fine sea salt

⅛ teaspoon freshly ground black pepper

Heat 1 tablespoon of the oil in a medium skillet over medium-low heat. Add the shallots and cook 2 minutes. Add the garlic and continue to cook until shallots are transparent, about 1 minute. Cool.

Combine the tomato paste or minced tomatoes, ricotta, olives, parsley, and thyme in a medium bowl. Add the shallot mixture and toss well. Stir in salt and pepper.

Brush dough with remaining 2 tablespoons olive oil. Spread ricotta mixture evenly over *focaccia*.

Makes enough for 1 focaccia

GARLIC AND TOASTED ALMOND TOPPING

1 cup (4½ ounces) slivered almonds

6 cloves garlic, finely chopped

3 tablespoons olive oil

Coarse salt

Combine the almonds and garlic in a medium bowl. Toss with 1 tablespoon oil, then add salt to taste.

Brush the dough with the remaining 2 tablespoons oil. Spread almond mixture evenly over dough.

Makes enough for 2 focaccia

TRULY TUSCAN BREAD

Allow 10 to 24 hours to ferment the first *poolish*.
Allow 8 hours to ferment the second *poolish*.
Total preparation and baking time (not including fermenting the 2 *poolish*):
11 hours, 30 minutes

This is a robust round bread from Northern Italy that has the texture of a sourdough bread but none of the sour bite. Italian bakers ferment this dough over a two-day period, building the *poolish* very slowly. The long and slow fermentation produces a high loaf with deep golden color, a thick crust, and a moist light crumb full of large air pockets and rich grain flavor. I love eating this bread dipped in olive oil and sprinkled with salt, or as an accompaniment to fresh tomato salad. Many bakers believe that a Tuscan bread must be saltless, but I found in my travels that many Florentine bakers *do* add salt and I do, too.

Makes 2 round 10-inch loaves

FIRST *POOLISH*

Spring water (75°F.)	½ cup	4 fluid ounces
Moist or dry yeast	pinch	
20% bran wheat flour*	¾ cup	4 ounces

SECOND *POOLISH*

Spring water (75°F.)	1 cup	8 fluid ounces
Moist or dry yeast	pinch	
20% bran wheat flour*	2½ cups	12 ounces

FINAL DOUGH

Spring water	1½ cups	12 fluid ounces
Moist yeast	1 teaspoon	about ¼ ounce
or dry yeast	½ teaspoon	about ⅛ ounce
20% bran wheat flour*	5½–6½ cups	27–32 ounces
Salt	1 teaspoon	

---

* See Flours (pages 42–49). These are good approximate measures. You may use more or less depending on the weight and absorbency of your flour.

MAKE AND FERMENT THE FIRST *POOLISH* (allow 10 to 24 hours) Combine the water and yeast in a medium bowl. Let stand 1 minute, then stir with a wooden spoon until yeast is dissolved. Add the bran flour and stir until the consistency of a thick batter. Continue stirring for about 100 strokes or until the strands of gluten come off the spoon when you press the back of the spoon against the bowl. Scrape down the sides of the bowl with a rubber spatula. Cover with a clean damp towel or plastic wrap, and place in the refrigerator for at least 10 and up to 24 hours.

MAKE AND FERMENT THE SECOND *POOLISH* (allow 8 hours) Add water and yeast to the *poolish*. Stir with a wooden spoon until *poolish* becomes loose. Stir in 2 cups (10 ounces) of the flour, mixing with a wooden spoon until well combined. Turn out onto a well-floured surface and knead, adding enough of the remaining flour to make a soft dough, about 5 minutes. Form into a ball and place dough in a lightly oiled 4-quart bowl. Cover with a clean damp towel or plastic wrap and place in refrigerator for 8 hours.

WARM THE *POOLISH* AND MIX AND KNEAD THE FINAL DOUGH (2½ hours) Place the bowl with the *poolish* in a warm (80°–85°F.) place until the *poolish* comes to room temperature, about 2 hours.

Measure the ingredients and calculate the necessary temperatures (see page 58). Add the water and squeeze the *poolish* through your fingers until it is broken up and the mixture is a loose and thin consistency. Add the yeast and 1 cup (5 ounces) of the flour; stir until well combined. Add the salt and enough of the remaining flour to make a thick mass that is difficult to stir. Turn out onto a well-floured surface. Knead, adding more of the remaining flour when needed, until dough is soft and smooth, 15 to 17 minutes. (Or make in a heavy-duty mixer; see page 67.) The dough is ready when a small amount pulled from the mass springs back quickly (see Kneading, page 66).

FERMENT THE DOUGH (3 to 4 hours) Shape the dough into a ball and let it rest on a lightly floured surface while you scrape, clean, and lightly oil the large bowl. Place the dough in the bowl and turn the dough to coat the top with oil. Take the dough's temperature: the ideal is 78°F. (see page 58). Cover with a clean damp towel or plastic wrap and put in a moderately warm (74°–80°F.) draft-free place until doubled in volume.

(continued)

Note: If the dough temperature is higher than 78°F., put it in a cooler than 78°F. place like the refrigerator, until the dough cools to 78°F. If it is lower than 78°F., put it in a warmer than 78°F. place until the dough warms to 78°F. The point is to try to keep the dough at 78°F. during its fermentation. If you do have to move the dough, be gentle and don't jostle it, or the dough may deflate.

FERMENT A SECOND TIME (2 to 3 hours) Deflate the dough by pushing down in the center and pulling up on the sides. Form into a ball, return to the bowl, and cover again with a clean damp towel or plastic wrap. Place in a moderately warm (74°–80°F.) draft-free place until again doubled in volume.

DIVIDE AND SHAPE THE DOUGH INTO LOAVES (10 minutes) Deflate the dough by pushing down in the center and pulling up on the sides. Transfer the dough to a lightly floured work surface and knead briefly. Cut into 2 equal pieces. Flatten each with the heel of your hand using firm direct strokes. Shape each piece into a tight ball for round loaves (see Taking Shape, page 68).

PROOF THE LOAVES (1½ to 2 hours) Line 2 bowls or baskets about 8 inches in diameter and 3 inches deep with well-floured towels, and place the loaves smooth side down in each bowl. Cover with a clean damp towel or plastic wrap. Put in a moderately warm (74°–80°F.) draft-free place until increased in volume about 1½ times, or until a slight indentation remains when the dough is pressed with a fingertip.

BAKE THE LOAVES (30 minutes) Forty-five minutes to 1 hour before baking, preheat the oven and homemade hearth or baking stone on the center rack of the oven (see Equipment, page 52) to 425°F.

The oven rack must be in the center of the oven. If it is in the lower third of the oven, the bottoms of the breads may burn, and if it is in the upper third, the top crusts may burn.

Gently invert the loaves from the baskets or bowls onto a floured peel so that they are right side up. Using a very sharp, serrated knife or a single-edged razor blade, score the loaves by making quick shallow cuts ¼ to ½ inch deep along the surface.

Using the peel, slide the loaves one at a time onto the hearth and quickly spray the inner walls and floor of the oven with cold water from a spritzer bottle. If there's an electric light bulb in the oven, avoid spraying it directly—it may burst. Spray for several seconds until steam has filled the oven. Quickly close the door to trap the steam and bake 3 minutes. Spray again in the same way, closing the door immediately so that steam doesn't escape. Bake until loaves are a rich caramel color and the crust is firm, another 25 to 30 minutes.

To test the loaves for doneness, remove and hold the loaves upside down. Strike the bottoms firmly with your finger. If the sound is hollow, the breads are done. If it doesn't sound hollow, bake 5 minutes longer. Cool completely on a wire rack.

TRULY TUSCAN BREAD

Task	Approximate Time	Comments
Prepreparation	24 hr. 8 hr.	Ferment *poolish* #1. Ferment *poolish* #2.
Preparation	5 min.	Warm *poolish* to room temperature. Calculate temperatures. Assemble ingredients. Mix.
Knead	15 min.	Take temperature of final dough.
Ferment	4 hr.	Moderate: 74°–80°F. until doubled in volume.
Ferment	3 hr.	Moderate: Until doubled.
Divide	5 min.	Deflate and cut into 2 equal portions.
Shape	5 min.	Flatten with heel of hand. Form balls for round loaves. Place in well-floured towel-lined baskets or bowls.
Proof	1 hr., 30 min.	Moderate: 74°–80°F. until increased 1½ × in volume.
Bake	30 min.	With steam. 425°F.
Cool	20 min.	On rack or in baskets.

Cumulative Total Time: 11 hr., 50 min.

THE
BAKER'S
SECRET WEAPON
A BREAD AND WAR STORY

've been traveling recently and consulting for a supermarket chain that is building bakeries within its stores. The company is so willing to produce high-quality fresh breads that it has hired consultants—bakers like myself—from all over the world. On a recent trip to company headquarters I met an older baker from Germany who had come to teach the market bakers about the science of bread baking.

"I'm a little surprised to be here," he confided one morning. "The last time I did bread business with Americans was during the war." He and I were having coffee in the supermarket's brand-new café. The old German told me that as a very young soldier he was taken prisoner by the Allies and sent to a POW camp.

"That's when you did bread business?" I asked.

"In a manner," he said. "I was assigned to the bakers' unit. We baked the bread for the entire POW camp. There were a lot of prisoners to feed because the war was old. But there were also a lot of bakers—older prisoners who had been there a long time. When I came along they didn't really need another baker, so they decided to make use of my young and innocent looks. It became my job to deal with the American GIs who guarded the camp."

"Every day we baked extra hot rolls, more than the camp needed. This was, of course, on the sly. My job was to gather up the rolls as soon as they came from the oven and run as fast as I could to the sentry posts of the camp while they were still hot. Then I'd barter with the GIs—hot bread for cigarettes. The Americans were easy to deal with because they trusted my boyish appearance, but more important, they were hungry for the friendliness of hot bread. I did very good business if I kept the bread hot.

"I would then bring the cigarettes back to the older guys, who would use them to trade for other favors and services in the camp. The value of all things changes in prison, you know. On a good day, I could trade bread for 300 cigarettes."

A baking-equipment salesman from a Brooklyn, New York, company was sitting at a table next to us, listening. "I baked during the war, too," he said, without any invitation. "I was sergeant in charge of the baking unit that moved with the front-line American troops as the Allies advanced through Italy. It was a big pain in the you know what," he said. "We'd have to break down the oven, the tent, and pack the equipment each time the front advanced. But the brass was smart," he said, smiling at us and raising a pointed finger. "They knew how fresh hot bread made the troops feel. Like somebody cared about them. Hot bread was a great morale booster even though it was never very good."

I asked him why it wasn't good, and he answered quickly. "The flour. It was so refined that there wasn't much life left in it."

The German baker nodded. "Yes, I remember, that's the flour we had to work with."

"Anything less refined would have spoiled too easily," the salesman said defensively. "The funny thing is," he continued, "well, maybe not funny like humorous," he said looking cautiously at the German, "but the fact is that the flour ended up being kind of an element of torture for the German POW bakers who traveled with our unit and who did most of the baking."

The German baker looked at him intently.

"How so?" I asked.

"Well, these POWs were real tough soldiers," the salesman said. "They never grumbled about anything—never showed pain or fear about being with us on the front lines. I mean when you think they could have been wiped out any day by their own soldiers. But, anyway, every day without letup they complained about only one thing— our flour! That was their only complaint. Drove me nuts. They said it was too white. These big, tough guys would shield their eyes like the sun was shining too bright and say it hurt their eyes.

"You can imagine what they thought about the bread!" he said.

The German baker laughed out loud. "Too white and too tasteless! Sure, I remember. I wasn't on your front lines but I remember the bread!"

"But our GIs didn't complain," said the salesman. "The bread was hot, and it was there for them twice a day, every day. They never said much about it, but who ever does? About bread, I mean. I know it helped them. They were hard fighting troops."

We finished our coffees, and I told them I'd never thought much about bread being a secret weapon during wartime.

"You can bet it sure is," said the salesman. "Ask anybody who was there."

I looked at the German baker. He smiled. "He's right you know. It was everybody's secret weapon. Everybody's secret."

BAKERS' FAVORITES

A COLLECTION OF FAVORITE BREADS, INCLUDING CAROL'S QUICK BREADS

ROSE LEVY BERANBAUM'S JEWISH RYE BREAD

Allow 5 hours to ferment the *poolish*.
Total preparation and baking time (not including the *poolish*):
5 hours, 45 minutes

Although she is most noted for her best-selling book, *The Cake Bible*, Rose Levy Beranbaum is more than a master of cakes. She is a bread baker whose expertise up until now has been tasted only by her family and friends. I'm proud to include her delicious Jewish Rye Bread, a robust loaf with a wheaty flavor and a light taste of rye. It resembles the freshly baked loaf her father would bring home from his favorite bakery in the Bronx, New York, when she was a girl. The crumb is lavishly packed with caraway seeds and the texture is chewy but not dense.

Rose's grandmother taught her one of the best ways I've ever heard of for enjoying a fresh slice of rye bread. "She would spread a slice thickly with unsalted butter," she says of her grandmother, "then pave the top with rounds of sliced red radish. To this day it is my favorite way to eat rye bread with one possible exception—when I bake it myself, I get the first slice while it is still warm from the oven."

Makes 2 round 10-inch loaves

POOLISH

Spring water (75°F.)	3 cups	24 fluid ounces
Moist yeast	1 tablespoon	¾ ounce
or dry yeast	1½ teaspoons	³⁄₁₆ ounce
Sugar	2 tablespoons	¼ ounce
Organic white flour with germ*	3 cups	15 ounces

FINAL DOUGH

Rye flour,* medium ground	2 cups	9¾ ounces
Caraway seeds	¼ cup	1 ounce
Vegetable oil	1 tablespoon	
Fine sea salt	1 tablespoon	¾ ounce
Sugar	1 tablespoon	1 ounce
Organic white flour with germ*	3 cups	15 ounces

---

* See Flours (pages 42–49). These are good approximate measures. You may use more or less depending on the weight and absorbency of your flours.

MAKE AND FERMENT THE *POLISH* (allow 5 hours) Combine the water, yeast, and sugar in a 6-quart bowl. Let stand 1 minute, then stir with a wooden spoon until yeast and sugar are dissolved. Add the white flour and stir until the consistency of a thick batter. Continue stirring for about 100 strokes or until the strands of gluten come off the spoon when you press the back of the spoon against the bowl. Scrape down the sides of the bowl with a rubber spatula. Cover with a clean damp towel or plastic wrap, and put in a moderately warm (74°–80°F.) draft-free place until it is bubbly and increased in volume. (The *polish* can be refrigerated overnight. Allow to stand at room temperature for 2 hours before proceeding.)

MIX AND KNEAD THE FINAL DOUGH (20 minutes) Measure the ingredients and calculate the necessary temperatures (see page 58). Transfer the *polish* to a 6-quart bowl. Add the rye flour, caraway seeds, oil, salt, and sugar. Stir with a wooden spoon until well combined. Add enough of the white flour to make a thick mass that is difficult to stir. Turn out onto a well-floured surface. Knead, adding more of the remaining flour when needed until dough is soft and smooth, 15 to 17 minutes. The dough is ready when a small amount pulled from the mass springs back quickly (see Kneading, page 66).

FERMENT THE DOUGH (2 hours) Shape the dough into a ball and let it rest on a lightly floured surface while you scrape, clean, and lightly butter the large bowl. Place the dough in the bowl and turn the dough to coat the top with butter. Take the dough's temperature: the ideal is 78°F. (see page 58). Cover with a clean damp towel or plastic wrap and put in a moderately warm (74°–80°F.) draft-free place until doubled in volume.

> *Note: If the dough temperature is higher than 78°F., put it in a cooler than 78°F. place like the refrigerator, until the dough cools to 78°F. If it is lower than 78°F., put it in a warmer than 78°F. place until the dough warms to 78°F. The point is to try to keep the dough at 78°F. during its fermentation. If you do have to move the dough, be gentle and don't jostle it, or the dough may deflate.*

FERMENT THE DOUGH A SECOND TIME (45 minutes) Deflate the dough by pulling up on the sides and pushing down in the cen-

(continued)

ter. Re-form into a ball, return to the bowl, and cover again with a clean damp towel or plastic wrap. Put in a moderately warm (74°–80°F.) draft-free place until doubled in volume.

FERMENT THE DOUGH A THIRD TIME (45 minutes) Deflate again, shape into a ball, return to bowl, and cover again. Put in a moderately warm (74°–80°F.) place until doubled again.

DIVIDE AND SHAPE THE DOUGH INTO LOAVES (10 minutes) Deflate the dough by pushing down in the center and pulling up on the sides. Transfer the dough to a lightly floured work surface and knead briefly. Cut the dough into 2 equal pieces. Flatten each with the heel of your hand using firm direct strokes. Shape each piece into a tight ball for round loaves (see Taking Shape, page 68).

PROOF THE LOAVES (1 hour) Place the loaves on a lightly floured board. Cover with a clean, damp towel or plastic wrap and put in a moderately warm (74°–80°F.) draft-free place until doubled in volume.

BAKE THE LOAVES (45 minutes) Forty-five minutes to 1 hour before baking, preheat the oven and homemade hearth or baking stone on the center rack of the oven (see Equipment, page 52) to 450°F.

The oven rack must be in the center of the oven. If it is in the lower third of the oven, the bottoms of the breads may burn, and if it is in the upper third, the top crusts may burn.

Using a very sharp, serrated knife or a single-edged razor blade, score the loaves by making quick shallow cuts ¼ to ½ inch deep along the surface. Using the peel, slide the loaves one at a time onto the hearth and quickly spray the inner walls and floor of the oven with cold water from a spritzer bottle. If there's an electric light bulb in the oven, avoid spraying it directly—it may burst. Spray for several seconds until steam has filled the oven. Quickly close the door to trap the steam and bake 3 minutes. Spray again in the same way, closing the door immediately so that steam doesn't escape. Bake 12 minutes. Reduce heat to 400°F. and bake until loaves are a rich caramel color and the crust is firm, another 15 to 20 minutes.

To test the loaves for doneness, remove and hold the loaves upside down. Strike the bottoms firmly with your finger. If the sound is hollow, the breads are done. If it doesn't sound hollow, bake 5 minutes longer. Cool completely on wire racks.

ROSE LEVY BERANBAUM'S JEWISH RYE BREAD

Task	Approximate Time	Comments
Prepreparation		Ferment *poolish*.
Preparation	5 min.	Calculate temperatures. Assemble ingredients. Mix.
Knead	15 min.	Take temperature of final dough.
Ferment	2 hr.	Moderate: 74°–80°F. until doubled in volume.
Ferment #2	45 min.	Moderate: 74°–80° until doubled.
Ferment #3	45 min.	Moderate: 74°–80°F. until doubled.
Divide and shape	10 min.	Deflate and cut into 2 equal portions. Flatten with heel of hand. Form balls for round loaves. Place on floured board.
Proof	1 hr.	Moderate: 74°–80°F. until doubled.
Bake	45 min.	With steam. 450°–400°F.
Cool	20 min.	On rack or in baskets.

Cumulative Total Time: 6 hr., 5 min.

SARDINIAN FLATBREAD

Total preparation and baking time:
35 minutes

On a visit to France a few years ago, I had the opportunity to meet with one of my favorite food writers, Patricia Wells. We spoke of, among other things, breads from other countries. She mentioned this bread and rattled off a recipe. I couldn't get it out of my mind; it sounded so simple and so good.

Semolina is getting easier to find these days. Any gourmet shop should carry it.

Makes 6 to 8 round 6-inch breads

Organic white flour with germ*	3/4 cup	4 ounces
Semolina	3/4 cup	4 ounces
Fine sea salt	1 teaspoon	
Spring water, cold	1 cup	8 fluid ounces

*See Flours (pages 42–49). This is a good approximate measure. You may use more or less depending on the weight and absorbency of your flour.

MIX AND KNEAD THE FINAL DOUGH (10 minutes) Combine the flour, semolina, and salt in a medium flat-bottom bowl. Make a well in the center and gradually stir in the water to make a soft dough. Knead in the bowl until the dough is smooth, soft, and elastic, 8 minutes.

(5 minutes)Shape the dough into a ball in the bowl. Cover with a clean damp towel and let it rest in a moderately warm (74°–80° F.) draft-free place.

DIVIDE THE DOUGH AND SHAPE THE BREADS (5 minutes) Cut the dough into 8 equal pieces about 2 ounces each and roll each piece into a smooth ball, about the size of a tangerine. Place the balls of dough on a well-semolina-floured board and flatten each with your fingertips. Using a rolling pin, roll each into a disk 6½ inches in diameter, turning the bread as you roll.

BAKE THE BREADS (12 minutes) Preheat a griddle or heavy skillet over medium heat. Bake the breads one at a time, keeping the remaining dough covered with a clean damp towel. Bake until the bottoms are lightly golden and you can see bubbles on the top side, about 1½ minutes. Using tongs, flip the bread and bake until the other side is lightly browned, about 10 seconds. Remove to a platter and keep warm.

For a crisp, crunchy bread, remove the bread from the griddle and place directly on a gas burner on medium heat for 10 seconds. Serve immediately.

SARDINIAN FLATBREAD

Task	Approximate Time	Comments
Preparation	5 min.	Assemble ingredients. Mix.
Knead	5 min.	In the bowl.
Rest	5 min.	Moderate: 74°–80°F.
Divide and shape	5 min.	In 8 equal pieces 2 ounces each. In tight balls.
Bake	12 min.	Preheated grill.

Cumulative Total Time: 32 min.

CHAPATI

Total preparation and baking time:
40 minutes

This is the basic bread of India. It is typically baked on one side on a griddle, then placed directly over an open flame, which makes it puff up to form a pocket, perfect for stuffing. When I visited India, the mother of the family that I stayed with made chapati with just about every meal. The breads contain no oil or salt and are a perfect accompaniment to a spicy dish as well as a special treat with leftovers. My friend Nadar makes a beautiful presentation by taking the hot chapati, placing a pat of butter in the center, folding it in half, and then in half again, making a triangle. He places them in a beautiful basket lined with a simple napkin. By the time everyone is seated, the butter has melted and the chapati is used as a delicious dipper for all of the lovely dishes he has prepared.

Makes ten 6-inch breads

| Whole wheat flour,* preferably coarse ground | 2 cups | 11 ounces |
| Spring water, cold | 1¼ cups | 10 fluid ounces |

*See Flours (pages 42–49). This is a good approximate measure. You may use more or less depending on the weight and absorbency of your flour.

MIX AND KNEAD THE FINAL DOUGH (15 minutes) Place the flour in a large flat-bottom bowl. Make a well in the center and gradually stir in 1 cup (8 ounces) of the water to make a fairly stiff dough. Knead in the bowl until the dough is smooth, soft, and elastic, about 5 minutes.

Add the remaining water and continue kneading. This is a slow, messy, and sticky step. As the dough absorbs the water it becomes silky and, although it will remain sticky, it will be extremely elastic. Keep kneading until all the water is absorbed. The dough is well kneaded when you hold it in your hand for a minute and it sticks to your palm.

REST (5 minutes) Shape the dough into a ball in the bowl. Cover with a clean damp towel and let it rest in a moderately warm (74°–80° F.) draft-free place.

DIVIDE THE DOUGH AND SHAPE THE BREADS (5 minutes) Cut the dough into 10 equal pieces about 2 ounces each and roll each into a smooth ball, about the size of a tangerine. Place the balls of dough on a well-floured board and flatten each with your fingertips. Using a rolling pin, roll each into a disk 6½ inches in diameter, turning the bread as you roll.

BAKE THE BREADS (15 minutes) Preheat a griddle or heavy skillet over medium heat. Bake the breads one at a time, keeping the remaining dough covered with a clean damp towel. Bake until the bottoms are lightly golden and you can see bubbles on the top side, about 1½ minutes. Using tongs, flip the bread and bake until the other side is lightly browned for about 10 seconds. Remove to a platter and keep warm.

For a very puffy chapati, remove the bread from the griddle and place directly on a gas burner on medium heat, 10 seconds. Serve warm.

CHAPATI

Task	Approximate Time	Comments
Preparation	5 min.	Assemble ingredients. Mix.
Knead	10 min.	In the bowl.
Rest	5 min.	Moderate: 74°–80°F.
Divide and shape	5 min.	In 10 equal pieces 2 ounces each. In tight balls.
Bake	15 min.	Preheated grill.

Cumulative Total Time: 40 min.

MY BEST BAGELS

> Total preparation and baking time (including fermentation):
> 3 hours, 5 minutes

These are chewy and delicious bagels with shining crusts and a sweet yeasty taste. Don't overboil; that's the secret. Just thirty seconds on each side is enough to invigorate the yeast cells in the dough and give you a high and plump bagel when baked in the oven. If desired, after brushing the tops of the bagels with egg white, sprinkle them with poppy seeds, sesame seeds, or minced dried onions.

Makes 10 bagels

Spring water	1¼ cups	10 fluid ounces
Moist yeast	4 teaspoons	2½ ounces
or dry yeast	4 teaspoons	2½ ounces
Whole wheat flour,* preferably coarse ground	½ cup	2¾ ounces
Fine sea salt	1 tablespoon	¾ ounces
Organic all-purpose white flour*	2½–3 cups	12½–15 ounces
Barley malt syrup (see Note)	2 tablespoons	
1 egg white, lightly beaten		

---

* See Flours (pages 42–49). These are good approximate measures. You may use a little more or less depending on the weight and absorbency of your flours.

> <u>Note:</u> *Barley malt syrup is available in natural foods stores.*
> *Do not use diastalic malt syrup, which is too strong.*

MIX AND KNEAD THE FINAL DOUGH (20 minutes) Measure the ingredients and calculate the necessary temperatures (see page 58). Combine the water and yeast in a 4-quart bowl. Let stand 1 minute, then stir with a wooden spoon until the yeast is dissolved. Add the whole wheat flour, salt, and enough of the white flour to make a thick mass that is difficult to stir. Turn out onto a lightly floured surface. Knead vigorously, adding more of the remaining flour when needed until dough is soft and smooth, 15 to 17 minutes. This dough will remain somewhat sticky and soft even when well kneaded. The dough is ready when a small amount pulled from the mass springs back quickly (see Kneading, page 68).

FERMENT THE DOUGH (1 to 1½ hours) Shape the dough into a ball and let it rest on a lightly floured surface while you scrape, clean, and lightly oil the large bowl. Place the dough in the bowl and turn the dough to coat the top with oil. Take the dough's temperature: the ideal is 78°F. (see page 58). Cover with a clean damp towel or plastic wrap and put in a moderately warm (74°–80°F.) draft-free place until doubled in volume, and a slight indentation remains after pressing the dough with a fingertip.

> *Note: If the dough temperature is higher than 78°F., put it in a cooler than 78°F. place like the refrigerator, until the dough cools to 78°F. If it is lower than 78°F., put it in a warmer than 78°F. place until the dough warms to 78°F. The point is to try to keep the dough at 78°F. during its fermentation. If you do have to move the dough, be gentle and don't jostle it, or the dough may deflate.*

DIVIDE THE DOUGH AND REST (15 minutes) Deflate the dough by pushing down in the center and pulling up on the sides. Turn onto a lightly floured surface and knead briefly. Cut the dough into 10 pieces about 2½ ounces each. Flatten each with the heel of your hand and shape into a tight 1½-inch ball. Place on a lightly floured board, cover with a clean damp towel or plastic wrap and put in a moderately warm (70°–80°F.) draft-free place for 10 minutes.

SHAPE THE BAGELS AND REST (20 minutes) Roll and stretch each ball into a log 8 inches long. Wrap around your fingers to form a ring. Pinch the ends together, then roll seam on work surface board. Place on a board, cover with a clean damp towel or plastic wrap and put in a moderately warm (74°–80°F.) draft-free place for 10 minutes.

POACH AND BAKE THE BAGELS (35 minutes) Forty-five minutes to 1 hour before baking, preheat the oven and homemade hearth or baking stone on the center rack of the oven (see Equipment, page 52) to 425°F.

The oven rack must be in the center of the oven. If it is in the lower third of the oven, the bottoms of the bagels may burn, and if it is in the upper third, the top crusts may burn.

(continued)

Combine about 3 quarts water and the barley malt syrup in a large saucepan. Heat to boiling, then reduce to a light simmer. Place the bagels, 2 or 3 at a time, into the simmering water, turning after 30 seconds for each side. Remove with a slotted spoon and drain on paper toweling. Repeat the process until all the bagels have been poached and drained.

Sprinkle a large baking sheet with cornmeal and place the bagels 1½ inches apart. Brush with beaten egg white and bake until lightly golden, 15 to 20 minutes.

Cool on a wire rack.

MY BEST BAGELS

Task	Approximate Time	Comments
Preparation	5 min.	Assemble ingredients. Mix.
Knead	15 min.	Take temperature of final dough.
Ferment	1 hr., 30 min.	Moderate: 74°–80°F. until doubled.
Divide and shape	5 min.	In 10 equal pieces 3½ ounces each. In tight balls.
Rest	10 min.	Moderate: 74°–80°F.
Shape	10 min.	Into rings.
Rest	10 min.	Moderate: 74°–80°F.
Boil	5 min.	
Bake	20 min.	425°F.
Cool	15 min.	On rack or in basket.

Cumulative Total Time: 3 hr., 5 min.

MY BEST BIALY

Total preparation and baking time (including fermentation):
4 hours, 5 minutes

I love this savory yeast roll almost as much as I love bagels. The recipe was developed by Jewish bakers in Bialystok, Poland, and was made popular by immigrants living in New York City.

Makes 8 bialys

Spring water (75°F.)	¾ cup plus 2 tablespoons	7 fluid ounces
Moist yeast	2½ teaspoons	¾ ounce
or dry yeast	1¼ teaspoons	⁶⁄₁₆ ounce
Sugar	1 teaspoon	
Whole wheat flour	½ cup	2½ ounces
Fine sea salt	1 teaspoon	
Organic all-purpose white flour*	2 cups	10 ounces
1 small onion, minced	½ cup	4 ounces
Poppy seeds	2 teaspoons	
Vegetable oil	1½ teaspoons	

---

* See Flours (pages 42–49). This is a good approximate measure. You may use more or less depending on the weight and absorbency of your flour.

MIX AND KNEAD THE FINAL DOUGH (20 minutes) Combine the water, yeast, and sugar in a large bowl, and stir with a wooden spoon until well combined. Let stand until it bubbles, about 10 minutes. Add the whole wheat flour and salt; stir until well combined. Add enough of the white flour to make a thick mass that is difficult to stir. Turn out onto a lightly floured surface and knead, adding more of the remaining flour as needed. This dough remains sticky so flour your hands frequently. Continue kneading until dough is smooth and very soft and a little dough when pulled from the mass springs back quickly, about 15 minutes. (Or make in a heavy-duty mixer; see page 67.)

FERMENT THE DOUGH (1 to 1½ hours) Shape the dough into a ball and let it rest on a lightly floured surface while you scrape, clean, and lightly oil the large bowl. Place the dough in the bowl and take its temperature. The ideal is 78°F. (see page 58). Cover with a clean

(continued)

damp towel or plastic wrap and put in a moderately warm (74°–80°F.) draft-free place until doubled in volume.

> *Note: If the dough temperature is higher than 78°F., put it in a cooler than 78°F. place. If it is lower than 78°F., put it in a warmer than 78°F. place. The point is to try to keep the dough at 78°F. during its fermentation. If you do have to move the dough, be gentle and don't jostle it, or the dough may deflate.*

FERMENT THE DOUGH A SECOND TIME (45 minutes) Deflate the dough by pushing down in the center and pulling up on the sides. Cover again with a clean damp towel or plastic wrap and put in a moderately warm (74°–80°F.) draft-free place until doubled in volume.

DIVIDE THE DOUGH AND REST (15 minutes) Deflate the dough and turn out onto a lightly floured surface. Knead briefly. Cut the dough into 8 equal pieces about 2 ounces each. Flatten each with the heel of your hand and shape into a 1½-inch tight ball. Cover with a clean damp towel or plastic wrap and put in a moderately warm (74°–80°F.) draft-free place for 10 minutes.

SHAPE AND PROOF THE BIALYS (30 minutes) Place the balls of dough on a well-floured board. With well-floured hands, flatten each into a 4-inch disk. Cover with a clean damp towel or plastic wrap and put in a moderately warm (74°–80°F.) draft-free place until almost doubled in volume.

FILL THE BIALYS AND PROOF A SECOND TIME (30 minutes) Combine onion, poppy seeds, and oil in a small bowl. Press on the center of the disks to create a 1½-inch-wide well and fill each with about 1 tablespoon of the onion filling, pressing the filling to adhere to the dough. Cover with a clean damp towel or plastic wrap and put in a moderately warm (74°–80°F.) draft-free place until doubled in volume.

BAKE THE BIALYS (15 minutes)

Forty-five minutes to 1 hour before baking, preheat the oven and homemade hearth or baking stone on the center rack of the oven (see Equipment, page 52) to 400°F.

The oven rack must be in the center of the oven. If it is in the lower third of the oven, the bottoms of the bialys may burn, and if it is in the upper third, the top crusts may burn.

Using the floured peel, slide the bialys a few at a time onto the hearth. Quickly spray the inner walls and floor of the oven with cold water from a spritzer bottle. If there's an electric light bulb in the oven, avoid spraying it directly—it may burst. Spray for several seconds until steam has filled the oven. Quickly close the door to trap the steam and bake 3 minutes. Spray again in the same way, closing the door immediately so that steam doesn't escape. Bake until bialys are lightly browned, 12 to 15 minutes. *Do not overbake.* The bialys should remain chewy not crisp. Cool on a wire rack.

MY BEST BIALY

Task	Approximate Time	Comments
Preparation	5 min.	Assemble ingredients. Mix.
Knead	15 min.	Take temperature of final dough.
Ferment	1 hr., 30 min.	Moderate: 74°–80°F. until doubled.
Ferment	45 min.	Moderate.
Divide and shape	5 min.	In 8 equal pieces 2 ounces each. In tight balls.
Rest	10 min.	Moderate: 74°–80°F.
Shape Proof #1	30 min.	Into disks. Moderate: 74°–80°F.
Fill and Proof #2	30 min.	Press wide wells. Spoon on filling. Moderate: 74°–80°F.
Bake	15 min.	With steam. 400°F.
Cool	10 min.	On rack.

Cumulative Total Time: 4 hr., 15 min.

MY BEST PITA BREAD

Total preparation and baking time:
2 hours, 50 minutes

Of all the flatbreads I make, this is one of the most versatile. It puffs up beautifully in the oven and forms thick crusts that separate nicely for pocket sandwiches.

The bread has a sweet wheat flavor and a chewy texture that tastes best warm from the oven. If you want to keep the pitas soft for enjoying later, wrap each in foil as it comes from the oven.

Makes 14 round 6-inch breads

Spring water	1½ cups	12 fluid ounces
Moist yeast	½ teaspoon	⅛ ounce
or dry yeast	¼ teaspoon	1/16 ounce
Organic all-purpose white flour*	3¼–3¾ cups	17–19 ounces
Fine sea salt	1 teaspoon	

* See Flours (pages 42–49). This is an approximate measure. You may use more or less depending on the weight and absorbency of your flour.

MIX AND KNEAD THE FINAL DOUGH (15 minutes) Combine the water and yeast in a large bowl. Let stand 5 minutes, then stir with a wooden spoon until yeast dissolves. Add 1 cup (5 ounces) of the flour and the salt; stir until well combined. Add enough of the remaining flour to make a thick mass that is difficult to stir. Turn out onto a lightly floured surface and knead, adding more of the remaining flour as needed, until the dough is smooth, soft, and elastic, 5 minutes. (Or make in a heavy-duty mixer; see page 67.)

FERMENT THE DOUGH (1 to 1½ hours) Shape the dough into a ball and let rest on a lightly floured surface while you scrape, clean, and lightly oil the large bowl. Place the dough in the bowl and take its temperature. The ideal is 78°F. (see page 58). Cover with a clean damp towel or plastic wrap and place in a moderately warm (74°–80°F.) draft-free place until doubled in volume.

Note: If the dough temperature is higher than 78°F., put it in a cooler than 78°F. place. If it is lower than 78°F., put it in a warmer than 78°F. place. The point is to try to keep

the dough at 78°F. during its fermentation. If you do have
to move the dough, be gentle and don't jostle it, or the
dough may deflate.

DIVIDE THE DOUGH AND REST (35 minutes) Deflate the dough
by pulling up on the sides and pushing down in the center. Turn
onto a well-floured surface. Knead briefly. Cut the dough into 14
equal pieces about 2 ounces each. Flatten each with the heel of your
hand and shape into a tight 1½-inch ball. Cover with a clean damp
towel or plastic wrap and put in a moderately warm (74°–80°F.) draft-
free place for 30 minutes.

SHAPE THE PITAS (35 minutes) Place the balls of dough on a well-
floured board and dust the top of each with flour. On a lightly floured
surface, roll each into a disk 6½ inches in diameter.

BAKE THE PITAS (about 5 minutes per batch) Forty-five minutes to
1 hour before baking, preheat the oven and homemade hearth or
baking stone on the center rack of the oven (see Equipment, page
52) to 400°F.

The oven rack must be in the center of the oven. If it is in the
lower third of the oven, the bottoms of the breads may burn, and if
it is in the upper third, the top crusts may burn.

Work with 4 pitas at a time, keeping the remaining pitas stacked
and separated by sheets of waxed paper and covered with a clean
damp towel. Using a lightly floured peel, slide the pitas onto the
hearth. Bake until the bottoms are lightly golden and the breads are
puffed up, about 4 minutes. For a crispy, crunchy pita, bake 1 minute
longer. Serve immediately or wrap each bread in foil to keep soft for
eating later.

(continued)

MY BEST PITA BREAD

Task	Approximate Time	Comments
Preparation	5 min.	Assemble ingredients. Mix.
Knead	15 min.	Take temperature of final dough.
Ferment	1½ hr.	Moderate: 74°–80°F. until doubled.
Divide and shape	5 min.	In 14 equal pieces 2 ounces each. In tight balls.
Rest	30 min.	Moderate: 74°–80°F.
Shape	5 min.	Roll into disks.
Bake	20 min.	400°F.
		Serve immediately.

Cumulative Total Time: 2 hr., 50 min.

CAROL'S QUICK ▪▪ BREADS ▪▪

I met Carol Guthrie when she came to Bread Alone to learn more about brick hearth baking. Carol's an avid and creative baker who helped me develop these quick but hearty and satisfying breads. Our Bread Alone pastry chef has adapted Carol's recipes for large yields and we serve them in the café with great success.

ANGEL BISCUITS

Allow dough to rest 1 hour and up to 2 days before baking.
Total preparation and baking time:
30 minutes

These are truly heavenly light and so easy to make. They are ideal for a buffet where you might have an assortment of breads. The dough can be kept refrigerated for several days and used as you need it for breakfast or supper biscuits.

Makes thirty 2-inch biscuits

Spring water (75°F.)	2 tablespoons	
Moist yeast	2 teaspoons	½ ounce
or dry yeast	1 teaspoon	⅛ ounce
Organic all-purpose white flour	5 cups	25 ounces
Sugar	¼ cup	1¾ ounces
Baking powder	3 teaspoons	
Baking soda	1 teaspoon	
Fine sea salt	1 teaspoon	
Solid vegetable shortening, chilled, cut into pieces	1 cup	8 ounces
Buttermilk, chilled	2 cups	16 fluid ounces

PREPARE THE DOUGH (10 minutes) Combine the water and yeast in a small bowl. Let stand 1 minute, then stir until dissolved. Set aside.

(*continued*)

Mix the flour, sugar, baking powder, baking soda, and salt in a large bowl. Using a pastry blender or 2 knives, cut in the shortening until mixture is the texture of coarse crumbs. Add the dissolved yeast and the buttermilk; stir just until well combined. Use your hands to knead lightly in the bowl to form a soft and sticky dough. Cover tightly with plastic wrap and refrigerate at least 1 hour and up to 2 days.

SHAPE THE BISCUITS (5 minutes) Preheat the oven to 450°F. Turn out the dough onto a lightly floured surface and knead briefly to revive the yeast. Roll out dough on a lightly-floured surface to about ½ inch thickness. Cut biscuits with a 2½-inch cutter and place 1 inch apart on ungreased baking sheets. Gather up dough scraps and knead briefly to combine; reroll until all the dough is cut out.

BAKE THE BISCUITS (12 to 15 minutes) Bake until just barely golden, 12 to 15 minutes. Serve immediately.

SAVORY DROP BISCUITS

> Total preparation and baking time:
> 45 minutes

When you want a savory bread with your meal and don't have much time, try these biscuits. They are delicious and take no time at all. Serve with soup, salad, afternoon tea, or supper.

Makes 15 biscuits

Unsalted butter, chilled	7 tablespoons	3½ ounces
1 medium onion, finely chopped	1 cup	5 ounces
Chopped fresh rosemary	2 teaspoons	
Organic white all-purpose flour	2 cups	10 ounces
Baking powder	2 teaspoons	
Baking soda	¼ teaspoon	
Salt	½ teaspoon	
Buttermilk, chilled	1 cup	8 fluid ounces

COOK AND COOL THE ONIONS (20 minutes) Melt 2 tablespoons (1 ounce) of the butter in a small skillet over medium-high heat. Add the onion and cook 3 minutes. Add the rosemary and continue cooking, stirring often, until onion is soft and golden, about 3 minutes more. Place in a wire sieve to drain well and cool completely.

Preheat the oven to 450°F.

MAKE THE DOUGH (10 minutes) Cut the remaining butter into ½-inch cubes. Mix the flour, baking powder, baking soda, and salt in a large bowl. With a pastry blender or 2 knives, cut in cubed butter until mixture is the texture of coarse crumbs. Add the onion mixture, using a fork or your fingers to work it in thoroughly. Pour in the buttermilk and stir just until a soft dough forms.

BAKE THE BISCUITS (15 minutes) Drop dough by heaping tablespoonfuls onto an ungreased baking sheet. Bake until just golden in color, about 12 to 15 minutes. Serve immediately.

VANILLA BEAN BUTTER LOAF

Total preparation and baking time:
1 hour, 40 minutes

It looks like an old-fashioned pound cake, but this loaf is very light. It is golden, rich, sweet, and delicious when cut thin and heaped with sliced strawberries or peaches. Madagascar vanilla beans are the most common, but if you locate plump, fragrant Tahiti beans, use only half a bean.

Makes one 9 by 5-inch loaf

1 vanilla bean		
Sugar	1¾ cups	1¼ ounces
Organic white all-purpose flour	2 cups	10 ounces
Baking powder	¾ teaspoon	
Fine sea salt	½ teaspoon	
Unsalted butter, softened	1 cup	8 ounces
5 large eggs		

MAKE THE VANILLA SUGAR (10 minutes) Butter and flour a 9 × 5 × 3-inch loaf pan. Position a rack in the center of the oven and preheat the oven to 325°F.

Cut the vanilla bean into 1-inch pieces and place with the sugar in the container of a food processor fitted with a steel blade or a blender. Process until the bean is finely ground. Sift sugar to remove any woody bits of bean, then set vanilla sugar aside. (Ideally, you will use a whole vanilla bean, seeds included. However, you may use the leftover vanilla bean, with the seeds removed, from Orange Vanilla Brioche—see page 243—to be frugal. The vanilla sugar can be made up to 2 weeks ahead, stored at room temperature.)

MAKE THE DOUGH (10 minutes) Mix the flour, baking powder, and salt in a large bowl. In another large bowl, and using a hand-held electric mixer, beat the butter at high speed until creamy, about 1 minute. Gradually add the vanilla sugar and beat until light in texture, about 2 additional minutes. Beat in the eggs one at a time. Gradually add the flour mixture and beat until just combined. *Do not overbeat.*

BAKE (1 hour, 35 minutes) Pour batter into the prepared pan and smooth the top with a rubber spatula. Bake on the center rack of the oven until sides of the cake have shrunk from the pan and a toothpick inserted in center comes out clean, about 1 hour, 20 minutes. Cool in the pan on a wire rack for 10 minutes, then remove and cool completely.

BANANA BUCKWHEAT BREAD

Total preparation and baking time:
1 hour, 20 minutes

This is a dark cakey bread with the earthy fragrance of buckwheat and the rich fruity flavor of banana. This easy to make loaf won highest praise from my friends who tested these recipes.

Makes one 9 by 5-inch loaf

Organic all-purpose white flour	2½ cups	12½ ounces
Buckwheat flour	1 cup	5 ounces
Baking powder	3 teaspoons	
Baking soda	¾ teaspoon	
Salt	1 teaspoon	
Shortening	¾ cup	6 ounces
Sugar	1½ cups	9½ ounces
3 large eggs		
Milk	¾ cup	6 fluid ounces
Mashed ripe bananas (about 6 medium)	2 cups	
Chopped pecans	1 cup	4 ounces

MAKE THE BATTER (15 minutes) Preheat the oven to 350°F. Lightly butter and flour one 9 × 5 × 3-inch loaf pan.

Mix the flours, baking powder, baking soda, and salt in a large bowl.

Using a hand-held electric mixer at high speed, cream the shortening and sugar in a large bowl until light. Add the eggs one at a time, beating well after each addition. Add the dry ingredients and the milk, alternating in thirds. Fold in the bananas and pecans.

BAKE (70 minutes) Pour batter into the prepared pan and bake until a toothpick inserted in center comes out clean, about 60 minutes. Cool on a cake rack for 10 minutes. Unmold and cool completely before slicing.

DRIED PEAR, PORT, AND POPPY SEED LOAF

> Total preparation and baking time:
> 1 hour, 35 minutes

Dried pears are one of my favorite foods. The sweetness of the port expands the full flavor of the pears; poppy seeds supply crunch.

Makes one 9 by 5-inch loaf

Dried pears, cut into ½-inch cubes	1 cup	5½ ounces
Port wine, such as Tawny or Vintage	3 tablespoons	
Organic all-purpose white flour	2¼ cups	11 ounces
Baking powder	¾ teaspoon	
Baking soda	½ teaspoon	
Salt	¼ teaspoon	
Poppy seeds	3 tablespoons	
Unsalted butter, softened	¾ cup	6 ounces
Sugar	1 cup	7 ounces
3 large eggs		
Vanilla extract	1 teaspoon	
Plain low-fat yogurt	⅔ cup	

MAKE THE BATTER (20 minutes) Preheat the oven to 350°F. Butter and flour a 9 × 5 × 3-inch loaf pan. Combine the pears and wine in a small bowl. Let stand 30 minutes; drain.

Mix the flour, baking powder, baking soda, salt, and poppy seeds in a medium bowl. Set aside. Using a hand-held electric mixer at high speed, beat the butter and sugar in a large bowl until light and fluffy, about 2 minutes. Add the eggs one at a time, beating well after each addition. Beat in the vanilla.

On low speed, add the dry ingredients and yogurt, alternating in thirds and scraping down the sides of the bowl, until just combined. Using a wooden spoon, stir in pears until just blended.

BAKE (1 hour, 15 minutes) Pour batter into the prepared pan and bake until a toothpick inserted in center comes out clean, about 1 hour, 10 minutes. Cool on a wire cake rack for 10 minutes. Unmold and cool completely.

LEMON ANISE TEA LOAF

Zesty lemon and anise play off one another and make this irresistible with hot tea or coffee. The recipe also is the basis for a terrific short-cake—simply spoon fresh blueberries over slices of the loaf and top with a dollop of whipped cream.

Makes one 9 by 5-inch loaf

Organic white all-purpose flour	3 cups	15 ounces
Baking powder	¾ teaspoon	
Baking soda	1 teaspoon	
Salt	1 teaspoon	
Anise seed, crushed	2 teaspoons	
Unsalted butter, melted and cooled	½ cup	4 ounces
Sugar	1 cup	7 ounces
Milk	1 cup	8 fluid ounces
Lemon juice	¼ cup	2 fluid ounces
Grated zest of 2 lemons	2 tablespoons	
Vanilla extract	1 teaspoon	
2 large eggs, lightly beaten		
Lemon juice and sugar	3 tablespoons each	
Spring water	5 teaspoons	

MAKE THE BATTER (15 minutes) Preheat the oven to 350°F. Butter and flour a 9 × 5 × 3-inch loaf pan.

Mix the flour, baking powder, baking soda, salt, and anise seed in a large bowl.

Beat the butter, sugar, milk, lemon juice and zest, vanilla, and eggs in a large bowl. Gradually add to the flour mixture and stir just until combined.

BAKE (45 minutes) Pour batter into the prepared pan and smooth the surface with a spatula. Bake until a toothpick inserted in center comes out clean, 30 to 40 minutes. Cool in pan 10 minutes.

MAKE THE SYRUP (5 minutes) Combine the lemon juice, sugar, and water in a small saucepan. Heat to boiling and boil 1 minute. Remove from heat.

GLAZE THE BREAD (5 minutes) Unmold the breads. Poke random holes in tops and sides of loaf with a cake tester or a toothpick. Brush lemon syrup over, then cool completely before slicing.

PROVOLONE SAGE CORN LOAF

Total preparation and baking time:
1 hour, 10 minutes

This is best eaten the day it's baked because the loaf will be a little dry and crumbly the second day. It's the most spicy of any bread in this collection: the flavors of cheese, pepper, and sage are strong and clear. The bread is a delicious partner to a corn chowder or simple soup.

Makes one 9 by 5-inch loaf

Organic white all-purpose flour	1½ cups	7½ ounces
Yellow cornmeal, plus extra for dusting	1 cup	
Salt	1 teaspoon	
Baking soda	½ teaspoon	
Baking powder	2 teaspoons	
Cayenne pepper	⅛ teaspoon	
Freshly ground black pepper	¾ teaspoon	
Chopped fresh sage	1 tablespoon	
Olive oil, preferably extra-virgin	¼ cup	2 fluid ounces
Buttermilk	1¼ cups	10 fluid ounces
2 large eggs, lightly beaten		
Shredded provolone cheese	1 cup	4 ounces
8 whole fresh sage leaves		

MAKE THE BATTER (20 minutes) Preheat the oven to 350°F. Lightly butter a 9 × 5 × 3-inch loaf pan. Sprinkle extra cornmeal in pan to coat sides and bottom evenly.

Mix the flour, cornmeal, salt, baking powder, baking soda, black and cayenne peppers, and chopped sage in a large bowl.

Combine the olive oil, buttermilk, and eggs in a small bowl; add to the flour mixture and stir with a wooden spoon until just combined. Stir in the cheese.

BAKE (50 minutes) Pour batter into prepared pan. Arrange the whole sage leaves in a decorative pattern on top. Bake until a toothpick inserted in the center comes out clean, 40 to 45 minutes.

Let stand in the pan 10 minutes, then unmold. Gently brush top of loaf with extra olive oil.

THE FAMOUS MASON

Andé is seventy-something. I've never felt brash enough to ask him the exact number. He is a mason who is the great-nephew and son of famous French brick masons who, for most of the nineteenth and early twentieth centuries, enjoyed a fine reputation as oven builders for the bakeries of Paris. It was André's great-uncle who began the business in 1860. For 100 years the name "Jean LeFort et Fils" on the iron plate that hung above an oven's door was a sign of high-quality work. But after World War II, the new technology of gas-fired and electric ovens became the way to higher and cheaper productivity. By 1960, a wood-fired brick oven was deemed so old-fashioned that only a few obstinate bakers held on to them, and a brick oven was never considered when a new bakery was to be built. The need for oven masons declined greatly, and André is now among a small handful of skilled masons who remain. Indeed, there are five such masons in all of Paris. André spends most of his time in semiretirement; only rarely is he called upon to repair an oven that his father built.

One spring I asked André to stay with me and my family and build a simple oven in my backyard. He was with us for six weeks, living in the studio above my garage. At 8:00 A.M. every day he began his work dressed in the bright blue uniform of a French laborer. He stopped at noon for lunch, usually soup and bread. Then he went back to work until 5:30.

Rumors began to fly that something odd was going on in my yard and pretty soon neighbors and friends were dropping by. I was honored to have a master craftsman at work. I watched him as often as I could. He held and examined each brick, slowly and carefully eying it for unevenness and cracks, then placed it atop the fresh mortar and tapped it into place. He worked slowly, not owing to his age but to the demands of his craft.

André doesn't look like a laborer. He is small, with a fragile and sensitive appearance. It has always seemed ironic to me that such a delicate-looking man would build the great fiery ovens for those barrel-chested bakers in France.

What André lacked in physical size, he made up for in reputation. In fact, the LeFort family were renowned for the beauty and durability of their ovens. The firm Jean LeFort et Fils was among only a few to build a snail-shell arch for the oven interior. It is painstaking work to lay the bricks in the spiral of a snail shell, but the result is an arch so strong it can last fifty years or more. André's father spent much of his life repairing ovens his uncle had built years prior, and until this last decade André spent much of his time attending to the work of his father.

Nowadays, instead of repairing a brick oven, most bakers abandon them and buy a modern oven. Landlords who buy old bakeries turn them into boutiques, demolishing the ovens and destroying the storefronts. With André in Paris I have watched a dump truck carry away the remains of yet another ancient oven.

"There goes another one," says André with an easy surrender in his voice. André examines the truck's cargo, looking for some characteristic that might reveal who built the oven and when. He searches for part of the chimney, a portion of the arch, a door handle—anything for a clue. Sometimes he thinks he knows the oven, but he's not sure, really. He hopes it's not the one he thinks it is, the one from around the corner. Do I mind if we go that way, just to see?

In my backyard, in the Catskill Mountains of New York State, is an oven with André's name embossed on the iron plate above the door. It took him three weeks to build the oven. It has become an object of curiosity and joy for my neighbors, and it is the center of any gathering we host. Firing it up as often as I can, I've baked sensational breads in it and dozens of pizzas. I've roasted hens, turkeys, and corn. It's an active, working monument to traditional wood-fired baking, to traditional bakers everywhere, and to the great oven masons of the past.

If you want a brick oven, it's very simple to get one. And you don't have to hire André LeFort to build it for you. Any competent mason can put one together with bricks, mortar, and a plan. Your breads—your whole life—will taste better.

APPENDIX
MAIL ORDER SOURCES

▓ KITCHEN EQUIPMENT ▓

The Chef's Catalogue
3915 Commercial Avenue
Northbrook, IL 60062
312-480-9400; 1-800-338-3232
KitchenAid mixers, baker's stones, wooden peels, scales.

The Baker's Catalogue (King Arthur Flour)
RR 2, Box 56
Norwich, VT 05055
1-800-827-6836
Best "one-call shopping" for the passionate baker: heavy steel loaf
pans, stoneware bowls, large cooling racks, dough scrapers, kitchen
scales, instant-read thermometers, wooden peels, baker's stones.

French Baking Machinery
RD 3, Box 799
Cranbury, MD 08512
(609) 860-0577
Call to mail order French willow bread baskets for proofing your
dough in authentic shapes.

Sassafras Enterprises, Inc.
1622 West Carroll Avenue
Chicago, IL 60612
1-800-537-4941
Reliable manufacturer of baker's stones and wooden peels.

Williams-Sonoma
P.O. Box 7456
San Francisco, CA 94120
415-421-4242
Well-known catalogue for baker's stones and kitchen scales, as well as high-quality baking pans.

FLOUR AND OTHER ▪▪ INGREDIENTS ▪▪

Arrowhead Mills
P.O. Box 866
Hereford, TX 79045
713-364-0730
The brand of stone-ground organic flour that many natural foods stores carry. They have a large variety of flours, as well as grains, beans, and seeds.

The Baker's Catalogue (King Arthur Flour)
RR 2, Box 56
Norwich, VT 05055
1-800-827-6836
Even though their flours aren't stone ground or organic, it's still a very good product, free of chemicals or bromates. Best of all, this East Coast mill is a great source for other baking ingredients, such as barley malt, dried cherries, vanilla beans and extract, and many different types of flour and grain.

Bread Alone
Route 28
Boiceville, NY 12412
914-657-3228
Call for our catalogue of whole-grain breads.

Brewster River Mill
Mill Street
Jeffersonville, VT 05464
802-644-2987
Stone-ground organic flours from a 1800 stone mill, along with excellent maple syrup. They carry whole wheat, white bread, buckwheat, and rye flours as well as cornmeal.

Community Mill and Bean
267 Route 89 South
Savannah, NY 13146
1-800-755-0554; 315-365-2664
This mill prides itself on milling to order by traditional stone grinding, so call here when you want *fresh* flour. While all of their flours
are excellent, the unbleached white flour with germ is particularly
fine.

The Fowlers Mill
12500 Fowlers Mill Road
Chardon, OH 44024
1-800-321-2024
Specialties are stone-ground whole wheat flour and buckwheat flour.

Great Grains Milling Company
P.O. Box 427
Scobey, MT 59263
406-783-5588
Great Mills is a good source to buy organic stone-ground 20 percent
reduced bran flour, which they call Golden Wheat Flour.

Great Valley Mills
RD 3, County Line Road
Box 1111
Barto, PA 19504
1-800-688-6455
The Kantoor family produces an impressive line of fine stone-ground
flours, but not all of them are certified organic. They also carry a full
line of mouth-watering smoked hams and turkeys for world-class
sandwiches.

Pamela's Products
156 Utah Avenue
South San Francisco, CA 94080
415-952-4546
The mail order source for the excellent Giusto's flours, many of which are organic and stone ground. (Pamela is Al Giusto's daughter.) Giusto's has been milling flours since 1940, and carries a huge variety of fabulous flours and grains. Their 20 percent reduced bran flour is called Old Mill, and it will probably become a favorite of yours.

1788 Tuthilltown Grist Mill
Albany Post Road
Gardiner, NY 12525
914-255-5695
Many tourists stop at the mill's shop to purchase products, but they mail order, too. One advantage is that they package in 1-, 2-, 5-, 10-, and 25-pound bags, but while stone ground, their flours aren't organic.

War Eagle Mill
Route 5, Box 411
Rogers, AR 72756
501-789-5343
Stone-ground flours and grains from certified organic ingredients are produced by this historic water-powered gristmill.

Walnut Acres
Penns Creek, PA 17862
1-800-433-3998
This is the Sears, Roebuck of the natural foods world, a soup-to-nuts catalogue that has organic stone-ground flours, home grain mills, seeds, grains, honeys, nuts, sugar-free preserves, and more.

Weisenberger Flour Mills
Box 215
Midway, KY 40347
606-254-5282
Not certified organic, but stone ground; their Unbleached All-Purpose Flour is very good.

INDEX

ABOUT THE AUTHORS

Daniel Leader is the owner and baker of the Bread Alone Bakery in New York's Catskill Mountains. Dan's food career began when, nine months short of his undergraduate philosophy degree from the University of Wisconsin, he realized his need to work with his hands as well as his mind. He enrolled at the Culinary Institute of America in Hyde Park, New York, graduated at the top of his class, and worked as a chef for some of New York City's hottest restaurants, La Grenouille and the Water Club. Then, after eight years of cooking food "too fancy to eat," he became obsessed with the idea of creating something wholesome, timeless, and beautiful. Great bread and Bread Alone were born. With two wood-fired brick ovens, he produces fifteen tons of fresh bread per week. Dan lives in Boiceville, New York, with his wife, Sharon, and four children, Liv, Nels, Octavia, and Noah.

Judith Blahnik is a freelance writer who enjoys collaborating with other writers and food enthusiasts. In addition to shaping *Bread Alone* with Dan Leader, she is coauthor of *Ruth and Skitch Henderson's Christmas in the Country* and she is currently at work on new collaborative projects which explore two of her favorite subjects— food and feelings, and baseball.

As a writer and researcher, Miss Blahnik worked for the late Bert Greene on his award-winning *Greene on Greens* and *The Grains Cookbook*. She attributes her curiosity about food and culture to the lively experience of knowing Mr. Greene. She likes living in Brooklyn, New York.